PREFACE

Two distinct yet vitally related objects have determined the contents and arrangement of the present revised and enlarged edition of *Sentences and Thinking: A Handbook of Composition and Revision.*

A HANDBOOK OF COMPOSITION

One of these objects is positive, constructive. Most "manuals of composition" really give scant attention to composition; assuming that the composition has already been written, they are concerned rather with the process of revision and rewriting. They tell the student far less about how-to-write than about how-not-to-write. In both doctrine and exercises they are in the main negative, destructive, as if success in writing consisted in the avoiding of errors. This inadequacy in the ordinary manuals of composition may partly be made good by the collateral use of a book of rhetoric — but only partly, because the manual and the rhetoric have no practical relation (cross reference between the two being impossible), and because the rhetoric can hardly give the full, reasoned discussion of the sentence and the abundant constructive exercises that are needed. Yet the sentence is, as everybody recognizes, the crux of the problem of sound writing. In Book I (Principles of Construction) we have accordingly attempted an extensive treatment of the sentence, in which all the matter has been carefully disposed in a logical sequence determined by one fundamental idea — the idea,

iii

119371

namely, that sentences and thinking, the expression and the thought, the form and the function, are organically related. In the light of this dominant conception, we have sought to present the doctrine of the sound sentence not arbitrarily but scientifically, not pedantically but reasonably. We have asked the student, not to learn a mass of "rules," but to think out the reasons behind the rules. It has been our conviction that, unless the student penetrates to the fundamental principles of expression, he will not only fail to learn how to write, but will even fail to learn how not to write. A mass of rules, no matter how painfully studied, cannot make a lasting impression on the human mind. In the republic of letters, blind obedience to mere autocratic prescription is likely to prove galling and ineffectual.

A HANDBOOK OF REVISION

Sentences and Thinking, however, is not only a handbook of composition; it is equally a handbook of revision. Whereas Book I (Principles of Construction) provides a coherent treatment of the principles of sentence making, Book II (Principles of Revision) provides a comprehensive reference manual for the revision and rewriting of themes. Many errors have been discussed with the brevity that their simplicity or rareness calls for; but in all cases of special difficulty or importance we have given an amount of attention exceptional in a book of this kind. Frequently, at the end of the discussion, the student is referred to specific pages in the first book, where the error may be reviewed in its logical context and from the constructive point of view. Exercises have been included in Book II as well as in Book I, but while those in the first book are predominantly constructive, those in the second are

EFFECTIVENESS

52 Archaic and Obsolete	53 Idiom	54 Provincialisms	55 Vulgarisms	56 Improprieties	**DICTION**
57 Colloquialisms	58 Slang	59 Glossary	60 Exact Diction	61 Emphatic Diction	
62 Euphony	63 Triteness	64 Enlarging Vocabulary	65 Wordiness		
66 Sentence Unity	67 Coördination	68 Straggling Sentence	69 Subordination	70 Overlapping Dependence	**UNITY**
71 Choppy Sentences	72 Incomplete Thought	73 Incomplete Constructions	74 Incomplete Comparisons	75 Miscellaneous Omissions	
76 Suspense	77 Climax	78 Balance	79 Good Repetition	80 Bad Repetition	**EMPHASIS**
81 Subordination for Emphasis	82 Weak Passive	83 Absolute Phrases	84 Emphatic Word Order	85 Awkward Word Order	
86 Fine Writing	87 Variety				
88 Parallelism	89 "And Which"	90 Correlatives	91 Connectives	92 Coherence Logical Order	**CLEARNESS**
93 Position of Modifiers	94 Dangling Modifiers	95 Reference of Pronouns	96 Mixed Figures	97 Mixed Constructions	
98 Split Constructions	99 Point of View	100 Repetition for Clearness			

SENTENCES AND THINKING

A Handbook of Composition and Revision

BY

NORMAN FOERSTER

PROFESSOR OF ENGLISH, UNIVERSITY OF NORTH CAROLINA

AND

J. M. STEADMAN, Jr.

PROFESSOR OF ENGLISH, EMORY UNIVERSITY

HOUGHTON MIFFLIN COMPANY

BOSTON   NEW YORK   CHICAGO   SAN FRANCISCO

The Riverside Press Cambridge

Revised and Enlarged Edition

PE1413
.F6
1923

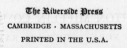

The Riverside Press

CAMBRIDGE · MASSACHUSETTS

PRINTED IN THE U.S.A.

PREFACE

revisory. In classifying the rules of the second book we have followed the valuable distinction between the permissible and the preferable, between "Correctness" and "Effectiveness," and each of these in turn is divided into four sections. Some of the sections under "Correctness," viz., Grammar, Punctuation, Mechanics, Spelling, may advisedly be assigned for study and recitation *before Book I is assigned*, in institutions where the students are markedly deficient in the rudiments of writing. With this object in view, we have given liberal space to grammar, a concealed ignorance of which is often accountable for what appear to be errors in composition.

The arrangement of the manual of errors, it will be noted, has been made the basis of the chart printed in the lining pages, which thus constitutes a logical index to this part of the book — or, rather, since cross reference links the two parts, to the entire book. By writing the numbers in the margin of the student's theme, the instructor will refer the student to a wealth of information, constructive as well as destructive, relating to his blunders and shortcomings. The completeness of this information will obviate a defect common in reference manuals — the annoyingly vague brevity of the discussion of an error to which the writer is repeatedly referred. While a bare statement, with an illustration or two, and perhaps a half dozen sentences for exercise in correction, may suffice for the best writers in a class, it will not serve for the deficient writers, who are likely to find such matter no more helpful when they are referred to it for the twentieth time than when they first consulted it. In the present text an important principle like subordination — the avoidance of the endless *and* — receives not only two pages in the manual of errors but also more than a dozen pages of doctrine and exercises in the constructive part of the book, which are made accessible by cross reference. It should be easy for the student to understand the nature of his mistakes and the means of revision; indeed, the book tells him as much as his instructor could tell him in personal conference. If he does not understand, the reason will ordinarily be a negligent haste, which may be remedied by the assignment of special exercises. We have provided a quantity of exercises sufficient to give the weak or negligent student frequent and varied practice.

The instructor should find it a very simple matter to get acquainted with the resources of the book. The chart provides a logical index for theme correction. The device of numbers superimposed on names, enabling the instructor to see the two as a single thing like a picture or Chinese symbol, will be found mnemonically useful. In addition to the chart there is another logical index, the analytical table of contents at the beginning of the book. There is also a full alphabetical index. We have aimed to make the book as convenient for the instructor as for the student, without distorting the truth in the interest of mechanical simplicity.

Cordial acknowledgments are due the many instructors, in colleges and universities in all sections of the country, who have generously contributed suggestions for the present completely revised and greatly enlarged edition of the book. All these suggestions have received grateful consideration. We are deeply indebted to Professor James Hinton, of Emory University; to Professor Harry W. Hastings, of New York State College for Teachers; to Professor Jacob Zeitlin, of the University of Illinois; and to Professor W. F. Thrall, of the University of North Carolina, who have read the entire manuscript of the new edition.

PREFACE

We desire also to thank Professor John A. Lester, of the Hill School, Pottstown, Pennsylvania, for the use of valuble matter on spelling, and Professor George Summey, Jr., of the Agricultural and Mechanical College of Texas, whose recent work on punctuation has become indispensable in any scientific consideration of this subject. Acknowledgments to various publishers have been made in the form of footnotes in the text.

CONTENTS

BOOK I: PRINCIPLES OF CONSTRUCTION

CHAPTER I. SENTENCES AND THINKING

Thought and Expression

Relation between the two 1–2
Organic and mechanic distinguished 2–3
Adequate paraphrase impossible 3–4
Adequate translation impossible 4
Style personal and not transferable 4
The sentence as an organic unit of thought 5–6
Matching the sentence to the thought 6–7
Style not only personal but human 7
Rhetoric concerned with human or universal expression . . 7–8

Subordination

Simple sentence 8
Compound sentence 9
Analogy of the living tree 10–11
Selection of the important thoughts 11–12
Expression of the subordinate thoughts 12
Table of connectives 13–15
Exercises 15–21

Parallelism

Logical sameness demands structural sameness . . 21–22
Sign of parallelism grammatical 22
Sign of parallelism the first word or phrase 23
Balance an extension of parallelism 23–24
Correlative conjunctions 24
Faulty and false parallelism 24–25
Exercises 25–30

Emphasis

Dependent on relative values 30–31
Italics 31
Improvement of the words 32
Making them stronger 32

CONTENTS

Making them more fresh 32
Making them more specific 32
Making them more concrete 33
Climax 33–34
Departure from the normal word order . . . 34–35
Important matter at the end of the sentence . . . 35
Pivotal words 35–37
Suspense 35–37
Periodic and loose sentence 37
Balance 38–40
Repetition 40–42
Repetition of pivotal words 40–41
Repetition not always desirable 42
Exercises 42–50

Variety
Result of the foregoing principles 51
No short cut possible 51–52
Exercise 52

Economy
Writing the transmission of thought 52–53
Tangled constructions 53–54
Mixed constructions 53–54
Misplaced modifiers 54
Mixed figures of speech 54–55
Unnecessary words 55–56
Unpleasant sounds 56–57
Exercises 57–60

Clearness
Blunders that beset even the clear thinker . . . 61
Reference
Reference of pronouns 61
Dangling participle 61–62
Dangling elliptical clause 62
Point of view
Change of subject 62
Logical agreement 63
Shift of tense 63–64
Transition 64
Three types of connectives 65
Clearness in diction
Ambiguous, vague, and obscure words 67

CONTENTS

Importance of a large vocabulary 68
Increasing the vocabulary 68–69
Exercises 70–76

CHAPTER II. SENTENCES, PARAGRAPHS, AND OUTLINES

The Summary Sentence
Summary sentence defined 77
Distinguished from the topic sentence 77
How to write a summary sentence 77–80

The Sentence in the Paragraph
Relation of sentence and paragraph 80–81
Topic sentence 81
Size of the paragraph 81–82
Five methods of development 82
Summary sentence 82–83
Transition 83

The Sentence in the Outline
Unity of the whole composition 83–84
Thesis sentence 84
How to write an outline in sentence form . . . 84–86
Exercises in summary sentence, paragraph, and outline . 86–87
Paragraphs for study 88–96

BOOK II: PRINCIPLES OF REVISION

CORRECTNESS: Grammar, Punctuation, Mechanics, Spelling

CHAPTER I. GRAMMAR

Introduction: Grammar and Composition
The function of grammar 97
Knowledge of grammar necessary to good composition . 97–98

1. Sentence Defined
Importance of knowing what a sentence is . . . 98–99
The sentence considered grammatically 99–100
Subject and predicate 99
Predication 99
Finite and non-finite verbs 99–100

xi

CONTENTS

Verbs and verbals distinguished 100
  Gerund 100
  Infinitive 100
  Participle 100
Phrase and clause distinguished from sentence . . . 101–03
  The phrase defined and distinguished from sentence . . 101
  The clause defined and distinguished from sentence . . 101
    Dependent clauses 102
    Independent clauses 102–03
Exercises:
A: Finding subject and predicate 103
B: (1) Phrase, dependent clause, and independent clause
    distinguished; parts of speech 104–05
  (2) Verbals distinguished from verbs 104–05
C: Simple, complex, and compound sentences 105

2. "Period Fault"
Definition and illustration 105
Types of "period fault"
  (a) Participial phrase mistaken for sentence 106
  (b) Appositive phrase mistaken for sentence 106
  (c) *That*-clause or infinitive phrase mistaken for sentence
                                      106–07
  (d) Subordinate clause mistaken for sentence . . 107
Exercise 107–08

3. "Comma Fault"
Definition and illustration 108–09
Methods of correction 109–10
  Substituting period for comma 109
  Other methods
    (1) Comma and coördinating of conjunction . . . 109
    (2) Semicolon without conjunction 109
    (3) Subordination 110
Differences between these methods of correction . . . 110
Exercise 110–11

4. Agreement
General rule for agreement 112
Agreement of subject and verb
  (a) Singular subject with plural modifier requires singular
    verb 112
  (b) Singular pronouns: *each, every, either,* etc., require
    singular verbs 112

CONTENTS

(c) Subject not changed in number when followed by *as well as*, *together with*, etc. 112

(d) Two or more subjects joined by *and* . . . 112–13

(e) Two or more singular subjects joined by *or, nor, and not,* or *but* 113

(f) Collective nouns 113

(g) Nouns plural in form but singular in number . . 113–14

(h) *It* and *there* as expletives 114

(i) Subject and predicate noun of different numbers . . 114

(j) Contracted verb forms 114

(k) Relative pronoun with plural antecedent . . 114

Agreement of Pronoun and Antecedent . . 115

(l) Singular pronouns must refer to singular antecedents: *each, every, either,* etc. 115

(m) Collective nouns may require either singular or plural pronoun 115

Exercise 116

5. Case

Definitions 116

Common errors in case

(a) Nominative case

(1) Nominative case of pronoun misused as object . 116

(2) Nominative case required after *than* or *as* in elliptical clauses 116–17

(b) Objective case

(1) Objective case wrongly used as predicate complement: *It is me* 117

(2) *Whoever, who,* etc., unaffected by preceding words 117

(3) Objective case wrongly used after prepositional phrases, *as to, in regard to,* governing a clause 117–18

(4) Objective case to be used as subject, object, or objective complement of infinitive . . 118

(c) Possessive case

Formation of possessive 118

Inflected possessive 118

Phrasal possessive 118

(d) Case of appositives 119

Exercise 119

6. Possessive with Gerund

Choice between possessive and objective . . . 119

Exercise 120

CONTENTS

7. Subjunctive Mode
Inflected and phrasal subjunctives 120
Uses of subjunctive
  (a) To express a wish or a regret 120
  (b) To indicate a strongly improbable condition or a pure
     supposition 120
  (c) To express a condition contrary to fact 121
Exercise 122

8. Tense
Tense forms and time of action 121–22
Uses of the several tenses
  (a) Present 122
  (b) Past 122
  (c) Future 123
  (d) Present perfect 123
  (e) Past perfect 123–24
  (f) Future perfect 124
  (g) Sequence of tenses 124
     Subordinate clauses 124
     Gnomic present 124
  (h) Tense of verbals
     (1) Perfect infinitive misused for present . . . 125
     (2) Present participle misused in expressing perfect
       or future time 125
  (i) Principal parts of verbs 125
Exercise 125

9. Shall and will
Development from independent verbs into auxiliaries of
  future; survival of original independent meanings . . 126
Development of meaning dependent upon person; different
  development in the different grammatical persons . . 127
Rules for the use of *shall* and *will*
  (a) Simple futurity 128
  (b) Determination, promise, etc. 128–29
  (c) Questions 129
  (d) Indirect discourse 130
  (e) *Should* and *would* 130–31
  (f) *Should* in all persons in subordinate clauses of con-
     tingency 131
Exercise 132

10. Essential and Non-essential Modifiers
  (a) Definition and illustration 132–33

CONTENTS

D. Other sentence elements
    (a) Title after a proper name 1
    (b) Explanatory dates and geographical names . 1
    (c) Suspended sentence elements 1
    (d) Strongly contrasted or transposed sentence
        elements 175–7

nnecessary Commas
General rule: No comma between closely related sentence
    elements 17
Unnecessary commas:
  (a) Comma between subject and verb or between verb and
    direct object 17
  (b) Comma after non-parenthetical introductory phrase . 177
  (c) Comma before first member of a series . . . 177
  (d) Comma after last member of a series . . . 177
  (e) Comma between intensive pronoun and antecedent . 177
  (f) Comma with essential modifier . . . 177
  (g) Comma before indirect quotation or a quoted title . 177
  (h) Comma between correlative conjunctions or between
    parts of a compound conjunction . . . 177
rcises
: General exercise in use of comma . . . 178–81
: Essential and non-essential modifiers 181

micolon
eneral rule 181
vo fundamental uses
Use I: Between independent clauses *not* joined by a simple
    conjunction the semicolon *must* be used . . 181
  (a) When no connective is used . . . 181
  (b) When an explanatory expression (*namely, for
    example, that is*, etc.), but no conjunction, is
    used 182
  (c) When a conjunctive adverb is used . 182
Use II: Between other sentence elements the semicolon
    may be used 182
    Choice between comma, semicolon, or period de-
    termined by considerations of
  (a) Rapidity of movement . . . 182–83
  (b) Emphasis 183
  (c) Clearness of word grouping . . . 183
    Compound sentences 183
    Complex sentences 184

(b) Tests 133–34
(c) Punctuation 134
Exercise 134–35

11. Adjective and Adverb
    Adjective, not adverb, after copulas 135–36
    Exercise 136

12 Conjunctions:
    Knowledge of different classes necessary to good writing
  (a) Coördinating conjunctions 137
  (b) Subordinating conjunctions 137–38
  (c) Conjunctive adverbs distinguished from pure conjunc-
    tions 138–39
      Exercise A: Practice in using conjunctions and con-
      junctive adverbs 140
  (d) Correlative conjunctions 140
  (e) Conjunctions and other parts of speech . . 140–41
      Exercise B: *Like, as,* and *as if* 141

13. Uses of *So*
  (a) Conjunctive adverbs distinguished from simple ad-
    verbs 141
  (b) Semicolon before *so* and other conjunctive adverbs . 142
  (c) *So* distinguished from *as . . . so* and *so . . . that* . 142
  (d) Compound sentence with conjunctive adverb unde-
    sirable 142
  (e) Misuse of *so* for *very, exceedingly*, etc. . 142
    Exercise 143

14. Classes of Pronouns
  (a) Classes of pronouns: 143–44
    (1) Personal, (2) Compound personal, (3) Relative,
    (4) Interrogative, (5) Demonstrative, (6) Indefinite,
    (7) Reciprocal
  (b) Syntactical uses 144
  (c) Common errors in the use of pronouns:
    (1) Lack of agreement with antecedent . . . 144
    (2) Reference 144
    (3) Confusion of personal and compound personal pro-
      nouns 144
    (4) *His, he,* and *him* improperly used for *one* and
      one's 144–45
    (5) *You* and *they* misused as indefinites . . . 145

CONTENTS

(6) *These*, *those*, and *it* used as indefinites . . . 145
(7) Confusion of the relatives *who*, *which*, and *that* . 145
Exercise 146

15. Clauses
  (a) Definitions and uses 146
  (b) Common errors
    (1) Subordinate clause used as sentence — "period fault" 146
    (2) Sentence used as noun clause 146
    (3) Two sentences written as one — "comma fault" . 147
    (4) Adverbial clause used as noun clause: *Reason is — because* 147
    (5) Overlapping dependence 147
    (6) Dangling elliptical clause 147
    (7) Misplaced clause 147
Exercises:
  A: Correcting errors in the use of clauses 147
  B: Composing sentences to illustrate the syntax of dependent clauses 147

16. Double Negative 148

17. Grammatical Terms
  Definitions and illustrations 148–61

CHAPTER II. PUNCTUATION

Introduction: The Purpose of Punctuation

  Punctuation organic, not mechanical 162
  Punctuation and grammar 162

18. Comma
  Distinction between one comma — to separate — and two commas — to group 162–63

19. One Comma to Separate
  I. The separative comma 163–69
    A. To prevent misreading by grouping words
    After preceding dependent clause 164–65
    Before the conjunction *for* 165
    B. To separate coördinate words, phrases, or clauses
      (a) Comma between members in a series
      When the members are not joined by a conjunction: *a, b, c* 165–66

xvi

When the last two m[...]
a, b, and c [...]
When all the memb[...]
junctions: *a, and b, a*[...]

  Note: Comma alwa[...]
  before "and Com[...]
  (b) To separate parts of a[...]
  Before *and* for clearne[...]
  Before *but, or, nor*, etc.[...]
  sis . . . . [...]
  (c) To separate indepen[...]
  simple conjunction[...]
  General rule . [...]
  Exception: short para[...]
  Comma before *but, n*[...]
  phasis . . . [...]
  Elliptical compound[...]
  (d) Comma with idioma[...]

20. Two Commas to Group
  II. Grouping, or enclosing, comma[...]
  Commas used *in pairs* with par[...]
  non-essential sentence elements[...]
    A. Independent parentheses[...]
      (a) Parenthetical sente[...]
      (b) Nominative absolu[...]
      (c) Direct address[...]
      (d) Interjections[...]
      (e) *Yes, no, indeed, s*[...]
      tence as a whole[...]
    B. Adverbial modifiers[...]
      (a) Introductory adv[...]
      predication: *indeed*[...]
      (b) Emphatic or summ[...]
      then, thus, therefor[...]
      (c) Non-essential adv[...]
    C. Adjective modifiers[...]
      (a) Non-essential adj[...]
      (b) Appositives[...]
      General rule[...]
      Exceptions .[...]
      Note: Punctu[...]
      such as, for e[...]

21. U[...]

E[...]

22. S[...]

xvii

CONTENTS

Misuse of semicolon
  General rule for avoiding misuse of semicolon . . . 184
  Special cases:
    (a) Between main clause and dependent clause . . 185
    (b) After salutations or before a direct quotation . . 185
  Exercise 185–86

23. Colon
  Uses of the colon:
    (a) Before a list, a formal appositive, or a formal or extended quotation 187
    (b) Between independent clauses when the second clause explains or amplifies the second 187
    (c) Before a direct quotation unaccompanied by a verb of saying 187–88
    (d) Miscellaneous uses 188
  Exercise 188–89

24. Period
    (a) After a declarative sentence 189–90
    (b) After abbreviations 190
  Exercises A and B: General exercises in punctuation . 190–92

25. Exclamation Point 192

26. Question Mark
    (a) After direct questions 193
    (b) After each element in compound question for separate emphasis 193
    (c) After doubtful words or facts 193
  Exercise 193–94

27. Dash
    (a) Before an interruption or a shift in construction . . 194
    (b) Before an emphatic or long parenthesis, or before a parenthesis with interior punctuation . . . 194
    (c) Before a summarizing expression or an emphatic appositive 194
    (d) Before any emphatic expression 195
    (e) The dash combined with other marks of punctuation 195
    (f) Misuse of the dash 195
  Exercise 195

CONTENTS

28. **Apostrophe**
  (a) To form the possessive of nouns 196
    (1) Nouns not ending in a sibilant sound . . . 196
    (2) Plural nouns ending in -*s* 196
    (3) Proper nouns ending in a sibilant sound . . 196
  (b) To mark omission of letters or figures . . . 196
  (c) To form the plural of letters, figures, etc. . . . 197
    Caution: No apostrophe in plural of nouns or posses-
      sive of pronouns 197
 Exercises
  A: Correction of errors in use of apostrophe 197
  B: Formation of possessive of proper names 197

29. **Parentheses and Brackets**
 Uses of parentheses
  (a) To enclose loosely attached, parenthetical expressions:
    choice between commas, dashes, curves, etc. . 197–98
  (b) To explain words or figures where accuracy is essential 198
  (c) To enclose figures of enumeration 198
  (d) Punctuation of parentheses 198–99
    Less than a complete sentence 198–99
    Complete sentences 199
 Uses of brackets
  (e) To mark an interpolation 199–200
  (f) To enclose a parenthesis within a parenthesis . . 200
 Exercise 200

30. **Dialogue and Quoted Matter**
  (a) Use of quotation marks
    (1) Before and after every direct quotation or part of a
      direct quotation 200–01
    (2) At the beginning of each paragraph, but at end of
      last paragraph only in extended quotations . 201
    (3) A quotation within a quotation . . . 201–02
  (b) Punctuation of direct quotations . . . . .
    (1) Quotation set off from accompanying verb of say-
      ing by comma or colon 202
    (2) Independent clauses not to be separated by comma
      without conjunction 202
    (3) Relative position of quotation marks and other
      marks of punctuation 200–03
  (c) Paragraphing of dialogue 203–04
 Exercise 204–05

CONTENTS

CHAPTER III. MECHANICS

31. Italics and Quotation Marks
    Uses of italics
      (a) To mark foreign words 206
      (b) To refer to a word or a letter as such 206
      (c) To emphasize a word 206
      (d) To mark the word *Resolved* in formal resolutions . 206
      (e) To indicate quoted titles of books, newspapers, magazines, etc. 206–07
    Uses of quotation marks
      (f) To mark a technical, ironical, or slang expression . 207
      (g) To define or translate a word 207
      (h) To indicate quoted titles of short poems, stories, essays, etc. 207
      (i) To enclose a direct quotation 207
      (j) To mark dialogue 208
    Exercise 208

32. Quoted Titles
      (a) Capitalization 209
      (b) Use of quotation marks 209
      (c) Use of italics 209
      (d) Articles in the title 209
    Exercise 209–10

33. Hyphen
      (a) To indicate syllable division 210
      (b) To separate parts of compound words 210

34. Syllabication
      (a) Hyphen always at end of line 210
      (b) Monosyllables not divided 210
      (c) Single letter not written as separate syllable . . 210–11
      (d) All syllables should be pronounceable 211
      (e) Single consonant between vowels stands in following syllable 211
      (f) Two consonants or double consonant usually divided . 211
      (g) Three consonants divided according to pronunciation groups 211
      (h) Compounds divided between component elements . . 211
      (i) Prefixes and suffixes as separate syllables . . . 211
    Exercise 211

CONTENTS

35. Capitals
Two fundamental uses:
   (1) To mark a new unit of thought 212
   (2) To designate proper nouns and adjectives . . . 212
Capitals to mark a new unit of thought or line of poetry
   (a) First word of every sentence, direct quotation, formal
      resolution 212
   (b) First word of every line of poetry 212
Capitals to designate proper nouns and adjectives
   (a) Proper nouns and adjectives 212
   (b) Words referring to God, Christ, the Trinity, etc. . 213
   (c) Titles of honor 213–14
   (d) Important words in quoted titles 214
Miscellaneous uses of capitals
   (a) I, O, A.D., etc. 214
   (b) Personified abstractions 214
   (c) *Whereas* and *Resolved* 214
Misuse of capitals
   (a) For emphasis 214
   (b) Names of seasons 214
   (c) *North, east, south, west,* etc. 214
   (d) Names of studies 214
   (e) Fragments of direct quotations 214
   (f) After a semicolon 214
   (g) Proper nouns that have become common nouns . . 214
Exercise 214

36. Abbreviations
   (a) (1) Titles: Mr., Rev., D.D.; and A.D., No., etc. . . 215
      (2) I.e., etc., e.g., viz. 215
   (b) Period with abbreviations 215
   (c) Improper abbreviations 215
   (d) Contractions to be avoided 215
Exercise 215–16

37. Representation of Numbers
   (a) Some numbers not to be spelled out 216
   (b) Some numbers to be spelled out 216
   (c) Sentence not to begin with figures 216
   (d) Omission of "and" in compound numbers . . . 216
   (e) Numbers usually not to be repeated in parenthesis . 216
   (f) Comma to group numbers 217
   (g) Hyphen in compound numbers below one hundred . 217
Exercise 217

CONTENTS

38. Manuscript Form
    (a) Legibility 217–18
    (b) Paging 218
    (c) Spacing 218
    (d) Indention 218
    (e) Erasures and corrections 218
    (f) Footnotes 218–19
    (g) Endorsement of theme 219
    (h) Correct form of title of theme 219–20
    (i) Writing verse 220–21

39. Punctuation Marks at Beginning of Line 221

40. Paragraphing 221

41. Outlining 221–22

CHAPTER IV. SPELLING

Introduction: Recording Errors 223–24

42. Pronunciation and Spelling
    List of words often mispronounced and misspelled . . 224
    Exercise 224

43. Confusion of Similar Forms or Sounds
    Groups of words commonly confused in spelling . . 225
    Exercise 225

44. Etymological Kinship
    Derivatives from the same root 226
    Prefixes likely to be confused 226
    Exercises:
    A: Derivatives from common Latin roots . . . 226–27
    B: Common prefixes 227
    C: Derivatives of English roots 227

45. *Ei* and *Ie*
    Rules for spelling 227
    Lists of common words with *ei* or *ie* 227–28
    Exercise 228

46. Doubling a Final Consonant
    Rules 228
    Examples 228–29

CONTENTS

Exercises:
A: Spelling the present participle of verb **229**
B: Spelling the present indicative third person singular . **229**

47. Dropping Final -*E*
General Rule **229**
Exceptions **230**
Exercise **230–31**

48. Final -*Y*
Consonant preceding -*y* **231**
Vowel preceding -*y* **231**
Exercise **231**

49. Plurals
(a) Plurals in -*s* or -*es* **232**
(b) Plurals of words ending in -*y* **232**
(c) Plurals of words ending in -*o* **232**
(d) Irregular plurals **232**
(e) Plurals of foreign words **232–33**
(f) Plurals of compound nouns **233**
(g) Plurals of letters, figures, signs **233**
Exercises:
A: Formation of plural from singular **233**
B: Formation of singular from plural **233**

50. Compound Words
General rule for use of hyphen **233–34**
Specific rules for use of hyphen **234–35**
(a) *Self, fellow*, etc., + another word **234**
(b) Preposition phrase forming a compound noun . **234**
(c) Two words preceding noun and used as single adjective **234**
(d) Compound numerals below a hundred . . . **234**
(e) Words that may be misread: *re-creation, recreation* . **234**
(f) *All* + another word **235**
Classes of words written solid
(a) Compound nouns composed of two other nouns . . **235**
    Real compounds: write solid **235**
    First word an adjective: write separately . . **235**
(b) Compounds of *any, every, no, some* + *body, thing, where,* etc. **235**
(c) Compound personal pronouns **235**
(d) Root + prefix or suffix: *ahead, kingdom* . . . **235**
(e) Derivative, or compound, prepositions . . . **235**

xxiv

CONTENTS

Lists of words written separately 235
List of words written solid or with hyphen 235–36
Exercise 236

51. Spelling List
A list of 400 words commonly misspelled 236–42

EFFECTIVENESS: Diction, Unity, Emphasis, Clearness

CHAPTER V. DICTION

Introduction: The Importance of Diction

Choice of words an index to personality 243–44
Choice of words determines personality 244
Diction concerned with correctness and effectiveness . . 244

CORRECT ENGLISH GOOD USE

Good Use defined 244–45
Good Use must be present, national, and reputable . . 245

Present Use

52. Archaic and Obsolete Words 245

National Use

53. Idiom 246

54. Provincialisms and Technical Words 246–47

Reputable Use

55. Vulgarisms, or Barbarisms 248

56. Improprieties
(a) Improprieties in meaning 248
(b) Improprieties in function 248–49

57. Colloquialisms 249

58. Slang
Term vaguely used 250
A definition of slang 250
Origin of slang 250–51

CONTENTS

Attitude towards slang determined by its characteristics . 251
The case against slang 251–52
Good Use a relative term 252
Exercises:
A: Idiom 253
B: Idiom 253
C: Collection of provincialisms 253
D: Correction of provincialisms 253
E: Vulgarisms and improprieties corrected . . . 253–54
F: Correct use of commonly misused words 254
G: Lists of vigorous and of objectionable slang . . . 254
H: Colloquialisms 254
I: Connotation 254

59. Glossary of Faulty Expression
A workable alphabetical list of words often misused . 255–69

EFFECTIVE DICTION

60. Exact Diction 269

61. Emphatic Diction 270

62. Euphony 270

63. Triteness
Definition 270
Illustrative list 270–71
Exercises:
A: Collection of trite expressions from reading . . 271
B: Collection of trite expressions from students' themes . 271
C: Detection and correction of trite expressions . . 271

64. Enlarging the Vocabulary 271

65. Wordiness
(a) Redundancy 271
(b) Tautology 271–72
(c) Verbosity 272

CHAPTER VI. UNITY

66. Sentence Unity
Logical and grammatical unity 273
Tests of sentence unity
I. Undercompleteness 273

xxvi

CONTENTS

II. Overcompleteness 273–74
Remedy for lack of unity 274
Exercise 274–75

67. **Coördination**
    (a) Excessive coördination 275
    (b) Illogical or obscure coördination 275
    (c) False coördination 276

68. **Straggling Compound Sentences** 276–77

69. **Subordination**
    (a) False subordination 277
    (b) Upside-down subordination 278
    (c) Faulty subordination — using the wrong connective 278–79
    (d) Overlapping subordination 279

70. **Overlapping Dependence** 279
Exercise 279–80

71. **Choppy Sentences** 280
Exercise 280–81

72. **Incomplete Thought** 281
Exercise 281–82

73. **Incomplete Constructions** 282
Exercise 282–83

74. **Comparisons Incomplete or Illogical**
    (a) Omission of *than* or *as* in double comparisons . . . 283
    (b) Omission of standard of comparison 283
    (c) Omission of one term of comparison 284
    (d) Comparison of things inconsistent or incapable of comparison 284
    (e) Careless use of *than any other, than any of, of all, all other,* etc. 284
    (f) Use of noun as both singular and plural . . . 284
    (g) Use of comparative for more than two or of superlative for less than two 284–85
Exercise 285

75. **Omissions — Miscellaneous**
    (a) Omission of part of a verb phrase 285

CONTENTS

(b) Omission of *to be* when used as both principal and auxiliary verb 285

(c) Omission of verb in a sentence containing a singular and a plural subject 286

(d) Omission of article, pronoun, subordinating conjunction, etc. 286

(e) Omission of preposition necessary to grammatical completeness 286–87

(f) Omission of article in literary titles 287

(g) Omission of *than* or *as* in comparisons 287

(h) General omission of words essential to logical agreement of sentence 287

Exercise 287–88

CHAPTER VII.   EMPHASIS

76. Suspense 289

Exercise 289

77. Climax 290

Exercise 290

78. Balance 290

79. Repetition — Good 290

80. Repetition — Bad

(a) Monotonous repetition of same word or phrase . . 291

(b) Repetition of conjunction *that* 291

(c) Repetition of same or of similar sounds 291

(d) Repetition of same idea 291

(e) Monotonous sentence structure 292

Caution: real and artificial variety 292

Exercise 292

81. Subordination for Emphasis 292–93

82. Weak Passive Voice 293–94

Exercise 294

83. Absolute Phrases .

(a) Phrases containing a perfect participle or a personal pronoun 294

(b) Absolute phrase at end of sentence awkward and weak . 295

(c) Punctuation of absolute phrases 295

CONTENTS

84. **Emphatic Word Order** 295

85. **Awkward Word Order**
    (a) Faulty arrangement of words 295
    (b) Omissions of words necessary to smoothness or clearness
        of expression 295
    (c) Repetition of the same words, constructions, or sounds . 295
    (d) Clumsy grammatical constructions
        (1) Absolute construction 296
        (2) "Thus causing" participle 296
        (3) Passive voice 296
        (4) Suspended preposition 296
        (5) *There* as expletive 296
        (6) Split constructions 296
  Exercise 296

86. **Fine or Overcareful Writing** 297

87. **Variety** 297–98

CHAPTER VIII.   CLEARNESS

88. **Parallelism** 299

89. **"And Which"** 299
  Exercise 300

90. **Correlatives** 300

91. **Connectives and Transition** 300–01

92. **Coherence and Logical Order**
    (a) Logical sequence of ideas 301
    (b) Completeness of thought 301
    (c) Logical word order 301–02
    (d) Logical agreements of parts of sentence . . . 302
  Exercise 302

93. **Position of Modifiers**
    (a) "Squinting," or "cross-eyed," modifiers . . . 303
    (b) Misplaced relative clauses 304
    (c) *However, therefore, thus,* etc. 304
    (d) Other sentence elements 304–05
  Exercise 305

CONTENTS

94. Dangling Modifiers: Elliptical Clause, Gerund, Participle
    (a) Dangling participles or gerunds 305–06
    (b) Dangling elliptical clauses 306–07

95. Reference of Pronouns
    (a) Double reference 307
    (b) Vague reference of *this, that, which*, etc. 308
    (c) Reference to unexpressed antecedent 309
    (d) Reference to inconspicuous or parenthetical antecedent . 309
    (e) *Same* or *said* misused for *it, this, that, the above-mentioned* 310
    (f) Inconsistency or shift in number between pronoun and
       antecedent 310

96. Mixed Figures 310
    Exercise 310

97. Mixed Constructions 311
    Exercise 311

98. Split Constructions
    (a) Split infinitive 312
    (b) Separation of subject and verb, verb and object, preposi-
       tion and object 312
    (c) Separation of parts of a verb phrase 312
    Exercise 312–13

99. Point of View
    (a) Shift in subject, voice or mood 313
    (b) Shift in tense 313
    (c) Shift from formal to colloquial style 313
    (d) Shift from indirect to direct discourse 313–14
    (e) Shift in number, person, or class of pronouns . . . 314

100. Repetition for Clearness 314
    Exercise 314–15

INDEX 317

SENTENCES AND THINKING

A Handbook of Composition and Revision

For a man to write well, there are required three necessaries: to read the best authors, observe the best speakers, and much exercise of his own style. — JONSON

There is no way of writing well and also of writing easily. — TROLLOPE

To write well a man should have a natural facility and an acquired difficulty. — JOUBERT

When you can with difficulty say anything clearly, simply, and emphatically, then, provided that the difficulty is not apparent to the reader, that is style. When you can do it easily, that is genius. — LORD DUNSANY

Practice is nine-tenths. — EMERSON

SENTENCES AND THINKING

∴

BOOK I: PRINCIPLES OF CONSTRUCTION

CHAPTER I

SENTENCES AND THINKING

Lay hold of the subject, and the words will follow. — CATO

The style of an author is the true image of his mind. He who would write clearly ought first to think clearly, and whoever would have a grand style must first have a grand character. — GOETHE

The difficulty of literature is not to write, but to write what you mean; not to affect your reader, but to affect him precisely as you wish. — STEVENSON

Thought and speech are inseparable from each other. Matter and expression are parts of one: style is a thinking out into language. — NEWMAN

To finish and complete your thought! — how long it takes, how rare it is, what an immense delight! . . . As soon as a thought has reached its full perfection, the word springs into being, offers itself, and clothes the thought. — JOUBERT

THOUGHT AND EXPRESSION

OUR problem may be stated very simply: given, a thought or feeling; required, words that will express this thought or feeling and convey it to the reader unchanged. The solution may be stated just as simply: the words required for the expression of the thought or feeling are the words inherent in the thought or feeling itself. They are not cunningly devised by the writer, invented and arranged by him with a view to impressing the reader; he does nothing but find them. They were there in his mind the moment that he experienced the thought, and his task is merely to hold the thought firm before his mind's eye till the words spontaneously flash into being. When the words thus reveal themselves, he says, "That's what I mean," and writes it. He has expressed himself, embodied his thought in words, made it visible and comprehensible by all men.

Expression, in other words, should be organic, not mechanic. "The form is mechanic," says Coleridge, "when on any given material we impress a predetermined form" — as when the gardener trims a cedar tree in order to force it into the unnatural form of a pyramid. "The organic form, on the other hand, is innate; it shapes, as it develops itself from within, and the fulness of its development is one and the same with the perfection of its outward form. Such as the life is, such is the form. Nature, the prime genial artist, inexhaustible in diverse powers, is equally inexhaustible in forms; each exterior is the physiognomy of the being within, — its true image." The tree as Nature makes it, the cedar, the pine, the oak, the willow, assumes its proper shape as it develops itself from within. The mature tree, in all its beauty, is already implicit in the seed — in the acorn resides all the grandeur of the oak. The kernel idea attains its necessary expression in the mature organism.

It is the same when the artist is not Nature but man. Shakspere in *Macbeth*, Keats in his sonnet "On First Looking into Chapman's Homer," Lincoln in his "Gettysburg Address," did not plan their compositions with rule and compass and cleverly arrange fine words, — did not work mechanically, — but, having a given idea to express, they allowed it to grow from within, nourishing it with a mental and spiritual attention, till it was ready to issue as a work of art. Since they worked organically, the resulting form

2

became the only possible form for the particular thought
that they had: "Such as the life is, such is the form." Assuming that they completely expressed what they meant to
express, we may say that they could not alter, and that we
could not alter, a single word without expressing something
else. Strictly speaking, the only way of explaining what a
literary composition contains is to repeat it word for word;
the poem, the address, means what it says, and nothing
else. This is equally true of the whole and of every part.
We cannot adequately paraphrase a single line, give its
meaning in other words than the author employed. Does
Shakspere's line

> To be or not to be, that is the question,

mean exactly the same thing as

> To exist or not to exist — which is preferable?

or

> Shall I end my life?

or

> Shall I commit suicide?

Does the first of these mean no more than the last — does it
not, for one thing, contain more feeling? Again, to take
another example, does Pope's line

> Hope springs eternal in the human breast,

contain the very same thought as

> Hope is deeply rooted in man,

or

> Man is never without hope,

or

> Men are always hopeful,

or

> People never stop hoping?

No doubt the meanings are closely similar; but they are not identical, and could not be unless the words were identical. There are not various ways of saying the same thing. And what is true of paraphrase, is true of translation. Speaking of foreign classics, Thoreau says that he must read them in the original because there are no translations. There are so-called "translations," to be sure, but on account of the organic unity of thought and expression, they necessarily fail to reproduce exactly the author's meaning. The only way to read Homer is to read Homer, not Pope's translation, or Bryant's, or any other. For a good book, as Milton says, is "the precious life-blood of a master-spirit," to be known only by direct communion.

As it is impossible to paraphrase, as it is impossible to translate, so, once more, it is impossible to reproduce an author's style. "Style," it has often been said, "is the man himself." By this is usually meant that each man's manner of expression is a reflection of his individuality, of that in him which renders him different from all other men, and which renders him inimitable. The only way to write like Addison, or Burke, or Carlyle, is to be Addison, or Burke, or Carlyle. Within certain important limits, which we shall consider presently, each writer must achieve his own personal manner of expression, his own style, reflecting his personal mode of thought and feeling. He does not think and feel precisely like any other man, and consequently he should not write precisely like any other man. He should be original in the right sense of the word, obedient to his vision of truth and beauty, never in the false sense of posing for what he is not, cultivating a superficial oddity.

Thought and expression, then, are merely two aspects of the same thing, whether we refer to the whole poem, short story, or expository article, or to the individual sentences that compose it. *Sentences and Thinking,* the title of this little book, is intended to suggest this organic nature of the sentence.

What is a sentence? It is *a group of words expressing a complete thought or feeling.*[1] It must express *a* thought, *one* thought, not part of a thought, nor more than a thought. Thus, when a student wrote:

> Observing and obeying his laws.

— he wrote as a sentence what is obviously only part of a thought. It should have been joined with the rest of his thought:

> Milton believed that man should be humble, obedient, and thankful toward God, observing and obeying his laws.

That is a complete, if rather ill expressed, thought. Again, when another student wrote:

> At last, on the 4th of August, England declared war on Germany, where I spent six weeks some years ago.

— he wrote as a sentence what is plainly more than a complete thought. "Where I spent six weeks some years ago" is an irrelevant addition to the thought and should be struck out or included where it does fit. Similarly, when a student wrote:

> I know that he will do it, in all these years he has never broken a definite promise.

— he wrote as a sentence what is really two sentences:

> I know that he will do it. In all these years he has never broken a definite promise.

[1] Thought and feeling are, indeed, extremely hard to distinguish, as is indicated by the Latin verb *sentire,* which means both "to think" and "to feel," and from which we derive our word *sentence.*

SENTENCES AND THINKING

The fundamental requirement of the sentence is that it express one complete thought, neither more nor less; or, as the grammarians say, it must have unity.

Remembering, then, that a sentence must contain but one complete thought, we constantly face the perplexing question: precisely what group of words will *express* this thought? Only the writer can answer with certainty, and he only when he has fully mastered his thought. Even the best writers are inclined to set down groups of words before they have mastered their thought, so that their expression is more or less distorted, does not quite faithfully reflect their thought; and inferior writers are almost steadily satisfied with words that will "do" — words that roughly represent the thought or perhaps merely hint at it. When we read a sentence that is vague and feeble, we may safely assume that the writer's thought was vague and feeble. When we read a sentence that is clear and strong, we may be sure that the writer's thought was clear and strong. "A sentence should read as if the author, had he held a plough instead of a pen, could have drawn a furrow deep and straight to the end." It will not do to excuse oneself by saying that one has a thought but cannot express it; if one really *has* it, possesses it, one can express it readily enough, since it will virtually express itself. When a sentence imperfectly represents a writer's intention, the thing to do is either to rewrite it entirely, seeking afresh the group of words that matches the thought, or to revise it, altering the words or their arrangement until the result is a fully expressed thought. In either case, success depends upon one's ability to recollect the thought, or to perceive it even more vividly than at first. The student who will exert himself to rewrite or revise in this spirit need never humiliate himself by confessing that he does not know what he means.

THOUGHT AND EXPRESSION

To write expressive sentences, therefore, we are to lean on the thought, deriving from it the power of utterance. The sentence is an organism, of which the soul is the thought, and the body the words. It is an embodied thought.

Yet it would be fatal for the student of composition to assume, from the foregoing explanation of the organic nature of the sentence, that all the rules of syntax and rhetoric are superfluous, that all he needs to do is to contemplate his thoughts and depend upon them for the sentences that will convey them to other men. For, after all, the sentence organism has certain definite laws that may be learned and applied. While it is true that the thought determines the expression, that *my* thought requires *my* expression, it is also true, happily, that in the main all men think alike. Style, as we have said, is the man; but style is also Man. We are all individuals, but individuals of the same species. Broadly speaking, our thoughts are those of all other men; if they were not, other men could not understand us. Even more, no doubt, our *ways* of thinking, the logical modes in which our minds work, are human rather than personal. And while the personal element in expression may safely be trusted to take care of itself, this impersonal element requires of us a severe discipline. We have a choice, indeed, between two disciplines. We may make our writing human rather than merely individual, in the first place, as many of the great writers have done, by reading widely and intensively in the work of the masters of English prose, familiarizing ourselves with the modes of expression of successful craftsmen like Addison and Burke and Carlyle and the leading writers of our own time, till at last we attain an intimate sense of the principles of expression and find ourselves, unconsciously perhaps, applying these principles in our own writing. There is no better, or more delightful, way of learning to write than this; but it demands a vast amount of reading. Most of us will prefer to combine this method with the second discipline. That is, we shall read as much as our time permits, and seek our main discipline in the study and practice of rhetoric. The technique of writing as expounded by the grammarians and rhetoricians is not an arbitrary statement of opinion, but, far otherwise, a codification of the habitual usage of the best writers. Rhetoric aims to formulate the universally valid principles of expression, to tell how it is in the nature of the human mind to express itself in language. As the natural sciences seek to define the laws of physical nature, so rhetoric seeks to define the laws of expression in relation to thought.

In the following pages, it will be our task to study and apply some of the most important of these laws; and first, the law of subordination.

SUBORDINATION

A SENTENCE, we have seen, is a group of words expressing a complete thought. A complete thought may contain any number of constituent thoughts.

When a sentence contains only one thought, it is a *simple sentence;* for example:

The man stands in the doorway.

We usually think, so to speak, in simple sentences, — our thoughts coming, not in bundles, but successively and singly. The following might represent a train of thought:

The man stands in the doorway. He is tall. Perhaps the doorway is low. His figure is shadowy. His clothes are dark. The house is dark within. One cannot distinguish the man's features.

SUBORDINATION

Obviously, that would be a hopelessly monotonous and ineffective way of expressing oneself on paper, no matter how accurately it represents our effortless, undirected thinking. The first step that one naturally takes in endeavoring to avoid this jerky, incoherent manner of writing is the binding together of closely related ideas, tying them in bundles. So one writes:

> The man is tall, or else the doorway is low. His clothes are dark, and the house is dark within. Etc.

In each of these two sentences, we have united two ideas by using a coördinating conjunction that expresses the relation of the constituent thoughts to each other, — *or* expressing alternation, *and* addition. The result in each case is a *compound sentence:* it presents a complete thought composed of two independent constituent thoughts.

Frequently, — in telling a story, for instance, — we express our thoughts in the form of compound sentences containing a large number of constituent thoughts. Thus:

> The street was bare, and not a soul was visible, and the horse and buggy went crashing on, and then we saw a child just round the curve. It seemed doomed, and we were frantic with horror, but suddenly we saw a man in a dark doorway, but we didn't recognize him, and he blocked the way, and he turned out to be our friend Martin.

Here are two compound sentences, one containing four, the other six, constituent thoughts. Each is a correct sentence, because the result in each case is one complete thought — first, the runaway horse was about to crush to death a child, and second, the child was unexpectedly saved by our friend Martin. But although these compound sentences are correct, they are only a little less monotonous and ineffective than that insufferable string of brief simple sentences with which we began.

Why is this so? We have bound our thoughts in bundles, so that they might be regarded as orderly groups, but the result is still crude. What more can be done?

The difficulty is that our bundles are like piles of logs of the same girth, neatly placed side by side and on top of each other, and capable of the addition of as many more of the same size as one cares to put on the pile. Adding a few logs to our second pile, we get this result:

> *It stood there looking at a bright pebble*, and *it didn't move at all*, and *it seemed doomed*, and *we were filled with horror*, and *some of us turned pale as death*, but *suddenly we saw a man in a dark doorway*, but *he had doubtless been there right along*, but *we hadn't noticed him before*, and *he came out like a flash*, and *he blocked the way*, and *it was Martin*. (The principal clauses have been italicized.)

Now, we do not want piles of dead logs, but living trees. Our sentences should not be built mechanically; they should grow, as organisms grow. The tree might well be taken as the symbol of a skillfully constructed sentence.

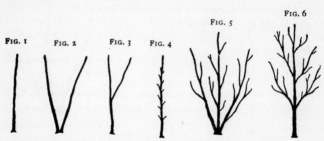

FIG. 1   FIG. 2   FIG. 3   FIG. 4   FIG. 5   FIG. 6

FIGURE 1.   THE SIMPLE SENTENCE, RUDIMENTARY FORM
FIGURE 2.   THE COMPOUND SENTENCE, RUDIMENTARY FORM
FIGURE 3.   THE COMPLEX SENTENCE, RUDIMENTARY FORM
FIGURE 4.   THE SIMPLE SENTENCE HIGHLY DEVELOPED
FIGURE 5.   THE COMPOUND SENTENCE HIGHLY DEVELOPED
FIGURE 6.   THE COMPLEX SENTENCE HIGHLY DEVELOPED

SUBORDINATION

A sentence may contain, like the sentence above, many constituent thoughts, but of these thoughts perhaps one will stand out as the main thought (the trunk), which divides into several subordinate thoughts (large branches), which again divide into subordinate thoughts (small branches), etc. Our sentence, if rewritten on this principle, might read as follows:

> Standing there looking at a pebble, quite motionless, and apparently doomed, *the child filled us with* such *horror* that some of us turned pale as death; but *suddenly we saw a man in a dark doorway*, whom we hadn't noticed before (though he had doubtless been there right along) and who, coming out like a flash, blocked the way — *it was Martin!* (The principal clauses have been italicized.)

Here instead of eleven independent thoughts, we have three:

(1) The child filled us with horror.
(2) Suddenly we saw a man in a dark doorway.
(3) It was Martin.

All of the other thoughts are subordinate:

to (1): (*a*) Standing there looking at a pebble.
(*b*) Quite motionless.
(*c*) Apparently doomed.
(*d*) Such that some of us turned pale as death.

to (2): (*a*) Whom we hadn't noticed before.
(*b*) Though he had doubtless been there right along.
(*c*) Coming out like a flash.
(*d*) Who blocked the way.

to (3): None.

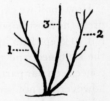

FIGURE 7. REPRESENTS THE STRUCTURE OF THE SENTENCE ABOVE

In general, the skillful writer is he who composes his sentences so that they abound in subordination, — in dependent constituent thoughts, — who in each group of thoughts infallibly picks out the most important for expression in the main clause or clauses and puts the subordinate thoughts in subordinate clauses and phrases.

How shall we find the important thoughts? This question confronts even the most experienced writer. We have, let us say, a thought to express that is composed of a number of constituent thoughts; we are aware of the fact that some are more important than others — that is almost bound to be the case; but how shall we find the chief among them, the trunk? There are but two methods: first, we may experiment, by writing our thoughts in various ways, till we succeed in putting emphasis on the chief among them (when the sentence perfectly expresses our thought we may be quite certain that the emphasis is properly distributed); or, second, we may reflect, i.e., experiment mentally, reviewing the constituent parts of the whole thought until we see them so clearly that the subordinate ideas fall into the background and the most important idea or ideas stand forth luminously.

How shall we express the subordinate thoughts? To express the most important thoughts is fairly easy — we have but to keep them in the foreground of the mind as we write the sentence, and they will find expression without much concern on our part. To express the subordinate thoughts, however, is not so easy. They are not so vivid in our minds, — they are remote and blurred, like the background of a landscape, — and they demand skill in phrasing on account of the large number of relationships that may exist between a subordinate clause and a principal clause, — time, condition, cause, purpose, result, concession, relativity, comparison, means, reference, consecutiveness, correlation, adversity, — relations that are to be expressed by the appropriate connective or by the use of a special construction. If, for example, the relation be condition, we might combine these two thoughts —

>It rains
>I will not go

— either by the use of a connective:

>If it rains, I will not go;

or by the use of a special construction:

>Should it rain, I would not go.

Fortunately, the English language is rich in connectives that express the various logical relationships. When there are a half dozen connectives for us to choose among, we ought to be able to recall one immediately, and to recall the most suitable one after a little reflection. Most people have only a handful of connectives at their command, but their poverty is not due to that of the English language. Following is a table that includes some of the most useful connectives:

CONDITION
>if
>in case that
>provided that
>unless

TIME
>when
>before
>after
>while
>since
>till
>until
>as

13

whenever
as long as
as often as
as soon as

PLACE

where
wherever
whence
whither

CONCESSION

though
although
while
even if
in spite of
notwithstanding

CAUSE

since
as
because
inasmuch as
in that
now that

PURPOSE

that
so that
in order that
for the purpose of
with a view to

RESULT

that
so that
but that
so..........that
such..........that

COMPARISON

than
as..........as
so..........as

SUBORDINATION

MANNER

     as
     as if
     as though

RELATION

     as
     who
     which
     what
     that
     whoever
     whichever
     whatever

Exercise 1, Subordination. Subordinate one statement to the other in as many ways as possible:

1. I saw her.
   I waved my handkerchief.
2. I completed the task.
   I went to bed.
3. I worked most of the night.
   I was sleepy the next day.
4. Theodore Roosevelt was a New Yorker.
   He was clearly one of our greatest Presidents.
5. Everybody knows that Becky Sharp is a character in *Vanity Fair*.
   This novel was written by Thackeray.
6. I have never seen a famous oil painting.
   I live in a remote part of the mountains.
7. The water of the town is very pure.
   It comes from natural mountain springs.
8. The mining camp was ten miles away.
   He had come from the camp that morning.
9. King Alfred was the most important political figure of the Old English period.
   He was also a patron of literature.
10. We arrived at the camp early in the spring.
    We wanted to choose the best site for our cabin.

15

11. English shows in its vocabulary and phraseology a very strong influence of the Bible.

    It shows a greater influence of the Bible than does any other great European language.

Exercise 2, Subordination. Write a list of the phrases and clauses in a given selection that indicate (1) Condition, (2) Time, (3) Place, (4) Concession, (5) Cause, (6) Purpose, (7) Result, (8) Comparison, (9) Manner, and (10) Relation.

Exercise 3, Subordination. Rewrite the following sentences in such a manner as to express the leading thoughts in independent clauses and the subordinate thoughts in subordinate clauses or other subordinate constructions. Remember that the substitution of conjunctive adverbs for coördinating conjunctions will not subordinate one clause to the other (see pp. 138–139).

1. He was an inventor and as such he proved very successful.
2. It was a pretty place, and so we thought we would camp there.
3. Holt is more energetic as well as abler than the other men, and he may be counted on to succeed.
4. We walked about three miles east, and there we found we had come to the end of the path; a steep hill rose up in front of us.
5. Some think that the man who reads the most books and remembers the most facts is the best educated man, but this is true only for the ones who intend to teach; they alone are educated in their kind of work.
6. The coal is brought in wagons, and it is afterwards shoveled into baskets, and it is then carried into the cellar.
7. I came to college with no idea of what I should do, but since I entered, I have decided to practice law, and next year I shall go to a law school and shall prepare myself for my profession.
8. This town got its name from Captain John Smith and is more than one hundred years old, but the inhabitants number only about eighteen hundred.

9. It had rained all the morning and it was raining harder that afternoon, and we decided not to go on the camping trip.

10. The next year I attended school at Jameson and was very successful in all my work but Latin, and I dropped it.

11. Statestown has a great many stores, and all of them do good business.

12. After I entered college, it was two days before classes started; so I didn't know how to pass the time, but it did not take me long to get acquainted with the boys, and after the first few days I began to enjoy my college life.

13. Our town has a good government, and it hardly needs the jail, but there is a small one.

14. We were riding along laughing and talking, and all at once a tire blew out, but we had all the tools with us and it did not take us long to repair it.

15. He was quite different from his companions, and it turned out that he was a nobleman, but he had suffered a great misfortune and had been driven into the army.

16. In the schools of France the ideal of writing well is constantly held before the pupil, and this is the case in both the lower and the higher classes, and so the pupil takes pride in writing well, but in America we have no such tradition, and this is one reason why the American college freshman writes badly.

17. He walked about an hour and then reached Blueville; this is a little village eight miles from Cordon.

18. She became uneasy, and was afraid that something had befallen him, and she wanted to go in search, but had been told never to go further than that sign, and so she had to wait.

19. As boys we had been even intimate associates, but I really knew very little of my friend; his reserve had always been excessive and habitual; and so I was not able to determine beforehand what his actions would be.

20. We were walking along the road, which was very hot and dusty, and we were talking about things in general and we were not expecting anything unusual to happen, but we were surprised at the strange sight that met our eyes when we turned a bend in the road.

21. She lived in a mercantile town and she had caught some-

thing of the spirit of the place and so she determined to venture a little in the great lottery of commerce, and soon there appeared in her window a grand array of dolls; these represented kings, queens, clowns, and other familiar types.

Exercise 4, Subordination. Combine each of the following groups of statements into one compact sentence:

1. Braddock feared a surprise attack. He left his main force behind. They were to guard the camp.

2. John Milton was an English poet. He was born in London. He was born in 1608. His first teacher was the Puritan Thomas Young.

3. The house stood on a hill. It was a high hill. The hill was covered with trees. The trees were oaks. They were very old and beautiful trees. The house was always shaded.

4. I went to a play last night. The play was *Cæsar and Cleopatra.* It was written by Shaw. The play was very interesting. The characters were good. The speeches were witty. I spent a most enjoyable evening.

5. Pope was of a tender constitution. He was of a delicate constitution. He was so from birth. But he is said to have shown two characteristics. One was a remarkable gentleness of disposition. Another was a remarkable sweetness of disposition.

6. The house was totally dark. It was like its neighbors. He tapped a few times. He heard a movement overhead. A door was opened. A voice asked who was there. It was a cautious voice. A woman was speaking. She was speaking to him.

7. William Wordsworth was born at Cockermouth. This place is in Cumberland. He went to school at Hawkshead. This school was in the very heart of the English Lake District. This district is very beautiful.

8. Another man followed. He was a stout man. He was a square-built man. He was intelligent looking. And he looked kind. He announced himself as leader of an emigrant party. This party was encamped ahead of us. It was about a mile in advance of our party.

9. The maple tree is a tree medium in size, generally being

about forty or fifty feet tall. It is a broad bushy tree. But it does not begin to branch out until about ten feet from the ground. The foliage of the tree is of large, broad, green leaves. In the autumn of the year, however, the foliage turns to a most beautiful golden and red color. On account of its shape and heavy foliage, the maple is one of our best shade trees. And it is very popular for this reason. (Use more than one sentence here if you think it desirable to do so.)

Exercise 5, Subordination. Rewrite the following paragraphs, changing to subordinate clauses as many as possible of the principal clauses (according to the probable logical relationships), and using connectives freely:

We were certain that the sun, when it rose, would show us how to proceed, but we were destined to be disappointed; a thick gray screen of clouds made it impossible to tell where the sun was. We had given up all hope of making sure of the points of the compass, and we debated: should we take the road to the left of the cabin, or should we take the one to the right? I wanted to bring the debate to an end; so I pulled out a coin and called eagerly, "Heads left, tails right!" I had my enthusiasm all to myself. The debate went on. Arguments were adduced, but they were always promptly refuted. We had grown hoarse at length, and the sun suddenly disclosed itself through the pines on the hill. (Student's Theme.)

The remainder of that night I paced to and fro on the smooth highway, and I reflected on the future and the past. My thoughts at first dwelled tenderly on those who were just gone, and then took a more manly temper as I considered what remained for me to do. Day came upon the inland mountain-tops, and the fowls began to cry and the smoke of homesteads to arise in the brown bosom of the moors, and then I turned my face homeward and went down the path to where the roof of Durrisdeer shone in the morning by the sea. (Adapted from the chapter entitled "The Enemy in the House," — some eight pages from the end, — in Stevenson's *Master of Ballantrae;*

the exercise, when completed, might well be compared with the original passage.)

And then they put their spears in the rests, and came together with their horses as fast as they might run, and either smote other in the midst of [in the middle of] their shields, that both their horses' backs brast [broke] under them, and the knights were both astonied [stunned], and as soon as they might avoid their horses, they took their shields afore them, and drew out their swords, and came together eagerly, and either gave other many strong strokes, for there might neither shields nor harness hold their strokes. (From Malory's *Morte D'Arthur*, Bk. VI, Ch. VIII; everything archaic in the passage should be modernized.)

Exercise 6, Subordination. Narrate a simple incident that can be dealt with adequately in a page or two, and then rewrite it, changing to subordinate clauses as many as possible of the principal clauses.

Exercise 7, Subordination. Write a paragraph of 100 to 200 words, and then rewrite it, using no *ands* or *buts* between clauses, and not allowing the average length of the sentences to run below fifteen words.

Exercise 8, Subordination. Correct the faulty subordination[1] in the following sentences. Do not divide the sentences unless it is necessary to do so.

1. He stooped down to tie his shoe when he noticed a most strange sight.
2. Everybody was eating as the sound of a drum was suddenly heard.
3. Henderson looked at it all and a sickening chill striking his soul.
4. A plan, which had most disastrous consequences, was then suggested.
5. For many days he had vainly searched for the lost trail,

[1] See **Subordination, 69.**

    thereby causing himself great weariness of body and loss of time and money.

6. He was disturbed by his friend's strange silence, being puzzled by the reticence of the man he had known so intimately.

7. There were three steps in the process. Having cut thin strips of wood, he fastened them together with wire, and then he placed these side by side in the grooves.

8. While Raphael lived during the Renaissance, Gainsborough lived in the eighteenth century.

9. There was one important difference between the two brothers: John was tall and slender, though James was stout and heavy.

10. He bent several iron rods together, with which he constructed the framework of his trap.

PARALLELISM

LET us follow out our principle that the structure of the sentence depends on the nature of the thought to be expressed, and observe how it applies to one or two important matters of sentence construction. We have seen that when any parts of our sentence-thought are *different* in rank, — when some are chief and others are subordinate, — we must, in order to be strictly truthful, express this logical difference through a structural difference. It naturally follows that when any parts of our sentence-thought are of the *same* rank, are logically coördinate, we must express this logical sameness through a structural sameness. For example, let us suppose that we desire to express a complete thought composed of two parts logically coördinate. We shall then write a compound sentence containing two clauses:

    The postmaster-general was Mr. Burleson, and the attorney general was Mr. Palmer.

If our thought has three parts, we shall write:

    I came, I saw, I conquered.

In these cases, subordination would positively distort the thought; it would not be quite the truth to say:

> Having come, I saw, I conquered.
>
> The postmaster-general was Mr. Burleson, the attorney-general being Mr. Palmer.

If we now suppose that we desire to express a complete thought composed of three constituent thoughts, one main thought and two subordinate thoughts, we shall of course put the main thought into the principal clause, and the subordinate thoughts into parallel subordinate clauses:

> If the rain stops, and if the roads are good enough, we shall drive on to Bridgton in the morning.

The first two thoughts have been expressed in the form of conditional clauses introduced by *if*, because they are related to the third and main thought in precisely the same way: our driving on to Bridgton is dependent on two contingencies. Since the subordinate ideas are parallel, they are put into parallel constructions. It would not do to say:

> Should the rain stop, and if the roads are good enough, we shall drive on to Bridgton in the morning.

Should is a verb, whereas *if* is a conjunction. There could be no parallelism until we changed our verb and conjunction to either two verbs or two conjunctions.

Two practical suggestions, if borne in mind, will help in the detection and correction of faulty parallelism. First, remember that the sign of parallelism is *grammatical* — we should have two (or more) participles, two infinitives, two pronouns, two prepositions, etc. If the principle of parallelism gives us trouble, we may be reasonably certain that the cause of the trouble is our shabby acquaintance with grammatical forms. In this event, the obvious remedy is to go back to our grammar and to study carefully, among

other things, the parts of speech. Before we can master
the parallel construction, we must be able to state the part
of speech of every word in any sentence.

Secondly, fix your attention on the first word or phrase.
This is always made the sign of parallelism. Provided that
we have two clauses introduced by *if* or two clauses introduced by *should*, we may be sure that they are parallel even
if the latter parts of the clauses differ. For example, in the
sentence already given —

> If the rain stops, and if the roads are good enough, we
> shall drive on to Bridgton in the morning.

— the phrase *good enough* follows the *are* of the second
clause, whereas the verb *stops* of the first clause stands
alone; and yet the two clauses are regarded as parallel in
construction, just as two lines may be parallel without being of the same length. In many cases of parallelism, the
similarity in grammatical forms affects only the first word
or two, as in this sentence:

> He said that it ought not to be done, and that he, for his part,
> had no interest in it.

Sometimes, however, the two constructions are parallel
throughout, as in this sentence from an essay of Arnold's:

> To know Italian *belles lettres* is not to know Italy, and to
> know English *belles lettres* is not to know England.

Here the two members, being equivalent, form a balanced
as well as a parallel construction. The principle of balance
is simply an extension or intensification of the principle of
parallelism. Neither parallelism nor balance is restricted
to a single sentence; either, indeed, may affect any number
of successive sentences. Here is a familiar illustration from
Julius Cæsar:

> Who is here so base that would be a bondman? If any, speak; for him have I offended. Who is here so rude that would not be a Roman? If any, speak; for him have I offended. Who is here so vile that will not love his country? If any, speak; for him have I offended.

One of the most useful types of balanced construction is that in which the balance rests on correlative conjunctions — conjunctions used in pairs to connect sentence elements of equal rank. (A list of them is given on page 140.) For example:

> Sincerity is of the utmost importance, not only in the choice of subject, but also in the execution of every detail.
> Both the choice of subject and the execution of every detail should be entirely sincere.

Note that the grammatical forms following the correlatives in these sentences are the same: "not only *in* . . . but also *in*"; "Both *the choice* . . . and *the execution*."

To the foregoing discussion of the principle of parallelism, a word of warning must be added. After we have become familiar with the parallel construction, and have observed how often the use of it immediately clarifies a murky thought, we may be inclined to resort to it on occasions when the thought does not lend itself to this mode of expression. Thus, in the following sentence:

> When he reached the city, and when we remember how unaccustomed he was to its noise and turmoil, he naturally began to question his decision.

— we have written a construction that is undoubtedly parallel, but that has no right to be! The two thoughts expressed in the two *when*-clauses are not parallel thoughts. Our difficulty is not that we have written a *faulty* parallel construction (one in which the construction fails to mirror the parallelism of the thought), but that we have written a

PARALLELISM

false parallel construction (one in which the thought does not justify parallelism in construction). So long as we remember the possibility of committing this blunder, we may employ parallelism to our heart's content.

Exercise 9, Parallelism. Point out the parallel constructions in the following sentences and passages, stating in each case whether the constructions begin with infinitives, or participles, or gerund phrases, or conjunctions, etc. Use sentence 1 as a model.

1. (*a*) Shouting at the top of his voice, and (*b*) gesticulating frantically, he made us stare at him in amazement. (Participles)
2. The accident occurred because the streets were slippery and because the driver was reckless.
3. He wore a soft hat, a military cape, and mud-bespattered boots.
4. He told us to walk a mile west, to turn north by the Buckstown turnpike, and to proceed as far as the railroad bridge.
5. Since he refuses to come, and since there is no one to force him to come, I suppose we shall have to get along without him.
6. I met him three times, — at the club, on the street, and on the ferry, — but he refused to look at me.
7. While the recollection of Mary's cruelties was still fresh, while the power of the Catholic party still inspired apprehension, while Spain still retained ascendency and aspired to universal dominion, all the reformed sects knew that they had a strong common interest and a deadly common enemy. (*Macaulay.*)
8. It has been sworn on the tomb of Washington. It has been sworn on the tomb of our allied soldiers, fallen in a sacred cause. It has been sworn by the bedside of our wounded men. It has been sworn on the heads of our orphan children. It has been sworn on cradles and on tombs. It has been sworn! (*Viviani.*)
9. It is for you now to take your part in the great process of reconciling liberty and discipline. Liberty alone scatters in

the air its power; discipline alone is a matter for slaves, dull, sodden slaves. But the highest attainment of the people of a free country, the highest attainment of civilization, is the reconciliation of liberty and discipline; discipline conscious of freedom, and liberty capable of discipline. (*Root.*)

10. Some books are to be tasted, others to be swallowed, and some few to be chewed and digested — that is, some books are to be read only in parts, others to be read, but not curiously, and some few to be read wholly, and with diligence and attention. . . . Reading maketh a full man, conference a ready man, and writing an exact man. And therefore if a man write little he had need have a great memory; if he confer little he had need have a present wit; and if he read little he had need have much cunning to seem to know that he doth not. Histories make men wise; poets, witty; the mathematics, subtle; natural philosophy, deep; moral, grave; logic and rhetoric, able to contend. (*Bacon.*)

Exercise 10, Parallelism. Consider the value of parallelism in Lincoln's famous letter to Horace Greeley, August 22, 1862.

Exercise 11, Parallelism. Using the following matter, write sentences, like the model below, containing as many varieties of parallelism or balance as possible.

1. How to use a dictionary.
   Model:
   When you look up a word in the dictionary, it is advisable (1) first to determine the pronunciation, (2) next to examine the derivation of the word, (3) then to read through all the definitions, and (4) finally to concentrate attention on the definition that fits the context. (*Adverbs followed by infinitives.*)
   You have not used your dictionary to the best advantage unless you have (1) determined the pronunciation of the word, (2) examined its derivation, (3) read through all the definitions, and (4) concentrated your attention on the definition that fits the context. (*Past participles.*)
   (1) When you have determined the pronunciation, (2)

when you have examined the derivation, (3) when you have read through all the definitions, and (4) when you have concentrated your attention on the definition that fits the context, then only have you used your dictionary as it really ought to be used. (*Subordinate clauses in common dependence and introduced by the same subordinating conjunction.*)

2. A contrast between your college and another college.
3. Reasons why a Freshman is superior to a Sophomore.
4. A summary of the mode of instruction in theme writing in your high school.
5. The chief distinctions of your town or county.
6. A summary account of how you spend your evenings.
7. The value of the study of Latin, or Spanish, or German.
8. Several underlying causes of the World War.
9. Why America is indebted to France.
10. A contrast between autocracy and democracy.

Exercise 12, Parallelism. Write a one-sentence summary (about as long as the model below), in parallel construction, of two of the following poems and short stories. Each sentence must contain only one main subject and one main predicate — that is, it must be a simple or a complex sentence, not a compound sentence. Use the example below as a model, but try to employ varieties of parallelism other than those it contains.

Poems: "Sir Patrick Spens," "Chevy Chase," "Lord Lovel." Milton's "Comus." Burns's "Cotter's Saturday Night." Tennyson's "Locksley Hall." Browning's "Incident of the French Camp," "How they Brought the Good News from Ghent to Aix," "Hervé Riel." Noyes's "Highwayman."

Stories: Irving's "Legend of Sleepy Hollow." Poe's "Cask of Amontillado," "A Descent into the Maelstrom," "Masque of the Red Death." Hawthorne's "Great Stone Face," "Birthmark." Bret Harte's "Luck of Roaring Camp." Hale's "Man Without a Country." Miss Jewett's "Fame's Little Day." O. Henry's "Phœbe," "Gift of the Magi," "A Municipal Report." Hardy's "Three Strangers." Maupassant's "Necklace," "Piece of String." Björnson's "Father."

SENTENCES AND THINKING

Model.

"As Toilsome I Wander'd Virginia's Woods" is a poem by Whitman telling how, as he roamed through the autumn woods of Virginia, he noticed at the foot of a tree the grave of a soldier; how he imagined the circumstances of the burial — the death of the wounded soldier during the retreat, the halt at midday, the quick preparation of a grave, the nailing of a tablet on the tree bearing these scrawled words, — *Bold, cautious, true, and my loving comrade;* and how, in the years that followed, the image flashed before him abruptly, when alone or in the street, of that unknown soldier's grave in the woods of Virginia, with its rude inscription, — *Bold, cautious, true, and my loving comrade.*[1]

Exercise 13, Parallelism. Write a one-sentence description, in parallel construction, of any two of the following pictures (obtainable, if need be, in the University Prints, the Perry Pictures, and similar series):

Willard, "The Spirit of '76." Leutze, "Washington Crossing the Delaware." Boughton, "Pilgrims Going to Church." Millais, "The Boyhood of Raleigh." Thompson, "Charge of the Scotch Grays at Waterloo." Turner, "The Fighting Téméraire." Millet, "The Man with the Hoe," "The Gleaners," "The Angelus," "The Sower." Bonheur, "The Horse Fair," "Ploughing." Poynter, "Atalanta's Race." Raphael, "The Sistine Madonna." Holman Hunt, "The Light of the World," "Finding of Christ in the Temple." Leonardo da Vinci, "The Last Supper."

---

[1] Charting the parallel members affords an excellent test of the parallelism of your summary sentence. Our example may be diagrammed as follows:

"As Toilsome"...is a poem telling
  1) how..........he noticed
  2) how..........he imagined the
    circumstances: a) the death
                   b) the halt
                   c) the quick preparation
                   d) the nailing
  3) how..........the image flashed

PARALLELISM

Model.

"Fog Warning" is a painting by Winslow Homer showing, in the foreground, a fisherman in a dory riding a great wave; behind him, to the right, a sailing ship perhaps a mile away; and, beyond the ship and along the horizon, a dark, streaming cloud that warns the fisherman, as he looks over his shoulder, of the perils of isolation in the fog.

Exercise 14, Parallelism. Detect and correct faulty parallelisms in these sentences:

1. The crowd began singing and to beat time to the music.
2. He said that the peasants are lazy, uneducated, and that they are intensely conservative.
3. I knew my friends had arrived and that they were safe.
4. He sees that the laws are carried out and the machinery of the government working well.
5. The first reason was that he stood for what the people wanted, and the second was because he was the representative of the strongest party.
6. It is a democracy because the individualistic spirit is present and the people having control of the government.
7. They soon became stronger in character and in wisdom, and also in prosperity.
8. Independence inspired the people with a new courage, a new hope, and a determination that was also new.
9. At that time I had the hope of becoming a doctor and probably specialize in some branch of medicine.
10. Patience is no longer a virtue, further endurance is cowardice, it would be slavery to submit to Prussian demands.
11. Some of these books are required, others are recommended, and there are others that are only suggested.
12. The house, old and dust-covered, and which had not been occupied for many years, at last had an occupant.
13. A dog, on hearing a peculiar noise and unable to understand exactly what it is, will at once start to find out the meaning of the noise.
14. Many people never see the beautiful and the glory in life.
15. Since it was getting late and the night air being chilly, we left as soon as we could.

16. The old man of eighty lies down at night just as peacefully, happy, and with his plans for another year's work as the young man does.

Exercise 15, Parallelism. Correct the faulty parallelisms, centering your attention on the grammatical forms that follow the correlative conjunctions:

1. He not only went to New York, but also to Washington.
2. Mr. Thompson both talked longer and more rapidly than I had expected.
3. They would neither dance nor would they play any of the card games.
4. Either you will report on time or be penalized for tardiness.
5. This nation not only has attained great things in science, but also it has achieved fame in the arts.
6. I believe neither in his wisdom nor trust in his honesty.

EMPHASIS

TELLING the truth we have found to be a very difficult task; nor have we yet come to the end of the matter. If we have learned to give the shades of our thought with approximate exactness by subordinating all subordinate matter, coördinating all coördinate matter, and making parallel all parallel matter, we have indeed been apt apprentices in the art of telling the truth; but mastery requires of us that we tell, not only the truth, but the whole truth. Absolute mastery we can scarcely hope to attain — that is reserved for the Homers, and Dantes, and Shaksperes, the great truth-tellers, who give us, if not all the truth, all the truth as they saw it. So far we lesser men cannot hope to go; but we should go as far as we can.

One obvious thing remains to be done. I may subordinate and coördinate faithfully without approximating the truth, simply because I have ignored relative values among my thoughts. The public speaker who gives two-thirds of his time to introductory remarks, and only one-third to his speech proper, is very far from telling the truth. The writer whose paragraph is top-heavy, who brings his paragraph to a conclusion suddenly because it is becoming alarmingly long, is not writing a truthful paragraph. The writer whose sentence does not mirror the symmetry of his thought (assuming that it has symmetry), whose sentence does not throw into relief what is important and leave in the background what is relatively unimportant, has not yet learned to write even an approximately truthful sentence. There are various ways of giving thoughts conspicuousness or emphasis.

Italics. School-girls writing letters, in which they are pleased to regard nearly everything as all-important, underline abundantly. In print, italics are equivalent to underlining. They are used sparingly by skillful writers, the volcanic Carlyle being a notable exception. In the following passage, for example, Carlyle has used italics for several words (including even part of a word) and capital letters for other words:

> He is a Columbus minded to sail to the indistinct country of NOWHERE, to the indistinct country of WHITHERWARD, by the *friendship* of those same waste-tumbling Water-Alps and howling waltz of All the Winds; not by conquest of them and in spite of them, but by friendship of them, when once *they* have made up their mind! He is the most original Columbus I ever saw. Nay, his problem is not an impossible one: he will infallibly *arrive* at that same country of NOWHERE; his indistinct Whitherward will be a *Thither*ward! In the Ocean Abysses and Locker of Davy Jones, there certainly enough do he and *his* ship's company, and all their cargo and navigations, at last find lodgement.

Carlyle, it should be remembered, had a better right than we to use these mechanical devices frequently, because he used them in addition to, not in place of, superior means of securing emphasis. What are these superior means?

Improvement of the Words. One of the best means, yet one of the least used by the student, is an improvement of the words. Words may be improved in several ways. (1) They may be made *stronger*, more intense, in meaning. If I write, "I shall be glad to come," and feel that I have not conveyed enough gladness, I may, indeed, simply italicize the important word — "I shall be *glad* to come." But I could express my pleasure more effectively by casting about for a stronger word than glad — possibly *delighted*. (2) They may be made more *fresh*. How quickly a word or phrase loses its effectiveness through repetition! "Weird," "busy as a bee," "along this line," "potent factor," and hundreds of other expressions have been used so often that they meet the ear dully. Slang is objectionable, among other reasons, because it is hackneyed. Journalistic expressions are objectionable for the same reason. So are colloquialisms. Whatever the character of the worn-out expression, the remedy consists in replacing it with one that is chosen, not because it comes to mind readily, but because it fits the context; if we will but resolutely endeavor to say what is in our minds, our words will be fresh and vital and not trite and lifeless. We do not mean "feathered songsters": we mean birds, or possibly wood thrushes. "He spoke with pep" is not only vulgar, but also stupidly vague: we mean, perhaps, that he spoke with passion or he spoke with energy, or with enthusiasm, or animation, or excitement, or bitterness, or elation, or what not. A word that really fits is always fresh. (3) They may be made more *specific*. We do most of our thinking in specific, not general, terms; even when class names are given, we often transform them mentally into individual members of the class. Therefore the statement "He went across the room" is much less emphatic than "He strode across the room" (or "hobbled," "ambled," "picked his way"); "He came soon after" than "He came in five minutes"; "It was a good sermon" than "It was a stirring sermon." (4) They may be made more *concrete*. In life, our thoughts are nearly always associated with definite images, pictures, colors, forms, sounds, and the like — these are the material that our minds work upon. Abstract thought, i.e., thought abstracted from sensuous experience, is as rare as it is difficult; always the human mind instinctively attaches itself to concrete things, to things that may be seen, heard, touched, smelt, tasted. Since this is so in life, it is equally so in literature, the expression of life. Accordingly, "eyes" is less effective than "gray eyes"; "attractively tinted clouds" than "wisps of salmon-pink clouds"; "the sound of a trumpet" than "the brassy blare of a trumpet"; "the roads meet at this point" than "the roads form a Y at this point." Though concreteness is commonest in descriptive writing, there is no kind of writing in which it is not a highly important element.

Climax. Assuming that the words chosen to express our thoughts are strong enough to bear our meaning, we have next to consider the emphatic ordering of them. When our thoughts are parallel but different in value — in intensity, in importance, in definiteness, in interest — we should indicate the gradations by the use of a climactic arrangement, an ascending series. The English word "climax" comes from a Greek word meaning "a ladder." In a ladder the rungs are, of course, placed one above the other, so that the climber progresses toward his object; similarly, in a sentence involving parallel members of differing values, the parallel members should be so placed that there is progress from those of lesser value to those of greater. "Your son is very ill — seriously ill — desperately ill" has emphasis because the order is climactic. We should have an anti-climax if we wrote, instead, "Your son is desperately ill — seriously ill — very ill." This would violate the rising intensity of the thoughts we are representing in language. Again, "The wind had ceased, the color faded out of the western sky, and a dozen whippoorwills began calling vociferously, till our ears throbbed with the sound," has emphasis through climax. In this case, instead of a rising intensity, we have an increase in both definiteness and interest. To have produced our whippoorwill concert first and then gone back to the bare fact of the wind's ceasing would have been to obliterate one thought through the splendor of another. As Herbert Spencer remarks, you cannot see the light of a fire after looking at the sun, but if you look at the fire first you can see both.

Departure from the Normal Word Order. Any deviation from the norm, whether in manners or in rhetoric, attracts attention. Any one who has learned to read has become so accustomed to a certain word order — subject, verb, and complement — that he notices, or feels unconsciously, every clear case of departure from this standard. For this reason these sentences —

> I picked him out from all the rest.
> We lesser men cannot go so far.
> I will crush to pieces whoever opposes me.

— are less emphatic than these:

> Him I picked out from all the rest.
> So far we lesser men cannot go.
> Who opposes me I will crush to pieces!

EMPHASIS

In practice, this principle means: If your sentence does not throw into relief your main thoughts, transpose some of the words and phrases experimentally until it does.

Placing Important Matter at the End of the Sentence. An excellent means of securing emphasis — one that can be resorted to in nearly every sentence, and that can be applied with ease — consists in placing important matter at the end of the sentence. The beginning of the sentence is also a conspicuous place, but since the end is much more conspicuous and since most writers cannot consciously attend to both, we shall find it advisable to concentrate our attention on the end. It is not hard to explain why the end is emphatic: upon reaching the period, the reader stops for a moment to reflect, to get his mental wind, before entering upon the next thought, and while he is pausing he notices most vividly what is nearest him — the last words of the sentence. In all sentences there are what we might term "pivotal words," on which the meaning of the sentence rests — the substantial words, as distinguished from the merely relational words. In the sentence, "I think, however, that his attitude is wrong," there are words that simply indicate relation, such as "that" and "is," and there are also words that contain the thought substance, such as "attitude" and "wrong," the latter being the most important and likewise the last word in the entire sentence. The sentence has emphasis. But place another word at the end, and observe how the sentence loses its ring:

I think that his attitude is wrong, however.
However, his attitude is wrong, I think.

The difference in arrangement is slight; the difference in effect is highly important. Again, when President Wilson wrote:

> A steadfast concert for peace can never be maintained except by a partnership of democratic nations.

— he rightly placed at the end the pivotal words, *democratic nations*. Tuck away these words in the interior of the sentence, and you spoil the effect:

> A steadfast concert for peace can never be maintained except by the democratic nations in partnership.

— which implies that *partnership* is the pivotal word.

When we have acquired the habit of reserving our important words for the close of the sentence, we are ready to extend this practice to the rest of the sentence. If the reader's mind pauses at the end of a sentence, it is also true that it pauses, more briefly, wherever there is punctuation within the sentence. Generally speaking, the punctuation marks off what we have called constituent thoughts. A sentence in which the logical divisions are not thus indicated is ordinarily not so easy to understand as a sentence in which the divisions are indicated by punctuation. The following sentence from Theodore Roosevelt's "Charter of Democracy" speech is an example:

> Let us remember, also, that Conservation does not stop with the natural resources, but that the principle of making the best use of all we have requires with equal or greater insistence that we shall stop the waste of human life in industry and prevent the waste of human welfare which flows from the unfair use of concentrated power and wealth in the hands of men whose eagerness for profits blinds them to the cost of what they do.

Here and there such a sentence, if emphatically phrased, is effective; ordinarily, however, it lacks emphasis because no words in it, save the last, are stressed, and the total result is more or less of a blur. Not content, then, with placing the pivotal words just before the period, we should make some effort to place other important words just before the commas and semicolons, as Roosevelt does in this sentence:

> We stand for applying the Constitution to the issues of to-day as Lincoln applied it to the issues of his day; Lincoln mind you, and not Buchanan, was the real upholder and preserver of the Constitution, for the true progressive, the progressive of the Lincoln stamp, is the only true constitutionalist, the only real conservative.

Suspense. Another principle, allied to that discussed above, serves the end of emphasis. The close of the sentence, we have found, is the most emphatic part of it; we can add still more to the emphasis at the close if we suspend the thought, keep the secret of the sentence, until we reach the last word. Examine the following sentences:

> The impulse of the English race toward moral development and self-conquest has manifested itself in Puritanism, and more powerfully than anywhere else.
> The impulse of the English race toward moral development and self-conquest has nowhere so powerfully manifested itself as in Puritanism.

The second sentence is stronger, not only because the pivotal word *Puritanism* is placed at the end, but also because our sense of grammatical completeness is not satisfied until we reach the concluding word. The meaning is suspended — the reader retains the thought expectantly — till illumination comes suddenly and brilliantly with the word *Puritanism*. A sentence in which grammatical completeness is thus reserved to the end is termed a *periodic sentence;* a sentence in which the thought is completed piecemeal is termed a *loose sentence*. In nearly all good writing, the loose sentence predominates; but no modern style is likely to be effective in which periodic sentences, or virtually periodic sentences, do not abound. Since a loose sentence may be composed as the writer proceeds, without much concern for what is coming, it is only too good a medium for the expression of flaccid thought — firm when composed by a skillful writer, it often sprawls at the touch of a slovenly writer. Though a style that is constantly periodic makes tiresome reading, a writer who is still serving his apprenticeship would not go far astray if he tried to employ the principle of suspense whenever an opportunity presented itself. When the meaning is suspended to the last words of the sentence, the writer is obliged to see his goal, however dimly, before he begins to write his sentence. That makes for well-knit sentences. A practical hint to utilize when one is trying to cast a sentence in a periodic mould is this: reserve the subject of the sentence for a position as near the end as possible, or, what often amounts to the same thing, put the subordinate clauses and phrases first and the principal clause last.

Balance. Emphasis is served, again, by the use of balance. We have already considered, in our study of parallelism, the need of expressing similar thoughts through similar constructions. We have now to consider the same need viewed as a matter of emphasis.

When our thoughts correspond to each other, we can best emphasize their correspondence by stating them in the form of a balanced sentence — a sentence, that is, in which the similarity of the constituent thoughts is manifested by the similarity of the syntax. Oftenest two ideas, or two sets of ideas, are placed side by side, as if the thoughts were being weighed in scales. These ideas, or sets of ideas, may agree with each other in either of two ways:

(1) They may agree through resemblance, as in the following instance from an essay by Dr. Johnson:

As we ought not to give way to fear, any more than indulgence to hope, because the objects both of fear and hope are yet uncertain, so we ought not to trust the representations of one more than of the other, because they are both equally fallacious; as hope enlarges happiness, fear aggravates calamity.

In the above sentence the object is to emphasize an analogy — a resemblance between things that are different.

But (2) the ideas may agree through unlikeness, by matching each other in their differences, as in this sentence from an essay by G. K. Chesterton:

All democrats object to men being disqualified by the accident of birth; tradition objects to their being disqualified by the accident of death.

Here the object is to emphasize a contrast, a sharply defined difference. Though the two thoughts may perhaps be regarded as of the same weight, the object is not to emphasize the identity of weight but the contrast between two equally weighty substances, as if one were a pound of iron and the other a pound of copper, or a pound of iron and a pound of feathers. Since this is the commoner and more emphatic type of balanced sentence, it will be well to inspect two or three other examples:

Talent is that which is in a man's power; genius is that in whose power a man is. (*Lowell.*)

The memory of other authors is kept alive by their works; but the memory of Johnson keeps many of his works alive. (*Macaulay.*)

Art must not aim at morality, else it is not art; but it must not violate morality, else it is not human.

In these sentences two ideas are set in violent contrast by the use of balance, as if the writer said, "This may look like that, but do not be deceived, for in their very likeness lurks a profound difference. It is true, they correspond part for part — but only as black and white, night and day, correspond." Accordingly, to make emphatic this difference between kindred things, the writer reveals their antithetical correspondence by a correspondence in sentence structure.

Repetition. A teacher summed up the art of teaching by saying, "First tell them you're going to tell them; then tell them, and then tell them that you've told them." Although the art of teaching certainly comprehends more than that, it would be hard to exaggerate the value of repetition in education or in any other activity in which knowledge or opinion is transmitted. What we have heard but once, we are very prone to forget. What we have heard often, we are likely to remember — and even to believe, whether it is plausible or not, as demagogues understand only too well. In a political speech, in a sermon, in an editorial, in a college lecture, we encounter again and again the same ideas, or facts, or emotions — sometimes repeated without variation, more often repeated with an interesting difference, with additions, that is, or with illustrations, or with comparisons, or with applications — until the ideas, facts, emotions have been driven home. In the composition of an effective paragraph, again, the same principle holds: the idea is nakedly stated, and then it is represented with detail, illustration, and the like, until the reader has received a clear and lasting impression. Even within the limit of a single sentence, there is room for emphasis through repetition.

One of the most valuable kinds of repetition is the repeated use of important words, of what we have termed "pivotal words." Observe the repetition in this fragment of *Sartor Resartus:*

Produce! Produce! Were it but the pitifullest infinitesimal

fraction of a *Product, produce* it, in God's name. 'Tis the utmost thou hast in thee: out with it, then. *Up, up!* Whatsoever thy hand findeth to *do, do* it with thy whole might. *Work*
while it is called Today, for the Night cometh, wherein no man
can *work.* (*Carlyle.*)

Although it is not the repetition in this passage that makes
it an impressive statement of the author's "Gospel of
Work," but the profound emotion out of which it springs,
yet the emotion would never be conveyed unless it were expressed, and in this case it is expressed partly by Biblical
allusion, partly by exclamation, partly also by repetition.
Another instance of emphasis (as well as clearness) through
repetition of important words is the following comment, by
Matthew Arnold, on the Scotch poems of Burns:

Let us boldly say that of much of this *poetry,* a *poetry* dealing
perpetually with *Scotch drink, Scotch religion,* and *Scotch manners,* a *Scotchman's* estimate is apt to be personal. A *Scotchman*
is used to this world of *Scotch drink, Scotch religion,* and *Scotch
manners;* he has a *tenderness* for it; he meets its *poet* half way.
In this *tender* mood he reads *poems* like the "Holy Fair" or
"Halloween." But this *world* of *Scotch drink, Scotch religion,*
and *Scotch manners* is against a *poet,* not for him, when it is not
a partial countryman who reads him, for in itself it is not a
beautiful world, and no one can deny that it is of advantage to a
poet to deal with a *beautiful world.* Burns's *world* of *Scotch
drink, Scotch religion,* and *Scotch manners* is often a harsh, a
sordid, a repulsive *world;* even the *world* of his "Cotter's Saturday Night" is not a *beautiful world.*

It is a little tiresome, this repetition of "Scotch drink,
Scotch religion, and Scotch manners," but it is effective:
nobody who has read attentively the essay in which it
occurs is likely to forget that Arnold regarded Burns's
world as an unlovely combination of Scotch drink, Scotch
religion, and Scotch manners.

One word more: it does not follow, from what has been said, that all repetition is good. Repetition is good when it serves a purpose, when it clarifies or emphasizes. It is bad when it occurs accidentally and without purpose, since then the reader, observing the repetition, consciously or unconsciously supposes that it serves a purpose, and not finding any purpose, any value in the repetition, feels that he has been misled and that the writer has failed to express himself adequately.

Exercise 16, Emphasis. Underline the pivotal words in the following sentences:

1. I have not read history without observing that the <u>greatest forces</u> in the world and the only <u>permanent forces</u> are the <u>moral forces</u>.
2. The French Revolution inaugurated a new movement not only for France, but for the whole world.
3. The teachers of morality discourse like angels, but they live like men.
4. No man can taste the fruits of autumn while he is delighting his scent with the flowers of the spring; no man can at the same time fill his cup from the source and from the mouth of the Nile.
5. The beginning and the end of what is the matter with us in these days is that we have forgotten God.
6. Ignorance, when it is voluntary, is criminal.
7. But the final value of action, like that of books, and better than books, is that it is a resource.
8. Government is a contrivance of human wisdom to provide for human wants.

Exercise 17, Emphasis. Of the following sentences, determine which are periodic, which are virtually periodic, and which are loose:

1. He has, we are glad to say, avoided both these extremes.
2. I came here to meet my friend, who was to return as soon as he had finished his business.

3. Although his reading was without plan, he learned much.
4. Whatsoever a man soweth, that shall he also reap.
5. I often saw the General, taking the liberty to call on him frequently.
6. He found the task so disagreeable that he soon gave up in disgust.
7. Finding it impossible to refuse, he consented, though with great reluctance.
8. Without further delay, he sprang from behind the garden wall silently.
9. With a trace of hysteria both began to laugh.
10. After reading all that has been written, and after thinking all that has been thought, on the topics of God and the soul, the man who has a right to say that he thinks at all, will find himself face to face with the conclusion that, on these topics, the most profound thought is that which can be the least easily distinguished from the most superficial sentiment. (*Poe.*)
11. What men allow themselves to wish, they will soon believe, and will be at last incited to execute what they please themselves with contriving.
12. This doubt troubled him, this terror, this fear.
13. From morning to night steadily had he worked.
14. Whatever the author might tell either his readers or himself, I am not convinced that the design was moral.
15. Columbus, who sailed across an ocean that was unknown to others, and who, though entreated by his sailors to discontinue the voyage, persevered until his end was gained, was a type of the persistent man.
16. Lincoln, who did not have the advantages of many people, but who made use of every possible opportunity to become educated, was a persistent worker also.
17. The moment this view of culture is seized, the moment it is regarded not solely as the endeavor to see things as they are, to draw towards a knowledge of the universal order which seems to be intended and aimed at in the world, and which it is a man's happiness to go along with or his misery to go counter to, — to learn, in short, the will of God, — the moment, I say, culture is considered not merely as the

endeavor to *see* and *learn* this, but as the endeavor also to make it *prevail*, the moral, social, and beneficent character of culture becomes manifest. (*Arnold.*)

18. And in like manner, what is called seeing the world, entering into active life, going into society, traveling, gaining acquaintance with the various classes of the community, coming into contact with the principles and modes of thought of various parties, interests, and races, their views, aims, habits, and manners, their religious creeds and forms of worship, — gaining experience how various yet how alike men are, how low-minded, how bad, how opposed, yet how confident in their opinions; all this exerts a perceptible influence upon the mind, which it is impossible to mistake, be it good or be it bad, and is popularly called its enlargement. (*Newman.*)

19. This flat, flourishing, easy country never could have looked more rich and prosperous, than in that opening summer of 1815, when its green fields and quiet cities were enlivened by multiplied red-coats: when its wide *chaussées* swarmed with brilliant English equipages; when its great canal-boats, gliding by rich pastures and pleasant quaint old villages, by old châteaux lying amongst old trees, were all crowded with well-to-do English travelers; when the soldier who drank at the village inn, not only drank, but paid his score; and Donald, the Highlander, billeted in the Flemish farm-house, rocked the baby's cradle, while Jean and Jeannette were out getting in the hay. (*Thackeray.*)

(See also the selections on pages 88–96.)

Exercise 18, Emphasis. Classify the sentences of one or two of your themes with regard to periodicity.

Exercise 19, Emphasis. Write six periodic or virtually periodic sentences, each sentence longer than the one before, beginning with one containing at least twelve words.

Exercise 20, Emphasis. Study the placing of pivotal words and other important words in an essay by Macaulay, an address by President Wilson, etc.

EMPHASIS

Exercise 21, Emphasis. Write ten sentences in which the pivotal words are placed at the end.

Exercise 22, Emphasis. Write ten sentences involving a departure from the natural word order.

Exercise 23, Emphasis. Convert all the periodic sentences in Exercise 17 into loose and the loose into periodic sentences.

Exercise 24, Emphasis. Make the following sentences more emphatic by improving the italicized words.

1. The minister preached a *good* sermon.
2. The view from Pike's Peak is *interesting*.
3. I think his robbery of the bank was *wrong*.
4. She is an *awfully nice* girl.
5. The trains *came together* with *a big noise*.
6. Thinking he was in France, I was *surprised* to see him walking down the village street.
7. I am *certainly sorry* to hear of your brother's death.
8. The way the author handles his plot will certainly *get* the reader's attention.
9. The *surprised* soldier at once *picked* up the bomb and *threw* it back into the enemy's trench.
10. Our team *sure* played a *horrid* game yesterday.
11. The *big fire* made the heavens *red as blood*.
12. The singer, who was arrayed in an *elegant* and *stunning* gown, possessed a *golden voice* of *rare charm*.
13. The landscape was *typical, so to speak,* of the *season of the year.*
14. We should show, *I think,* our *appreciation* of the *great sacrifices* of our World War veterans.
15. The Kent county *annals of crime have record* of another instance where the *red hand of murder* has been successful in its *heinous purpose,* and the *perpetrator of the dastardly crime* now awaits in the Kent county jail to see what punishment *those who sit in judgment will mete out* to him. In the *quiet and peaceful hours* of Wednesday morning,

when *time had two hours hence recorded the midnight hour and was rushing silently toward dawn*, Howard Green, colored, killed his wife, Ester A. Green, *in cold blood* at her home *on the outskirts of* Millington, with a shotgun, after a dispute over their daughter and other things. (*From a daily newspaper.*)

16. Truth is an *asset* that I *place a premium on*. If our state is to be *on a par* with her *sister states*, the student body, including the *fair maidens*, should be imbued with a love of truth. Everything *in the line of* falsehood must, if we are to be *abreast of the times*, be *done away with*. The very *individuals* who are *enthused* over the Honor System are sometimes just the ones we cannot *bank on*.

Exercise 25, Emphasis. For the italicized words in the following sentences substitute words more exact or specific:

1. Descriptions in a short story help to *bring about* the effect of the story.
2. The frightened deer *ran away* as soon as he *saw* the hunters.
3. The heavy body of the suffering *animal fell* to the floor.
4. This is a *splendid* site for a summer hotel.
5. The *very* fat old man *walked painfully* up the hill.
6. A queerly-deformed *individual* came forward and in his *funny* voice *said*, "Now, masters, what do you want?"
7. George Eliot allows her characters to grow. Godfrey Cass *gives* a good example.
8. Throughout the book the author *remains* close to the facts, and at times he *goes much* into details of real life.
9. The apparition *went* silently up the stairway.
10. In the city the spring comes earlier than it does in the country, and the *trees* in the sheltered squares sometimes *come* into blossom *some time* before their brethren in the open fields.
11. *Birds* called in the thickets where *one kind of tree* flamed amid *other trees*, with irregular splashes of *color*.
12. A few scattered clouds were *moving* in the *wind*, their shadows *coming down* the *brightly tinted* slopes.

EMPHASIS

Exercise 26, Emphasis. Improve the wording of the following descriptions. Avoid "fine writing."

1. It was a *fine* autumn landscape *all right*. The trees were *brightly colored,* and the river *could be seen running* through the meadows and woods. The *furry denizens of the forest* were getting ready for the snow and *old Boreas.* Down by the river *a bird could be heard* singing, and *another kind of bird* was hammering in the woods. Smoke was *coming* out of the chimney of a farmhouse *nestling* in the valley, beside which a few *trees stood like sentinels.*

2. Ten miles further up, Beverley Dam flings its giant rock-and-cement finger across the northern extremity of the valley. A mammoth lake limns its liquid outline against the sylvan slopes and furnishes a splendid scenic by-product amid this haunting habitat of swirling waters.

3. Verbally bidden a number of friends wended their way on last Saturday afternoon to the pretty cottage home of Mr. and Mrs. H., who, in her characteristic thoughtful way, arranged this social hour, to pay court to her household guests, Miss M., her great-aunt, Miss B., an aunt, and Miss S., a friend — all of Wisconsin. Guarding the portals and welcoming the incoming guest was Mrs. H. V., who in her sweet way directed them to the hostess and her trio of charming honorees. Informality everywhere reigned; just the usual attractiveness of the home found accent in great crystals of spring blossoms. Incidentally and with a careless care, the winsome Miss N. led the way to the dining room. A rare beauty board gleamed with crystal, centered with a huge bowl of "pink pinks" about which burned pink tapers under pink shades, casting a roseate hue over the cluny lace cover and the crystal bon-bon trays. At either end of the table were seated Mrs. A. P. and Mrs. J. D., pouring a delicious tea concoction from exquisite tea urns. In this and the tempting sandwich service were Miss A. and Miss V. chattingly presiding. Much pleasure was enjoyed both by the delightful little house-party and their many guests — both gowned in the very top notch of style and beauty. (*From a newspaper.*)

47

SENTENCES AND THINKING

Exercise 27, Emphasis. Try to account for the effectiveness of the diction in the following sentences:

1. There were no books, no music, and only a few newspapers in sight — a bare, blank, cold, drab-colored shelter from the rain, not a home. Nothing cosey, nothing heart warming; a grim and horrible shed.
2. The silken hair, too, had been suffered to grow all unheeded, and as, in its wild gossamer texture, it floated rather than fell over the face, I could not, even with effort, connect its arabesque expression with any idea of simple humanity.
3. Great torrents always seem angry, and great rivers too often sullen; but there is no anger, no disdain, in the Rhone . . . For all other rivers there is a surface, and an underneath, and a vaguely displeasing idea of the bottom. But the Rhone flows like one lambent jewel; its surface is nowhere, its ethereal self is everywhere, the iridescent rush and translucent strength of it blue to the shore, and radiant to the depth. Fifteen feet thick, of not flowing, but flying water.
4. After the fever of life, after wearinesses and sicknesses, fightings and despondings, languor and fretfulness, struggling and succeeding; after all the changes and chances of this troubled state, — at length comes death, at length the white throne of God, at length the beatific vision.
5. It is rather for us to be dedicated here to the great task remaining before us — that from these honored dead we take increased devotion to that cause for which they gave the last full measure of devotion; that we here highly resolve that these dead shall not have died in vain; that this nation, under God, shall have a new birth of freedom; and that government of the people, by the people, for the people, shall not perish from the earth.

Exercise 28, Emphasis. Complete the following sentences by using balance:

1. Whereas the French President is elected by the Chamber of Deputies and holds office for seven years, the American president . . . .

EMPHASIS

2. To retreat across the river would destroy the dawning hope of his soldiers; to remain where he was . . . .

3. He is shy, awkward, and blundering in his childhood, yet full of sensibility; he is a butt for the jeers and jokes of his companions, yet . . . .; he is . . . ., yet . . . .; he is . . . ., yet . . . .

4. There are many differences between knowledge and wisdom. Knowledge can be acquired by any one; wisdom comes not to all; knowledge . . . .

5. Man doth seek a triple pleasure; first a sensual, consisting in those things which very life itself requireth either as necessary supplements, or as beauties and ornaments thereof; then an intellectual, ...; and lastly a . . . .

Exercise 29, Emphasis. Rearrange the following sentences so as to secure balance:

1. But to read the *Diary* is a pleasure; it will always be a task to read the *Memoirs*.

2. Death is a port whereby we pass to joy; the lake of life drowneth all in pain.

3. The country was made by God, but man made the town.

4. If you see a thing too often, you no longer see it; a thing heard too often is no longer heard.

5. If Nature wishes to make a man estimable, she gives virtues; she gives success whenever she wishes to make him esteemed.

6. To ascertain and communicate facts is the object of science; the function of art consists in quickening our life into a higher consciousness through the feelings.

7. The Puritan prostrated himself in the dust before his Maker, but his foot was set on the neck of his king.

8. Queen Elizabeth could talk poetry with Spenser; she was able to discuss philosophy with Bruno; she and Lyly discussed Euphuism; the chivalry of Essex was enjoyed by her; and she was equally able to pore with Cecil over dispatches and treasury books.

Exercise 30, Emphasis. Copy several **examples of balance** from the speeches of Burke or the essays of G. K. Chesterton.

Exercise 31, Emphasis. Discuss the use of repetition as a means of attaining emphasis in the following sentences:

1. He will find one English book and one only, where, as in the *Iliad* itself, perfect plainness of speech is allied with perfect nobleness; and that book is the Bible.
2. Gentlemen may cry, Peace, Peace! — but there is no peace.
3. They are therefore not only devoted to liberty, but to liberty according to English ideas, and on English principles.
4. Never was there such a stir in Boston as on this occasion; never such a hurrying hither and thither about the streets; such popping of heads out of windows; such gathering of knots in the market-place.
5. Who kills a man kills a reasonable creature, God's image; but he who destroys a good book, kills reason itself, kills the image of God, as it were, in the eye.
6. Street after street, and all the folks asleep — street after street, all lighted up as if for a procession and all as empty as a church — till at last I got into that state of mind when a man listens and listens and begins to long for the sight of a policeman.
7. The violence of those outrages [those which lead to revolutions] will always be proportioned to the ferocity and ignorance of the people, and the ferocity and ignorance of the people will always be proportioned to the oppression and degradation under which they have been accustomed to live.
8. It is good sense, reason, which does all, — virtue, genius, soul, talent, and taste. — What is virtue? reason put in practice; — talent? reason expressed with brilliance; — soul? reason delicately put forth; — and genius is sublime reason.

Exercise 32, Emphasis. Collect several examples of emphasis through repetition from the Bible and from the works of any of the following: Arnold, Macaulay, Burke, Carlyle, and Irving.

VARIETY

THE need of variety in sentence construction is not a thing for the writer to worry about; let him worry abundantly about the need of subordination, parallelism, and emphasis, the three principles we have studied in the preceding pages, and if he worries to good purpose, learning how to apply them with certitude and ease, he will find that he has mysteriously acquired variety. Nobody thinks monotonously, not at least while he is alert enough to write, and it follows that if he really expresses his thinking, subordinating what is logically subordinate, making parallel what is logically parallel, and emphasizing what is logically emphatic, he will attain in his writing a large measure of variety. Inevitably he will have short sentences and long sentences ; simple, and compound, and complex sentences; "loose," and periodic, and balanced sentences; a fair sprinkling of interrogative and exclamatory sentences; refreshing departures from the normal word order. And if he has a well-defined personality, he will have in addition the variety of style that arises from the coloring of thought by individual temperament and character.

There is no quick way to secure variety — no short cut. If a writer, instead of trying to express his thought, aims directly at variety, he will never attain it, or, at best, will attain a kind of variety that he does not want, an artificial shadow of the real thing, an insufferably conscious manner of expression, drawing the reader's attention away from the thought to the verbal manipulations of the writer. He will write "Old Sol" to avoid repeating the word "sun"; he will write, "In the winters I went to school, and my summers were spent at my father's farm" (shifting the voice and subject) instead of simply writing, "In the winters I went to school, in the summers lived at my father's farm"; he will shift freely from the past tense to the historical present (a matter discussed on pp. 63–64); he will write short sentences where he ought to have long ones, and long sentences where he ought to have short ones, and since he probably cannot write long sentences without getting confused, he will occasionally produce a cumulative sentence that begins innocently but grows preposterously, like a giant snowball rolling down a slope. In his efforts to secure variety, he will perform every meretricious trick of style he can think of and violate all the principles of good writing.

Our conclusion, in a word, is this: if a writer observes that his work is monotonous, that a page of it is dull and that a book of it would be a torment, let him determine to gain the interest that springs from variety by struggling to express his thoughts and feelings as they are, by insisting that what is naturally subordinate, parallel, and emphatic be so rendered in his sentences.

Exercise 33, Variety. Analyze the variety in sentence structure in a given passage by pointing out (1) various types of subordination, (2) instances of parallelism, (3) emphatic diction, (4) the use of climax, (5) departures from the normal word order, (6) periodic sentences, (7) balanced sentences, (8) the range in sentence length.

ECONOMY

WRITING is not, of course, a private matter. When we speak of it as self-expression we do not mean that we write merely to amuse ourselves, to give our powers play. Sometimes we do write for such a motive; but at the same time, in the background of the mind, is an ever-present sense of the public. Unconsciously we are ever asking ourselves such questions as: "Will this be clear to the reader?" "Will he get the full force of this?" "Could this be misinterpreted?" Writing should be regarded, then, not as soliloquy, but as the transmission of thought from one mind to another. It is not an end in itself, but a means — a machine for the transmission of thought, as the wireless telegraph is.

It follows that good writing, like good machinery, must operate smoothly, with a minimum of friction. Economy demands that the thought be transferred in its entirety and without distortion. Any mode of writing that calls attention to itself violates the principle of economy. If the attention of the reader is attracted to offensive misspellings, to blunders in grammar, to misleading punctuation, to the use of slang, to excessive cleverness in phrasing, to the use of showy language, to monotony of sentence construction, the amount of attention given to the thought is diminished in proportion. It is as though, in telling a man where Squire Jones lives, we interspersed our directions with disturbing comments on the state of the weather and the high cost of living in these parts. Once more we must return to our fundamental principle: the truth, the whole truth, and nothing but the truth. It is the writer's message that we want, nothing more or less.

Tangled Constructions. When the structure of your sentence is involved, you are unconsciously asking the reader to untangle it, to recast it mentally, — to repair your machinery, — before he can quite grasp the meaning.

Tangled constructions arise from two chief causes:

(1) Mixed Constructions. A sentence is tangled whenever the writer fails to complete a construction that ought

to be completed, shifting without reason from one construction to another. For example:

> It was a rule in the classes of this pedantic professor that whenever a student used a slang expression in recitation for him to get a failure grade on the theme handed in that day.

The blunder, in such a sentence, can be readily revealed by looking for the main line of the sentence, or, what amounts to the same thing, eliminating for the moment all the branch lines. Thus:

> It was a rule (in the classes of this pedantic professor) that (whenever a student used a slang expression in recitation) for him to get a failure grade.

"It was a rule that for him to get a failure grade" is obviously intolerable; what the writer tried to say is, "It was a rule that he would get a failure grade."

(2) Misplaced Modifiers. A sentence is tangled, again, whenever the writer fails to place together matter that is logically, and therefore structurally, closely related. For example:

> The papers he then placed in her hand without a tremor for which he had so long struggled and so hopelessly till but the hour before.

The sense does not stand forth luminously, to say the least; in particular, we are uncertain whether that "for which he had struggled" was a tremor, or her hand, or the papers. Placing modifiers close to the members modified, we secure, instead, this result:

> Without a tremor he then placed in her hand the papers for which he had struggled so long and, till but the hour before, so hopelessly.

Mixed Figures. Akin to the tangled construction is the

mixed figure of speech. In this case however it is not the construction that is at fault; it is the thought itself, which begins with one comparison and then confuses the reader by unexpectedly shifting to a different comparison. At the time of the election of President Taft, for example, a prominent Middle Western newspaper displayed this headline:

Bryan Snowed under by Taft Landslide.

It is well enough to compare the vote for Mr. Taft with a heavy snowfall and with a landslide, but not with both at the same time. A mixed figure is like a photograph negative containing two pictures grotesquely blended; one picture at a time is an elementary rule in the art of writing as in the art of photography.

Unnecessary Words. When you use an unnecessary word or phrase, you are putting an obstacle, however slight, before the reader — are throwing sand on the machinery. Our words should be adequate, neither too few nor too many. The danger of using too few words is not serious, since to say a thing briefly is harder than to say it verbosely. The danger of using too many words must be constantly remembered by the writer who aims at skillful expression. Sometimes he can reduce the number of words by mere omission, as in this sentence:

Whenever I meet him he (always) greets me.
When (ever) I meet him, he always greets me.

At other times he can do it by rephrasing the thought more briefly:

He was very sorry to hear the bad news.
He was grieved to hear the news.
He was grieved at the news.

Or by change in construction, especially by the use of subordination instead of coördination:

> I hastened to the man and lifted him up.
> Hastening to the man, I lifted him up.

But the briefest is not always the best; brevity in the interest of economy is one thing, and brevity as a result of impatience is quite another. We must not use words unnecessarily, but we must use words enough to enable the reader to grasp our meaning and to remember it. Our thought must not be clouded with words, but it must be fully expressed with words that really serve the function of words — to clarify and enforce. Our trees must be free of dead wood, but they must also be fully developed.

Unpleasant Sounds. Again, when a writer uses combinations of words that are disagreeable to the ear, he is violating the principle of economy, because, as we have remarked, any mode of writing that calls attention to itself violates the principle of economy. Cacophony, or "bad sound," grates on the ear even when the reader does not audibly pronounce the words, and thus distracts his attention from the sense. When the poet Browning, who differed from normal humanity in having a considerable relish for discord, wished to ask whether the animal that has fed to repletion suffers from care and doubt, he wrote a vigorous but obtrusively harsh line:

> Irks care the crop-full bird? Frets doubt the maw-crammed beast?

Euphony is perhaps most frequently violated by the use of unpleasant *repetitions* of sound — by the use of such chance combinations as "the present president," "the visitor admired the vista," "a shrill trill," "he pitched hay all that day," and by the excessive use of the same consonant, as in this sentence:

> The *p*ale *p*rince *p*erceived a *p*erplexed ex*p*ression in the face of the *p*rincipal *s*peaker.

Exercise 34, Economy. Point out the cause of obscurity in the following sentences, and then recast the sentences in such a manner as to bring out clearly the intended meaning. Try to reproduce all the thought and to do so in a single sentence.

1. Germany was not long in seeing that by the acquisition of Alsace-Lorraine France would be reduced to a second-class power, and at the same time bring Germany to the front.

2. The Monroe Doctrine is a policy of the United States to regard the attempt of any European power to gain a foothold in the New World by conquest, or to acquire any new establishment in America by any means, will be considered as an unfriendly act to the United States.

3. When I remember how hard it was for me in those days early in the term to write a short theme, I marvel — even a one-page theme — I really marvel that I ever survived those days, when I consider how the words come trippingly from my pen now, these days, when writing is a simple matter to me, and the contrast is great.

4. When these acts of violence would reach the press and be immediately published only added fuel to the flames.

5. If it does not rain to-morrow, we shall drive on to Himmelsville, if the roads are good enough.

6. Because the Germans had taken possession of Russian provinces and had invaded the heart of Russia proved that the Germans were insincere in their promises.

7. He runs a hotel which there are not the best things in the world said about it.

8. The hot sun beat upon my neck which had been up for some time.

9. Every one thought the rebellion had been rooted out, but it was soon rekindled with renewed vigor.

10. I had to ask myself what man lay there with a sudden chill of apprehension.

11. The sound of the sea mounted to where I stood like a long sigh.

12. The pocketbook was returned with its contents though it was found by a farm hand, and, not being able to read, he gave it to his master.

13. I walked down the deserted road as the sun sank slowly and listened to the noises of the beach.

14. This world with all its trials is the furnace through which the soul must pass and be developed before it is ripe for the next world.

15. He seated himself in the chair as the committee entered and leaned back expectantly.

16. The object of the book as stated by the author is primarily for the entertainment of boys and girls.

17. Good nature is a characteristic American trait, and one which they often suffer for.

18. "Mr. Speaker, I smell a rat, but I propose to nip him in the bud." (*Congressional Record*)

19. I like this book because it deals with facts of which nearly all of us are familiar with.

20. I know of no better way to criticize this poem than Coleridge.

21. The book explains several ways that literature can help one in a style both logical and attractive.

22. Some students who live in town have to ride on the cars and with the poor car service they now get makes it rather disagreeable to go to and from college.

23. Longfellow's "Excelsior" is an idealistic poem which tells how a youth bore a banner, with the strange device "Excelsior" through ice and snow.

24. He is always sailing on the lake, a sport I am also very fond of.

25. He will deliver the things you want at once.

26. The slave was condemned to be eaten in the arena by the king of Rome.

27. I have read the book that you gave me with great interest.

28. He only wrote on one side of the paper.

ECONOMY

Exercise 35, Economy. Condense the phrasing in the following sentences and paragraphs without subtracting from the thought.

1. The wounded prisoner was suffering intensely from his painful wounds.
2. I know that I am right, for I saw the accident as an eyewitness.
3. With not a single opposing vote, he was unanimously elected president.
4. All the crowd rose together upon their feet with one accord and wildly waved their hats in their hands.
5. He is at the height of his power and will never be more powerful.
6. In place of the regular night service an afternoon service will be substituted instead.
7. The sharp sound of the wind, which is caused as it whirls through the tops of the trees, is the only disturbance of the tranquil quiescence of the garden.
8. I believe that I can do that work equally as well as he can.
9. Before I come I must first see how much money I have got in the bank.
10. A large crowd had congregated together before the house of the old widow woman.
11. We learned that it would take time to repair the automobile, and we walked to the nearest village, had some lunch, and we then returned to the scene of the accident, but the machine had not yet been repaired, and we tried to help the driver repair it, but our efforts were all in vain.
12. Near the road is an old house and it is now deserted and covered by dust, but it was once the home of the governor of the State, who lived there until the death of his wife, and who moved away about ten years ago.
13. Up to this time the efforts of the local custodians of the law to apprehend the men who make illicit whiskey near the town have proved absolutely unsuccessful, for they have not captured a single man, although it is commonly reported by everybody that there are hundreds of men engaged in the

lucrative and profitable business of making and selling whiskey, beer, brandy, and wines of every description.

14. On the edge of the road, at the point where it made a sharp turn before it led down the hill, there was standing a coach, and it looked black and very large in the white snow. The coach was crookedly imbedded in the snow, and there were no horses attached to it.

15. I was walking along a well-worn and much-used path which ran along a small creek, just as the setting sun was slowly sinking behind several clouds over the western horizon. The clouds were tinted a yellow-red by the rays of the setting sun, and the color of the clouds was reflected distinctly in the smooth surface of the water, turning its color to a very light pink. The trees were bare, as the leaves with their red color had fallen to the ground to protect it from the approaching winter which was near at hand.

Exercise 36, Economy. Comment on the repetition of sounds in the following sentences, stating whether you think the repetition is accidental or deliberate, undesirable or desirable.

1. The speaker discussed the source of the force of international law.
2. She acted like a rough boisterous boy.
3. I was silenced by his silent sullenness.
4. The men in gray will march to-day in the general procession.
5. The dogs barked, the pigs grunted, the cats caterwauled, and the cows lowed dismally.
6. Swaying slightly the gypsy shrilly shrieked her curses at us.
7. The girl turned slowly and stood quite quietly.
8. The summer soldier and the sunshine patriot will, in this crisis, shrink from the service of his country.
9. He told us to search there with the greatest care.
10. The elephant never trampled the life out of his owner on these occasions when the drunken man beat him, for he knew that after the beating, Deesa would embrace his trunk and weep and call him his love and his life and the liver of his soul, and give him some liquor.

CLEARNESS

THE principles of composition that we have considered should lead, if faithfully followed, to skillful writing, writing that is clear, emphatic, and varied — above all, clear. The principles of subordination, parallelism, emphasis, and economy call for clear thinking, and clear thinking, as we know, almost inevitably means clear writing. Conversely, it follows that if writing is vague, the thinking that preceded the writing was vague.

Yet there are certain syntactical pitfalls that waylay the writing of even a clear thinker, errors in sentence structure that human flesh — including such authors as Hawthorne and Thackeray — is heir to. It is the business of every writer to understand the nature of these errors and the readiest modes of correction.

Reference. (1) Reference of Pronouns. When we say, "The French nation is the most admirable in the world. They are the standard-bearers of civilization." — we are reproducing in expression an error in our thinking. *They* lacks an antecedent because we committed the error of supposing that we were talking about *the French* or *the French people.* We didn't know what we were talking about! The sentences should have read:

> The French nation is the most admirable in the world. It is the standard-bearer of civilization.

(2) Dangling Participle. The same error is involved in the case of the dangling participle. We should not write:

> Having eaten our lunch, the river trip was resumed.

Grammatically, the participial phrase must modify the subject of the governing clause; grammatically speaking, therefore, we are saying that the river trip ate our lunch! That was not in our minds, of course — then it should not be in our sentence. If *we* ate the lunch, *we* should be the subject of the governing clause:

> Having eaten our lunch, we resumed the river trip.

The participle *Having eaten*, instead of dangling in the air with nothing to attach itself to logically, is now securely fastened to its grammatical and logical master-word *we*.

(3) Dangling Elliptical Clause. Precisely the same thing happens in the case of the dangling elliptical clause, — a clause that is termed elliptical because its subject and predicate are omitted, and dangling because it is not properly fastened to the governing clause. For example:

> When four years old, my grandmother died.

Since *When four years old* is grammatically dependent on the subject of the governing clause, *grandmother*, we have unwittingly said that our grandparent died at the ripe old age of four. The simplest remedy in this case is to restore the omitted subject and predicate of the elliptical clause;

> When I was four years old, my grandmother died.

Point of View. (1) Change of Subject. When you are looking out over a landscape, you see everything that is visible from where you are standing, and nothing else. You do not see the other side of the barn, any more than you see the other side of the moon coming up over the barn. If you describe what you cannot see, you are false, false to your senses and to your mind. So when you write:

> In order to make the furnace burn harder, the lower door must be opened.

— you commit the same blunder, by regarding your

thought from the point of view, first, of a person, and secondly, of the door of the furnace. Sentences, of course, should be consistent in point of view, as our minds are when they are operating efficiently. We should adopt, in the sentence above, either the point of view of the person, or the point of view of the object:

> In order to make the furnace burn harder, you must open the lower door.
> In order that the furnace may be made to burn harder, the lower door must be opened.

(2) *Logical Agreement.* Other failures to observe the point of view are due to a variety of logical disagreements, as when, for instance, one says:

> Indian corn is now being grown in this country, and within the past ten years or so has developed to a considerable occupation

— in which the point of view is first that of the grain and then that of the occupation of raising the grain; or, again, when one gives a definition thus:

> "Infraction" is when you break a rule or law

— in which the writer begins by thinking of an act and then goes on as though he were thinking of the occasion of the act. An infraction is, of course, an act — not a *when!*

(3) *Shift of Tense.* In the writing of narration, uniformity in point of view is often violated by the abuse of the historical present tense, by the purposeless shifting from the past tense to the present. The historical present is a legitimate device when used by a skillful writer in a moment of high excitement during the narration of an event; though writing in the past tense, he is emotionally carried away by the reality of the action and spontaneously resorts, for the moment, to the present tense. On the basis

of our conception that what is in the mind should determine what is written on paper, this is as it should be. Too often, however, an unskillful writer, instead of looking to his thought and feeling, looks to the practiced writer for a hint to help him in writing cleverly, and in cold blood proceeds to confuse his tenses:

> The flames were mounting higher and higher, and we began to wonder whether they would reach the window where she stood. A fireman runs up with a shout, but she did not hear him, and just stood there. She stands for a long time, as if dazed, and then was hidden by the smoke. What shall we do?

The apprentice at the art of writing will do well to avoid this means of securing vividness altogether; he will be more likely to attain vividness if he uses one tense, either past or present, throughout.

Transition. Good writing is the expression of connected thinking. Stray thoughts set down one after another without relation could not be regarded as good writing, unless the thoughts were so fresh and penetrating, and so admirably phrased, that the reader would want to preserve them. Most of Emerson's essays are made up of such thoughts, first recorded in a notebook, then strung together on a fragile thread of thought and published as an essay: yet Emerson is called by Matthew Arnold the foremost prose writer of the nineteenth century. But most men, both greater and smaller than Emerson, think more connectedly, more logically, as we say, and are therefore bound to write otherwise. Connected thinking calls for connected writing. It is not enough that the thought should move logically from sentence to sentence; there must be an equivalent connection in the phrasing. It is logical to say:

I am glad to see the President powerful.   He has too much power.

But the signs of connected thinking are lacking.   We should say:

I am glad to see the President powerful.   But he has too much power.

I am glad to see the President powerful, but he has too much power.

The first statement may be called positive, the second negative, subtracting something from the first, somewhat as $4-1=3$.   Omission of a *but*, which often serves as the minus sign in writing, may, of course, be highly confusing.

We have at our disposal at least three types of connectives: we may repeat a word, generally a noun; we may use a pronoun or other reference word, such as *they* or *then;* or we may use a conjunction (see pp. 13–15) or a conjunctive adverb (see pp. 138–139).   A good writer, it is sometimes said, may be recognized most readily by the skill with which he employs connectives — the frequency and the discrimination with which he uses them.   One could not find a better receipt for avoiding vagueness than this: if possible, *link every sentence with the preceding sentence or sentences.*   Note the connectives in the following passage (those linking sentences have been printed in capital letters, those linking parts of sentences in italics):

On passing from a country in which free institutions are established to one where they do not exist, the traveller is struck by the change; *in the former* all is bustle and activity, *in the latter* everything is calm and motionless.   In THE ONE, melioration and progress are the general topics of inquiry; in THE OTHER, it seems as if the community only aspired to repose in the enjoyment of the advantages which it has acquired. NEVERTHELESS, the country which exerts itself so strenuously to promote its welfare is generally more wealthy and more prosperous than that which appears to be so contented with its lot; *and* when we compare them together, we can scarcely conceive how so many wants are daily felt in *the former*, while so few seem to occur in *the latter*.

If THIS remark is applicable to those free countries in which monarchical and aristocratic institutions subsist, it is still more striking with regard to democratic republics. In THESE States it is *not only* a portion of the people which is busied with the melioration of its social condition, *but* the whole community is engaged in the task; *and* it is not the exigencies and the convenience of a single class for which a provision is to be made, *but* the *exigencies and the convenience* of all ranks of life. (*Tocqueville*.)

Clearness in Diction. If writing is wanting in clearness, the cause may often be found, not in errors of reference, point of view, transition, and the like, but in an inaccurate use of individual words. We have already considered diction with respect to emphasis (pp. 32–33); we have now to consider diction with respect to clearness.

How often has an ambiguous word in a letter caused confusion or pain, the loss of time or money, the severance of a friendship! How often has a vague phrase in a state paper, or in a political speech, or in an editorial aroused a storm of protest and perhaps violent action! How often, in formal debate and in friendly discussion have protracted arguments resulted from the misunderstanding of a single word! It is well that our words should be emphatic; it is imperative that they be clear.

But what is clearness? The term is relative. A forest pool may be clear enough to permit one dimly to see the bottom; it may be so clear that one can make out certain objects at the bottom; it may be so clear that one can see the bottom with great distinctness; or it may be so clear that one is scarcely aware of the presence of the water.

Similarly, in composition, there are all degrees of clearness, from mere visibility to perfect transparency. When all the words precisely fit, when all the words accurately convey the intended meaning, the ideal of clearness in diction has been attained. It is not enough that the words roughly correspond to the thoughts, so that the reader may be said to "understand" the writer's sense; they should be so clear that he cannot by chance *mis*understand.

Failure in clearness of diction is caused by (1) *ambiguous words*, words that may have two meanings in the same context, such as "partially" in the sentence, "He dealt with the subject partially"; (2) *vague words*, words that may have more than two meanings, such as "nature," "equality," "democracy," when the use of such terms is not defined by the context or by actual definition; and (3) *obscure words*, words that are so ill-suited to the context that they apparently have no meaning at all, such as "procession" and "habitual" in the sentence, "I did not like the book: it seemed to me a queer procession, and the style anything but habitual."

The remedy for such failures in clearness lies, of course, in the use of the word that completely expresses the thought — a remedy far less simple than it seems. For, in the first place, clear expression follows only upon clear thinking, and clear thinking is a rare commodity, which can be purchased only at the price of such effort as few people are willing steadily to give. Most people write before they have clarified their thoughts, and then carelessly offer their muddy product to the public — or to the instructor in English. The act of writing, to be sure, helps vastly in the clarification of thought;[1] but it is not often that even the

---

[1] "Whenever on account of its vagueness, I am dissatisfied with a conception of the brain, I resort forthwith to the pen, for the purpose of ob-

most practiced authors are able to achieve a first draught that has a right to be regarded also as final; nearly always there must be rigorous revision, or the rewriting of parts, or the rewriting of the whole, or even the rewriting of the whole time and again till every word has the air of inevitability.

In the second place, clear expression is impossible unless the writer has a liberal stock of words, the means of expression. Indeed, it is impossible even to think, save in a rudimentary, animal fashion, without an abundance of words, since a thought totally without expression — without words to embody it — is scarcely a thought at all. For such crude thinking as suffices for everyday living, a small supply of words will meet our needs; but there is a wide difference between our ordinary simple, undeveloped thinking and the complex, lucidly outlined thinking required for the transference of ideas and feelings from the writer to other persons, and for such thinking we need a corresponding large supply of words — five or ten times as many. How can we obtain this large supply?

In a sense, we already possess it. We have a reading vocabulary, immensely larger than our writing vocabulary, a liberal stock of words more or less accurately understood when we encounter them but for the most part never used in our writing. This reading, or passive, vocabulary is a kind of hoard that we have laid up, gold coin buried in the cellar; it would be good business, to say the least, to place our savings in a bank or otherwise invest it. Words, like money, should be in circulation. From our ever-growing reserve of words earned by constant and attentive reading we should derive interest in the form of words added to our

taining, through its aid, the necessary form, consequence, and precision."
(Poe, *Marginalia*.) See also the Palmer paragraph, p. 89.

writing vocabulary, our active vocabulary. Most writers
would be amazed to learn how few words familiar in their
reading have a place in their writing, such common words
as *diminish, tranquil, hamper, alternative, recur, incredible.*
Do not be afraid of such words. They will not hurt you,
but serve you. They are better coin than the pennies you
have been using. If at first you are inclined to squander
them — to misuse them — repeated use will soon teach
you their true value.

Meanwhile, you may increase your writing vocabulary
by another means, the dictionary. If it repels you because
its vast wealth contrasts with your poverty, remember that
that wealth is entirely at your disposal. You are free to
take from it word after word, day after day, week after
week, until you find that you have a supply sufficient to enable you, to your keen delight, to utilize your intelligence.
It is a slow, but a fascinating process. Select a good dictionary, have it at hand always, and acquire the habit of using it. Look up new words in it; browse in it; master its arrangement — how it accounts for the growth of the word
literally from its *root* up. Observe the root of your word;
observe the variety of definitions showing the variety of
uses; observe the synonyms and wherein they differ from
your word; observe the standing of the word, whether colloquial, slang, dialect, etc. Even when you have done all
this, you have not reached the end, — beyond all that the
dictionary can tell you lies the connotation of the word, its
atmosphere, so to speak, too delicate, too elusive for deno-
tation, and to be learned only by familiarity with the word
as it recurs in your reading.

If you shrink from the effort of mastering words, bear in
mind that to write clearly you must think clearly, and that
to think clearly you must enlarge your vocabulary.

SENTENCES AND THINKING

Exercise 37, Clearness: Reference. Correct the faulty reference in the following sentences:

1. Kultur was a word used in Germany to indicate their ideal.
2. When six years old, my father took me to school.
3. Upon opening the door the door mat tripped me up.
4. The molten iron is very heavy, causing it to sink to the bottom.
5. While before the fireplace, the butler came in and handed him a letter.
6. After seeing that the tires were in order, the engine was started by him.
7. Turning a bend in the road, the little town could be plainly seen.
8. Never having seen the house, it was impossible for me to describe it.
9. Although very young, my grandfather asked me to go with him.
10. Entering the building, it was obvious that some one had been there recently.
11. Being in a test-tube, I could watch the crystals grow.
12. Looking back upon the events of this night, they now appear strangely unreal.
13. Upon questioning my sister, she showed a decided reluctance to explain.
14. While very young and tender, he carefully watched the plants grow.
15. After setting the vase in this insecure position, it naturally tumbled over when the door was slammed.
16. Sitting for three hours in the sun, my clothes became dry enough to walk home.
17. Hated and persecuted by the people of his time, one cannot help sympathizing with Shylock.
18. Although blest with a loving wife, she was too ambitious for the welfare of her husband.
19. Let every American uphold the President and do their part in averting disorder.
20. They had such different customs from those we now have that it is a curiosity.

21. On entering the porch, the eye is struck with the appearance of ease and comfort that characterized it.
22. The book shows us the obstacles the hero has overcome, which naturally makes the story more interesting.
23. The author gives us an insight into the man's nature. He has accomplished this by carefully selecting important incidents from his life.
24. In the reading of this book there were several ideas which impressed me.
25. Since having these facts presented to me so ably by the writer, they are more clearly fixed in my mind.
26. There is a plot to throw the Crown Prince into the sea. The Prime Minister is at the bottom of it.
27. Both lives were saddened by marrying one they did not love.
28. The speaker related many exciting things he had seen on the battlefield. This appeals to me because it recalls some of my own war experiences.
29. Everybody loves their mother.
30. These plays are all true tragedies, which was the author's favorite form.
31. Every one of them did as they pleased.
32. She led a very lonely life until one day when she learned how to remedy this.
33. The holder of the coupon when properly punched is entitled to one of our beautiful calendars.
34. Knowing that Lucas was associated with the Secret Service it was, to Mr. Simmons, a perfectly natural inquiry.

Exercise 38, Clearness: Point of View. Make the point of view in the following sentences consistent.

1. Girls fed the sheets in separately and they came out smooth and glossy at the other end of the machine.
2. To repair the furnace, it must be taken apart.
3. We walked through the older parts of the city, where many quaint old sights were seen.
4. I told him to come as soon as he can.
5. To have a fast game of baseball, the balls should be new.
6. I told him that I haven't read the book.
7. To avoid notoriety, the name of the hero is not given.

8. We went through the mechanical department, where many wonderful machines were seen.

9. We all put our shoulders to the wheel and soon the wagon was pulled out of the ditch.

10. In order to learn scientific farming, chemistry must be studied.

11. The Puritans hated bear-baiting, not because it gave pain to the bear, but because the spectators were given pleasure.

12. He had talent, but it did not seem to do him much good.

13. The Monroe Doctrine gave great encouragement to the young republics of South America, and they were enabled by it to develop their own systems of government.

14. To illustrate Hugo's vastness of knowledge, he wrote six chapters on the origin of the sewer of Paris.

15. *David Copperfield* is better than any of Dickens's novels.

16. He works in the law office, a profession I intend to enter when I have finished college.

17. Matthew Arnold is among the best examples in English literature of the long periodic sentence.

18. The work of the freshman year is harder than the sophomore.

19. The reason he dropped out of school is because he failed on two subjects.

20. The size of this boat is different from a schooner.

21. Lobbing is when you knock the tennis ball up very high.

22. He asked me did I think it would rain.

23. He threw a heavy ball about, which is good for the shoulder muscles.

24. A great deal of work must be done in order to conduct the business profitably.

25. Since we felt sure that he would come to the dinner, a place was reserved for him till the last minute.

26. If you have ever been young and went to church at night, you will sympathize with the heroine in this story.

Exercise 39, Clearness: Transition. Copy the paragraph on page 88 beginning, "Now there are some clear objects for choice . . . "; single underline the links within the sentence and double underline the links between sentences.

Exercise 40, Clearness: Transition. List all the connectives that occur in a theme or two that you have written, and then list the connectives in a passage of the same length from Burke or Arnold.

Exercise 41, Clearness: Transition. Choose from the list on pages 13–15 ten connectives that you rarely or never use, and write a passage, or several passages, in which you use them discriminatively.

Exercise 42, Clearness: Transition. Clip from a newspaper an editorial in which connectives are used with skill. Underline the connectives.

Exercise 43, Clearness: Transition. Write a theme of 150 words — preferably a comment — in which each sentence is linked with the preceding sentence or sentences.

Exercise 44, Clearness: Transition. Supply connectives in the following passage:

> The difference between popular and learned words may be easily seen in a few examples. We may describe a girl as "lively" or as "vivacious." In the .... case, we are using a native English formation from the familiar noun *life*. ...., we are using a Latin derivative which has precisely .... meaning. .... the atmosphere of the two words is quite different. No one ever got the adjective *lively* out of a book. .... is part of everybody's vocabulary. We cannot remember a time when we did not know it, and we feel sure that we learned it long before we were able to read. ...., we must have passed several years of our lives before learning the word *vivacious*. We may even remember the first time that we saw it in print or heard it from some grown-up friend who was talking over our childish heads. .... *lively* .... *vivacious* are good English words, ... *lively* is "popular" and *vivacious* is "learned."

SENTENCES AND THINKING

Exercise 45, Clearness: Diction. Point out and correct the ambiguity of diction in the following sentences:

1. He fixed the wheel on the floor.
2. I met a certain party at the library this morning.
3. He acts as if he is mad.
4. I want you to bring me the balance of my account at the bank.
5. At one time the fleets of England and Japan were incomparable.
6. Both men were not elected.
7. I want you to mind what I say.
8. No one was fond of the child because he was ugly and mean.
9. Every one loves their mother.

Exercise 46, Clearness: Diction. Point out and correct the vagueness or obscurity of diction in the following sentences:

1. Mr. Partelle aids his proof by giving examples.
2. This invention is a novice.
3. Three men furnish the main characters of the novel.
4. Sir Walter Scott's inmates were not literary men.
5. This was an incidence that excited much comment.
6. In *Glimpses of Unfamiliar Japan* Hearn's purpose was to naturalize Japan.
7. In this story the lost pocketbook was returned by a peasant, who was accused of being a colleague of M. Hauchecorne.
8. My brother's sickness at this unusually busy season got away with him.
9. They listened for a while to the great occasion with numerous acclamations.
10. From Homer to the present day an interest in other people has been man's absolving interest.

Exercise 47, Clearness: Diction. Define any ten of the following words and then compare your definition with the dictionary definition: *qualm, inimitable, irksome, travesty, sophistry, provident, salient, specious, germane, pertinacity, connoisseur, rejuvenate, efficacy, dexterity, candidate, petulant, tantalize, meander, charlatan, imperturbable, tantamount,*

74

egregious, ingenuous, effete, hackneyed, symmetry, colloquialism, clarify, panorama, centennial, cynical, expedite, gloaming, haggle, hazard, innuendo, instigate, loathsome, mercenary, monotone, platonic, quixotic, satyr, Utopian, vassal, yearn, yore, zealot.

Exercise 48, Clearness: Diction. With the aid of a dictionary distinguish between the following synonyms. Then write sentences each containing at least two of the synonyms from six selected groups. *Reticent, reserved, silent. Pertinent, relevant, apt, apposite, suitable. Male, masculine. Manly, manful, mannish, virile. Lively, animated, vivacious, sprightly, gay. Novel, new. Dress, attire, apparel, clothing, vesture, garb, raiment, costume. Ability, capacity. Apt, likely, liable. Crime, vice, sin. Divers, diverse. Right, privilege. Purpose, propose. Remember, recollect. Oral, verbal. Amateur, novice, tyro. Sole, solitary. Phase, aspect, kind. Apprehend, comprehend. Detract, defame, slander, vilify. Complete, finish. Shake, tremble, quaver, quiver, shiver. Cry, scream, yell, call, shriek, vociferate. Statement, narrative, account. Erudite, learned. Speech, oration. Brave, valorous. Horse, steed, nag, plug, charger, equine. Fat, corpulent. Truthful, veracious. Gift, donation. Shady, umbrageous.*

Exercise 49, Clearness: Diction. Find one or more synonyms for each of the following words and write sentences to bring out the exact difference in meaning between the synonyms: *alien, antagonize, cent, credible, decisive, egoism, euphemism, insult, likeness, healthy, phase, majority, part, rebellion, strategy, result, brightly.*

Exercise 50, Clearness: Diction. Collect ten new words recently observed in your reading. Use each correctly in a sentence.

SENTENCES AND THINKING

Exercise 51, Clearness: Diction. Look up the etymology of *unique, aggravate, ingenuous, horrid, acrid, expect, abortive, allow, alternative, calamity, involve, portion, proposition, veracity, anticipate,* and *conscious.* Point out and explain the misuse of these words in the following sentences:

1. He is the most unique man I have ever seen.
2. I was very much aggravated by his insolent remarks.
3. The shrewd old man gave a very ingenuous reply.
4. I think this book is horrid.
5. The tone of the article is extremely acrid.
6. I expect he has missed his train.
7. The attempt to wreck the train proved abortive.
8. He allowed he would join our hunting party.
9. We have before us the choice of three alternatives.
10. The loss of my purse was a sore calamity to me.
11. Several of our leading citizens have been involved in the crime.
12. In what portion of the city do you live?
13. When the hunter made the strange proposition that we spend the night in the little tent, I curtly refused.
14. We cannot doubt the veracity of these facts.
15. I don't anticipate that he got to his work on time this morning.
16. I was not conscious when he entered the room, for I was eagerly listening to an account of the football game.

Exercise 52, Clearness: Diction. Study the connotative or suggestive value of the diction in the following description of the poet Tennyson:

"A great shock of rough dusty-dark hair; bright-laughing hazel eyes; massive aquiline face, most massive yet most delicate; of sallow-brown complexion, almost Indian-looking; clothes cynically loose, free-and-easy; — smokes infinite tobacco." (Carlyle, in *The Correspondence of Carlyle and Emerson.*)

CHAPTER II

SENTENCES, PARAGRAPHS, AND OUTLINES

A whole is that which has a beginning, a middle, and an end. — ARIS-
TOTLE

Few write in the way in which an architect builds. . . . Most people write
only as though they were playing dominoes. — SCHOPENHAUER

THE SUMMARY SENTENCE

THE most profitable practice in the principles of subordination, parallelism, and emphasis will be found in the writing
of summary sentences. The summary sentence, as the
term is here used, is a sentence which expresses all the essential thought of a paragraph. Such a sentence is not ordinarily used in actual writing, though it sometimes occurs at
the end of a long or difficult passage, and though the topic
sentence is sometimes a virtual summary sentence.

Generally, the topic sentence is inadequate as a summary
of the thought of the paragraph, for the reason that it
merely *points to* the subject treated, without indicating
precisely *how* it is treated. It is often no more than the
label on a bottle; the summary sentence, on the other hand,
is always a distillation of the contents.

How should one set about the writing of a summary sentence? Given a paragraph, more or less misunderstood by
a hasty reader; wanted, a single, deft sentence that shall
embody the thought of the paragraph: obviously, the thing
cannot be done in a moment. Although the practiced
writer of summary sentences may sometimes compose his
sentence by merely reflecting on the substance of the para-

graph, the novice will probably find it necessary to go through a rather exacting analysis. A short paragraph from the War Message will afford an example.

> We have no quarrel with the German people. We have no feeling toward them but one of sympathy and friendship. It was not upon their impulse that their Government acted in entering this war. It was not with their previous knowledge or approval. It was a war determined upon as wars used to be determined upon in the old, unhappy days, when peoples were nowhere consulted by their rulers and wars were provoked and waged in the interest of dynasties or of little groups of ambitious men who were accustomed to use their fellowmen as pawns and tools.

(*1*) *What does the paragraph mean?* It goes without saying that one must know exactly what the thought is before one is in a position to express it in a sentence. The paragraph above happens to be a very simple one, so that its meaning will be clear on a second reading if it is not clear on the first. Often, however, certain difficulties must be overcome: (*a*) unusual words, (*b*) words used in unusual senses, (*c*) tangled or obscure sentences, (*d*) allusions. A good dictionary is an indispensable part of our equipment.

(*2*) *What is the topic sentence?* Now that we know what the paragraph means, we are prepared to begin to express its meaning. Let us choose, as a convenient skeleton for our summary sentence, the topic sentence. If the topic sentence is found to express all the important thought of the paragraph, we shall need to modify it very little; but ordinarily it will serve only as a starting-point. The topic sentence in our paragraph is the first sentence:

> We have no quarrel with the German people.

(*3*) *What additions to and subtractions from the topic sentence are to be made?* We can see at a glance that our topic sentence does not express all the important meaning of the paragraph. "We have no quarrel with the German people" — is that all that President Wilson is saying? By no means. After repeating the idea in the second sentence, he goes on, in the third and succeeding sentences, to explain *why* we have no quarrel with the German people. The topic sentence indicates *what he is talking about*, but *what he is saying* is another matter. The fact that the war was begun without the German people's knowledge or approval must be got into our summary sentence. It must be added; apparently there is nothing, in this case, to subtract. Let us add it then:

> We have no quarrel with the German people, and this is the case because the German Government began the war without their knowledge or approval.

(*4*) *Can the sentence be made periodic?* Since one thought in the paragraph is likely to be of more importance than all other thoughts, we shall rarely be able to accept a summary sentence that is cast in the mould of a compound sentence. We shall need a simple or a complex sentence, preferably periodic in structure. That means putting first our subordinate matter: "and this is the case because" etc. Reserving our main clause to the end, then, we may get some such result as this:

> Because the German Government began the war without their knowledge or approval, we have no quarrel with the German people.

Or, better:

> Because the Government began the war without the knowledge or approval of the German people, with them we have no quarrel.

(*5*) *Can the phrasing of the sentence be condensed?* There is always danger that a summary sentence will be cumbersomely long and involved. What we are seeking is the briefest, neatest form consistent with comprehensiveness. In the sentence above, no further condensation is necessary; several words have already been omitted — the first sentence numbering twenty-five words, the last one twenty-one.

(6) *Is there a connective?* Have we repeated one of the pivotal words or phrases of the preceding summary sentence, or used a suitable pronoun, or added a conjunction? In this case, the link is the word *Government*, which would occur in a good summary sentence of the preceding paragraph of the War Message. If possible, link every summary sentence to the preceding summary sentence by the use of some sign of transition in the thought. (See, once more, the discussion of transition, pp. 64–66.)

If these suggestions are faithfully followed, the student will not only learn to write acceptable summary sentences, but will strengthen his command of the principles of sentence and paragraph construction.

THE SENTENCE IN THE PARAGRAPH

AFTER writing a number of summary sentences, we are likely to discover that we have unconsciously acquired a vital sense of what constitutes a paragraph. At least, it has become perfectly clear to us that a paragraph is not a haphazard group of sentences, a motley crew without a leader, but a company in uniform, with an organization, a common purpose, and a captain. If we have really grasped this, we have learned much. What remains is to view a little more deliberately the purpose and organization of this company.

THE SENTENCE IN THE PARAGRAPH

As it is the purpose of an expository essay or article to explain something, so it is the purpose of an expository paragraph in such an essay to explain part of this something. Not any part however, but a certain very definite part; it must say all that needs to be said about this part of the subject, and it must say nothing else, unless by way of transition. Like a sentence, it must be complete in itself, and like a sentence, it must not contain foreign matter. The company of sentences that make up a paragraph must be a unit.

The leader of this unit is the topic sentence. Though it may occupy any position in the paragraph, and indeed is sometimes omitted altogether, in the vast majority of paragraphs it is placed at the beginning, because this is nearly always its logical place. Something is to be explained — what is that something? As the reader passes from paragraph to paragraph, the topic sentences inform him promptly as to the changes in subject-matter.

The subject having been stated in the topic sentence, it is the function of the rest of the paragraph to develop this subject as far as may be needful. The amount of the development depends, of course, on the subject. If the subject asserts that Americanism may be defined by the contents of four historical documents (see the initial paragraph on page 91), the paragraph will naturally concern itself with the four documents; but there might have been six documents, and then the paragraph would have been longer than it is. We do not want paragraphs to be long or short, large or small, but of the right size — the right size depending on the purpose of the paragraphs, just as in the planning of a house the right size of the rooms depends on the use of the rooms. The unpracticed writer who composes series of short, "scrappy" paragraphs is like an architect who plans a house with rooms so small that they are not suited to practical needs: or perhaps worse, he is like a man who employs no architect and uses no plan, but, constructing his house as the building proceeds, finds in the end that they are diminutive and confused. As for method in the development of a paragraph subject, this again depends upon the thought to be expressed, and varies, as human thought varies, to such an extent that it would take one a long time to find two paragraphs in which the method is identical. Certain types, however, may be distinguished, among them these:

a. Chronological arrangement — as in explanation of processes.
   (See the Burroughs paragraph, p. 90.)
b. Division — parts, causes, reasons, purposes, etc.
   (Eliot paragraph, p. 88, and first paragraph of "Americanism," p. 91.)
c. Examples — instances in support of a general statement.
   (Hawthorne paragraph, p. 89.)
d. Comparison or contrast.
   (Huxley paragraph, p. 90.)
e. Combinations of the above.
   (Palmer paragraph, p. 89.)

After the subject has been developed in some such manner, we may wish to add, at the close of the paragraph, a summary sentence more or less resembling the summary sentences discussed above (pp. 77–80). Since the function of a concluding summary sentence is to remind the reader of the content of the paragraph, it should be employed, of course, only when the paragraph is extraordinarily long or the thought extraordinarily complicated. In ordinary cases it is best to end with the last phase of the development, or with a sentence repeating the thought of the topic sentence, or with a transitional sentence that points forward to the next paragraph.

This brings us, finally, to the matter of transition. In our study of sentence construction, we have already observed (pp. 64–66) the need, not only of connected thinking, but also of the signs of connected thinking. What was there found to be true of the relation of sentence to sentence is quite as true of the relation of paragraph to paragraph. The writer knows the relation in advance; the reader does not. In the interest of economy of effort, the reader should be guided by a "but" or "yet," or "moreover," or "in the second place," or by the repetition of a word or phrase. Note, for example, that the second paragraph in "Americanism" (p. 91) begins with "These documents," a phrase which immediately links the thought of the paragraph with the thought of the paragraph preceding it. So important is this matter of transition that on occasion a writer composes a paragraph devoted wholly to the linking of what has been said with what is still to be said.

THE SENTENCE IN THE OUTLINE

THE requirement of unity, which we have studied in relation to the sentence and the paragraph, is equally essential in the composition as a whole. As it is the function of a sentence to express a single thought, and as it is the function of a paragraph to express a single thought embracing a company of constituent thoughts, so it is the function of the composition as a whole to express a single thought — a thought made up, it is true, of a great army of constituent thoughts, but yet a single thought. Thus, Cardinal Newman's lecture on "Knowledge Viewed in Relation to Professional Skill," containing about thirty-five pages and hundreds of sentences, is simply a full expression of this single thought:

> Since intellectual culture is useful in being an end in itself, and since it is useful in training men for membership in society and for professional study, a Liberal Education is superior in utility to an education which aims directly at skill in calling.

This is the thesis, the argument, the "point," of the lecture, and such a sentence might therefore be termed a *thesis sentence*. Every exposition and argument, and, in a somewhat different sense, every description and narration should so unmistakably be a unit that one could easily, if not rapidly, compose a thesis sentence representing its contents. A writer who is still training himself, indeed, would do well to compose such a sentence, not after, but *before* writing the whole composition. He will then have a plan, or outline, of his thought to prevent digression, to assure the treatment of all the leading parts of the thought, and to keep the central purpose so vividly in his mind that every sentence he writes will contribute something toward achieving it.

For a brief paper, one of not more than half a dozen pages, a carefully prepared thesis sentence may be a sufficient outline. For an extensive essay, however, a more detailed outline is often indispensable. Of the various types of outlines, we shall here consider only the one that is always adequate — that in which the thought is expressed exclusively in sentences and in which the arrangement is by symbols and indentation. For example, Newman's discourse contains four main divisions, which he very likely set down in a preliminary outline and which we might set down in an analytical outline in some such fashion as this:

THE SENTENCE IN THE OUTLINE

I. That the idea of a Liberal Education has not been accepted by all prominent men may be exemplified by the controversy between certain Edinburgh Reviewers and two defenders of Oxford.

II. We may easily combat the theory of Utility in education by maintaining that intellectual culture, in being its own end, is useful.

III. Taking "useful" to mean, not "what is good," but "what tends to good," we are again drawn to the conclusion that a Liberal Education is in a high degree useful.

IV. The fact that a Liberal Education is useful because it trains men for membership in society and for professional study may be enforced by quotations from the writings of the defenders of Oxford.

If a still more detailed outline is desired we may add, under each main heading, important subordinate matter. Thus, under main heading III we might indicate its three divisions (A, B, C) and in the case of the last of these (C) two further subdivisions (1, 2,) so that in its expanded form our outline of this section would be as follows:

III. Taking "useful" to mean, not "what is good," but "what tends to good," we are again drawn to the conclusion that a Liberal Education is in a high degree useful, for
A. What is good is always useful, since good is reproductive of good.
B. The usefulness of what is good may be illustrated by the parallel of bodily health.
C. A Liberal Education serves the following uses:
1. It leads to the formation of the good citizen.
2. It is the best aid to professional skill.

Note that everything has been cast into sentence form — that there are no loose ends, no mere phrases, but always sentences.

When the outline is complete, we are ready to write the thesis sentence. The simplest procedure is to combine the substance of the main headings. If the main headings are so numerous that not all can be woven into a single statement, eliminate those that are least important. Then, of those that remain, select the most important one. That is to become the main clause of the thesis sentence and the remaining headings are to become the subordinate clauses or phrases. If possible, let the sentence be periodic, or at least virtually so; that is, place the subordinate clauses first and the main clause last. (See once more the example on p. 84.) The thesis sentence may then be prefixed to the outline, just below the title.[1]

Exercise 53, Summary Sentence. Following the suggestions given in pp. 77–80, write summary sentences for the following paragraphs: (1) the first paragraph of "Americanism" (p. 91); (2) the Eliot paragraph (p. 88); (3) the Hawthorne paragraph (pp. 89–90); (4) the Huxley paragraph (pp. 90–91); (5) the Burroughs paragraph (p. 90); (6) the Palmer paragraph (p. 89); and (7) the Bourne paragraph (p. 88).

Exercise 54, Paragraph. Write five topic sentences that might be developed into paragraphs.

Exercise 55, Paragraph. Write a theme of three paragraphs, giving special attention to paragraph transition.

Exercise 56, Paragraph. Write a paragraph closing with a summary sentence.

Exercise 57, Paragraph. The following paragraphs are defective in construction. Read them attentively to detect the most serious defects. Then rewrite the paragraphs in such a way as to remedy these defects.

[1] For permission to reprint in this chapter, particularly in the last section, certain matter from *Outlines and Summaries*, by Norman Foerster (New York, 1915), the authors are indebted to the generosity of the publishers of that book, Messrs. Henry Holt & Co.

THE SENTENCE IN THE OUTLINE

WHAT STUDENTS READ

According to my observation, students read no good literature. Several of my friends enjoy the works of the greatest English novelists — Thackeray and Dickens particularly — and I know several students who occasionally read some of Shakspere's plays. Shakspere was born in 1564. Personally, I think a student who graduates from college without having read *King Lear* and *As You Like It* has missed a great deal of genuine pleasure and profit. Students who read Shakspere and Thackeray and Dickens, though they are not many in number, are certainly to be found in our universities. Thus it is clear that students do read some good literature.

Most of my friends read only two kinds of writing: first, what they find in their textbooks, and second, the short stories in the magazines. They buy or borrow copies of the current magazines, in which they find a large number of stories that have at least this merit (if it is a merit): that they are written by authors still living. Often these stories are extremely silly or extremely dull, and most of them are really less interesting than the short stories and the novels of many standard writers. One reason why students read fiction in the magazines rather than in good books is, I think, that they foolishly prefer to pay twenty cents for a magazine to paying seventy-five cents or a dollar for a good book. Some of them, however, read the works of standard authors.

Exercise 58, Outline. Prepare a one-page plan for a theme, using the sentence form for your outline. Make the sentences parallel if you can.

Exercise 59, Outline. Write a two- or three-page analytical outline of "Americanism" (pp. 91–96), observing carefully the following instructions: head your paper with the title, below the title write the thesis sentence, and below that the outline. In the outline, use the sentence form throughout; and be sure that your symbols and indentation conform to the examples on page 85.

PARAGRAPHS FOR STUDY

Now, there are some clear objects for choice here in college, for real choice, for discreet choice. I will mention only two. In the first place, choose those studies — there is a great range of them here — which will, through your interest in them, develop your working power. You know that it is only through work that you can achieve anything, either in college or in the world. Choose those studies on which you can work intensely with pleasure, with real satisfaction and happiness. That is the true guide to a wise choice. Choose that intellectual pursuit which will develop within you the power to do enthusiastic work, an internal motive power, not an external compulsion. Then, choose an ennobling companionship. You will find out in five minutes that this man stirs you to do good, that man to evil. Shun the latter; cling to the former. Choose companionship rightly; choose your whole surroundings so that they shall lift you up and not drag you down. Make these two choices wisely, and be faithful in labor, and you will succeed in college and in after life. (*Charles W. Eliot.*)

The failure of the melting pot, far from closing the great American democratic experiment, means that it has only just begun. Whatever American nationalism turns out to be, we see already that it will have a color richer and more exciting than our ideal has hitherto encompassed. In a world which has dreamed of internationalism, we find that we have all unawares been building up the first international nation. The voices which have cried for a tight and jealous nationalism of the European pattern are failing. From that ideal, however valiantly and disinterestedly it has been set for us, time and tendency have moved us further and further away. What we have achieved has been rather a cosmopolitan federation of national colonies, of foreign cultures, from whom the sting of devastating competition has been removed. America is already the world-federation in miniature, the continent where for the first time in history has been achieved that miracle of hope, the peaceful living side by side, with character substantially preserved, of the most heterogeneous peoples under the sun. Nowhere else has such contiguity been anything but the breeder of misery. Here, notwithstanding our tragic failures of adjustment, the outlines are already too clear not to give us a new vision and a new orientation of the American mind in the world. (*Randolph Bourne.*)

Why, then, do we hesitate to swell our words to meet our needs? It is a nonsense question. There is no reason. We are simply lazy; too lazy to make ourselves comfortable. We let our vocabularies be limited, and get along rawly without the refinements of human intercourse, without refinements in our own thoughts; for thoughts are almost as dependent on words as words on thoughts. For example, all exasperations we lump together as "aggravating," not considering whether they may not rather be displeasing, annoying, offensive, disgusting, irritating, or even maddening; and without observing too, that in our reckless usage we have burned up a word which might be convenient when we should need to mark some shading of the word "increase." Like the bad cook, we seize the frying pan whenever we need to fry, broil, roast, or stew, and then we wonder why all our dishes taste alike while in the next house the food is appetizing. It is all unnecessary. Enlarge the vocabulary. Let any one who wants to see himself grow, resolve to adopt two new words each week. It will not be long before the endless and enchanting variety of the world will begin to reflect itself in his speech, and in his mind as well. I know that when we use a word for the first time we are startled, as if a firecracker went off in our neighborhood. We look about hastily to see if any one has noticed. But finding that no one has, we may be emboldened. A word used three times slips off the tongue with entire naturalness. Then it is ours forever, and with it some phase of life which had been lacking hitherto. For each word presents its own point of view, discloses a special aspect of things, reports some little importance not otherwise conveyed, and so contributes its small emancipation to our tied-up minds and tongues. (*G. H. Palmer.*)

Insects are among the earliest births of spring. Multitudes of I know not what species appeared long ago on the surface of the snow. Clouds of them, almost too minute for sight, hover in a beam of sunshine, and vanish, as if annihilated, when they pass into the shade. A mosquito has already been heard to sound the small horror of his bugle horn. Wasps infest the sunny windows of the house. A bee entered one of the chambers with a prophecy

of flowers. Rare butterflies came before the snow was off, flaunt-
ing in the chill breeze, and looking forlorn and all astray, in spite
of the magnificence of their dark, velvet cloaks, with golden bor-
ders. (*Hawthorne.*)

The incomparable French natural-historian and felicitous
writer Henri Fabre has witnessed what I never have: he has seen
the caterpillar build its case or cocoon. In the instance which he
describes it was the small grub of one of the Psyches. The first
thing the creature did was to collect bits of felt or pith from the
cast-off garment of its mother. These it tied together with a
thread of its own silk, forming a band, or girdle, which it put
around its own body, uniting the ends. This ring was the start
and foundation of the sack in which it was to incase itself. The
band was placed well forward, so that the insect could reach its
edge, by bending its head up and down and around in all directions. Then it proceeded to widen the girdle by attaching parti-
cles of down to its edges. As the garment grew toward its head,
the weaver crept forward in it, thus causing it to cover more and
more of its body till in a few hours it covered all of it, and the sack
was complete, a very simple process, and, it would seem, the only
possible one. The head, with the flexible neck, which allowed it
to swing through the circle, was the loom that did the weaving,
the thread issuing from the spinneret on the lip. Did the silk
issue from the other end of the body, as we are likely to think it
does, the feat would be impossible. I suppose a woman might
knit herself into her sweater in the same way by holding the ball
of yarn in her bosom and turning the web around and fulling it
down instead of turning her body — all but her arms; here she
would be balked. To understand how a grub weaves itself a
close-fitting garment, closed at both ends, from its own hair, or
by what sleight of hand it attaches its cocoon to the end of a
branch, I suppose one would need to witness the process. (*Burroughs.*)

The vast results obtained by science are won by no mystical
faculties, by no mental processes, other than those which are
practised by every one of us in the humblest and meanest affairs
of life. A detective policeman discovers a burglar from the marks
made by his shoe, by a mental process identical with that by

which Cuvier restored the extinct animals of Montmartre from fragments of their bones. Nor does that process of induction and deduction by which a lady, finding a stain of a particular kind upon her dress, concludes that somebody has upset the inkstand thereon, differ in any way from that by which Adams and Leverrier discovered a new planet. The man of science, in fact, simply uses with scrupulous exactness the methods which we all habitually and at every moment use carelessly. (*Huxley.*)

AMERICANISM [1]

By Hartley B. Alexander

Four great historical documents, marking progressive epochs in our national history, give the essential definition of Americanism in politics. First is the Declaration of Independence, signed July 4, 1776, proclaiming the principles by which the United States justify their independence of European domination. Second is President Monroe's message to Congress, of December 2, 1823, announcing the right of the peoples of the western hemisphere to pursue their political destinies without interference from Old World powers. Third is Lincoln's memorial address at Gettysburg, November 19, 1863, in which the rights of Americans to their own continents are affirmed to be inalienably democratical, and without democracy to be forfeit. Fourth is the message delivered by President Wilson at the joint session of the two Houses of Congress, April 2, 1917, asserting the value of the democratical polity to the whole territorial world and the right to it of the entire human race.

These documents are not themselves causes of political conduct in any primary sense. Rather, each is a summary of contemporary political conviction — from which fact arises the height of their significance as expression of the political faith of America. It is certainly true that this faith has been clarified and invigorated by the fine intelligence of the expression; for more than to any other form of state, public intelligence is necessary to democracy. Nevertheless, as in every other form of state, the final sanction of government is the faith of the citizen; which is the im-

---

[1] Reprinted through the kind permission of the author and of the publishers of the *New Republic.*

pulse for that conduct whereof, in democracies, intelligence alone can set the pattern. The patterns of Americanism are its public utterances, with the four that have been mentioned in the stations of preëminence.

Out of each of these documents may be chosen phrases which serve as texts of their fuller meaning. "All men are created equal ... unalienable rights ... life, liberty, and the pursuit of happiness": this is the core of the Declaration of Independence, voicing in eighteenth century speech that belief of democrats in men's right to the self-responsible making of their own laws which is fundamental in our polity. It is true that this formal meaning of the pronouncement has received many material alterations in the course of a century of history (though none, certainly, that weaken the strength of the form); and among them, not the least, a vast extension of the meaning of "all men" and a profound complexification of the doctrine of "rights." The men who signed the Declaration, though their minds were broad with the morning, were yet but conscious rebels. What they felt was less the tyranny of the Old World than the independence of the New, and what they demanded was the right of free experimentation in lands unspoiled. The true foundation of the rights of man as they knew them was their own self-confidence in their own political sagacity. The beginning of American liberty was the commanding acceptance of responsibility.

The Declaration proclaimed America's right to try out democracy; the Monroe Doctrine proclaimed both the success of the experiment and the belligerent intention to broaden its territorial marches. "*The American continents, by the free and independent condition which they have assumed and maintain,* are henceforth not to be considered as subjects for future colonization by any European powers." The italicized phrase is the important one: it proclaims again the acceptance of responsibility, no longer for experiment, but for huge expansion. The Monroe Doctrine, in effect, established a greater Mason and Dixon's line, having the natural seas for its delineations. Unless history shall show greater consequences from President Wilson's War Message, it is the most ambitious political proclamation ever made effective. In its own consciousness the United States was no longer, as de Tocqueville and other sympathetic Europeans regarded it, merely an unexpected fruitful trial of precarious political theory; it was now confident and aggressive, with ambitions outpassing the grandiosities of emperors — and incidentally and immediately, defying emperors and their ambitions; for the direct occasion of Monroe's message was the threat of the Holy Alliance for the re-subjection of South America and the Russian threat of expansion in North America.

The truly arrogant pretentiousness of the Monroe Doctrine is best realized when we contrast the sparseness of the human population in the western hemisphere with the relatively crowded condition of the eastern: virtually, since the democratic faith was but meagerly represented in the Old World at that time, it was a demand from an insignificant minority among men that they be possessed of a third of the world. Certainly, such a demand could never have received any general recognition had it not been coupled with a free invitation to all European peoples to colonize America in every sense save the political; the convincing corollary to the Monroe Doctrine was the open door to immigrants. It may be remarked that the situation is not greatly changed to-day. The Americas are still the most sparsely populated of the great habitable areas of our globe; the Monroe Doctrine is still in force. But the test of its strength is to come not from Europe but from Asia. The real issue, before Americans and Europeans alike, is now whether, in the interests of political independence, the western hemisphere must not, and in fairness, open the doors of immigration to the Oriental. Can the Caucasian west preëmpt this virginal domain to the lasting exclusion of the congested east? What is the meaning of "all men" in our Declaration?

Lincoln's "Gettysburg Address" represents cognizance of the same fundamental problem from the angle of internal organization; it is, as it were, the conscious self-measurement of the New World polity in the glass of its own ideals. The speech looks back to the nation's beginnings, and, in a sense, it is a final re-affirmation of what Monroe had before affirmed: that the experimental stage of American democracy was passed, and that thenceforth, bulwarked by America, "government of the people, for the people, and by the people" should not perish from the earth. It affirmed this, not in view of external threat, but in the presence of internal; in effect stating that America could not tolerate from any group of its own people the formation and perpetuation of an oligarchical or other form of anti-democratical state, that democracy alone should be free to develop in the western hemisphere, for the very reason that democracy is imperiled by non-democratical neighbors. The address was, in short, an apostolic profession that democracy is convinced of its own righteousness, and is intolerant of all dangerous rivals.

Supporting this profession there was a profounder meaning than the ostensible one of territorial union and political unity. The meaning of "all men" still called for definition, and Lincoln could not use the word "people" in any cant sense. He had long before proclaimed that the nation could not endure half slave and half free; he well knew that the crux of the war was the slave question; and no man could have been wiselier conscious than he of the fact that the settlement of that question for freedom must mean ultimately a redefinition of "people" and a new conception of American citizenship. The United States had liberally welcomed Europeans of many tongues and complexions, who should be the making of its people; now it was ready to take into the body politic millions of that race which is most antipodal to the European. The enfranchisement of the American blacks is the most heroic act of political faith in history. True, the problem of readjustment has none of the simplicity which the idealists of that time dreamed it to have; it is a problem that now is and will long continue with us. But the faith that was in the Declaration and that forms the heart of Americanism to-day, faith in the civic nobility and therefore in the civic rights of all nature which we can call human, received in the enfranchisement of the Negroes its extreme attestation. From that time forward Americans could face the world, conscious that they had made themselves clean with their first professions. Race questions and class questions — as distinguished from questions of formal politics — will long continue to vex us, and eventually the Mongol problem will be huger than the Negro; but by implication all of these were settled, and not only for us, but for all democratical peoples, when our Civil War came to its issue. The civic man is henceforth of no preferred complexion and of no recognized caste — at least, this is now a fixed article in our American faith in a "government of the people": Americanism cannot be for "all men" in any lesser sense than for "men of all kindreds."

The Revolutionary War established the privilege of democracy in the New World. A mature generation later that privilege was converted into an aggressive right, balking the ambitious pretensions of the Cæsars of that day in respect to the two western continents. Another generation matured, and the Civil War marked the purification of democracy in its own house, and a final clear-conscious recognition of the uttermost intention of the term democracy. Now a third generation has matured and passed, and in a war outmeasuring all those that men have fought the United States is called once more, not only to stand for its political faith, but to expand the meaning of that faith. The stand and the expansion have both been made and (true to the genius of his nation) the President has given their meaning in a penetrating phrase. "The world must be made safe for democracy; its peace must be planted upon tested foundations of political liberty." *The World!* Here, indeed, is expansion; our globe has shrunk too small for democratic and autocratic states to subsist together, nor can Ocean herself constrain them in separation. Democracy has issued her final defiance to all the citadels of absolutism, proclaiming no longer her right to independence, nor merely her right to her own free field, but now her purposed supremacy in all fields and over all politics. Here is arrogance of pretension out-matching Monroe's, whose broad-limned compromise breaks futile, like the old compromises of North and South. Democracy is now claiming for herself no lesser thing than the world.

The new declaration is fittingly accompanied by a reaffirmation of the old. The "tested foundations of political liberty" refer us once again to the trial which our national history has given to our national faith, proudly asserting that we have passed the trial with triumph, and that the high self-confidence of the authors of the Declaration has been justified to their sons' sons. But more than this, the new declaration, like those which have preceded it, adds new meaning to the whole national faith. Our fight, said the President, is for the liberation of the world's peoples, "the German people included," — therein asserting the right of democracy to a kind of spiritual colonization, even in antagonistic lands. The assertion of such a right, unless it were the deepest of convictions, could only be the most incredible effrontery; and if conviction, it can have for its meaning naught save a new definition of "all men." Henceforth, the word "people" must include not merely men of all external complexions, but men of all internal complexions, not merely men of all classes, but men of all polities — and for the reason that there is but one true form of the truly human polity, and that is the democratical form. The faith that underlies such an assumption is prodigious; and it is in that faith that we are fighting, for it is the core of Americanism. Fighting, and at the same time watching and listening with an eager and amazing confidence for the first signs of response from the German people; for the President spoke only what all Americans in their hearts believe, when he said that our war is with institutions and not people.

Americanism has received its definition in four great documents. Three of these have been issued upon the occasion of great wars, and the fourth, for near a century, has been as distinctly belligerent in character as the mailed fist or the jangling sabre. Americanism is, obviously, no pacifist faith. But it is, none the less, a faith. It is a faith vast in its pretensions beyond all dreams of autocrats; and it is a faith, despite its century of trial, little justified by what has transpired in human history. Yet in the face of autocrats and of history, it is inwardly unshaken and serene, religious in its confidence, miraculous in its hopes. Its foundation is something more constraining than experience and far more compelling than reason; for its foundation is an inner light, which for us is like a revelation, showing as in an apocalypse the common humanity of "all men." Americanism is a faith that men have died for, and that men are dying for to-day — whether it be a madness or divinity that hath touched them with it.

BOOK II: PRINCIPLES OF REVISION

CORRECTNESS: Grammar, Punctuation, Mechanics, Spelling

CHAPTER I

GRAMMAR

A man's grammar, like Cæsar's wife, must not only be pure, but above suspicion of impurity. — Poe

INTRODUCTION: GRAMMAR AND COMPOSITION

The function of grammar is to codify the sounds, inflections, and syntax of words, to describe systematically the speech habits of the best writers and speakers. Since these speech habits are always undergoing some alterations, we may say that a living language evolves much like an organism; old words and constructions are abandoned, new words and constructions are added. Grammar, describing these evolving speech habits, also changes, only more slowly, more conservatively. It refuses to recognize modifications of the language until they have clearly established their title. Unless one is among the leading writers and speakers, therefore, the proper thing to do is obviously to abide by the "rules" of the latest code.

Too often, unfortunately, the study of the grammatical code has been divorced from the study of composition. Consequently, the college student of composition, who is supposed to have learned his grammar in the preparatory school, often finds himself embarrassed, in his efforts to write, by a surprisingly sketchy knowledge of grammar and of its relation to the problem of expression. He soon discovers that a large proportion of so-called errors in composition are actually errors in grammar, and that the only sure remedy for such errors is a thorough review of those principles of grammar that have a vital relation to composition.

Thus, when the student begins the study of parallelism, he finds that what appears to be a matter of rhetoric is fundamentally a matter of grammar, that parallel structure implies similarity of grammatical structure. Any difficulty that he may have in using the principle of parallelism is traceable to his ignorance of the parts of speech and their functions in a sentence. Again, when he writes:

> He said that he would come. Though his desire was obviously lukewarm.

— the fatal "period fault" is caused by his confusion of a subordinating conjunction, "though," with a coördinating conjunction, "but."

The student whose errors in composition are frequently caused by ignorance of grammar should study with the utmost attention the **Grammatical Terms,** pp. 148–161.

1 SENTENCE DEFINED

Importance of Knowing What a Sentence Is. The sentence, as the thought-unit, is the starting point for the study of composition. Although a knowledge of the grammatical structure of the sentence is less important than clear, logical, unified thinking, only a few rare spirits can dispense with a conscious understanding of grammar. Ordinary mortals cannot hope to write passable English without a definite knowledge of what a sentence is and without the ability to distinguish unerringly between sentence, phrase, and clause. Before defining these terms, let us look at several typical groups of words:

The man. The sun. The rim of the sun. Rises. Over the horizon. Is coming. Was visible. The rising sun. Was shining. Had been injured. When the sun rises. Began. To disappear. Which had just risen.

All of these words or groups of words leave us with a sense of incompleteness. They do not tell us anything; they merely suggest ideas or arouse our curiosity. Not one of them is a sentence.

The Sentence Considered Grammatically. If we choose from the group above a word or phrase that names something (a subject), and join to it a word or phrase asserting something about the thing named (a predicate), our sense of completeness is satisfied, and we have a sentence:

The sun rises.
The man had been injured.
The rim of the sun was visible over the horizon.

Such a combination of subject and predicate is called a *predication.* Every sentence must express a predication, must name something and assert something about the thing named. Furthermore, this predication must be independent in itself. Otherwise, it cannot satisfy our sense of completeness. We may, then, define a sentence as *a group of words containing a complete and independent predication.* This definition, viewed more specifically, means that every sentence must contain a subject — a noun or some expression used as a noun — and a predicate — which must contain a verb capable of making a complete and independent assertion.[1] Such a verb is called a *finite* verb. But not all forms of the verb fulfill this requirement; there are some *non-finite* forms, called *verbals,* which cannot predicate in-

[1] For the sake of simplicity no account is taken at this point of elliptical sentences, sentences in which the subject or the predicate is implied, not expressed.

dependently or completely. *Verbals* should be clearly distinguished from *verbs*.

Verbs and Verbals. Study the following groups of words:

The sun rising over the horizon.
Rising slowly over the horizon.
To rise over the horizon.
The sun rose.
The sun rose over the horizon.

It will be observed that only the last two groups of words constitute sentences. The other groups contain, not finite verbs, but *verbals*, that is, words derived from a verb, but performing the function of noun or adjective; words that name an action or describe some noun or its equivalent.

Verbals are of several kinds. A verbal noun (*gerund* or *infinitive*) is a word derived from a verb but used as a noun. A verbal adjective (*participle*) is a word derived from a verb but used as an adjective. Verbal nouns and adjectives differ from other nouns and adjectives only in derivation, not in use.

Consider the use of the underscored words in the following sentences:

The man <u>runs</u> over the hill every morning.
<u>Running</u> is a good exercise.
<u>To run</u> without stopping requires good lungs.
<u>Running</u> water is purer than stagnant water.

In the first sentence *runs* is a finite verb: it makes a complete and independent assertion about the subject; the group of words "makes sense." In the second and third sentences *running* and *to run* name something; they are used just as a simple noun, for example, *baseball*, or *tennis*, would be used. In the last sentence *running* describes *water* in precisely the same way as the simple adjective *stagnant* does. In the last three sentences the verbal is accompanied by a finite verb, *is*, *requires*, and *is*, which expresses the predication of the sentence. No group of words can stand alone as a sentence unless it contains a finite verb.

Phrases and Clauses Distinguished from Sentences. A *phrase* is a group of related words not containing a subject and a predicate and used as a single part of speech. Phrases may be used as the equivalents of nouns, verbs, adjectives, or adverbs.

Examples: The rim of the sun was visible. (Noun phrase.)

The rim of the sun was rising. (Verb phrase, auxiliary + infinitive or participle.)

The coat of many colors was destroyed. (Adjective phrase.)

The sun rose over the horizon. (Adverbial phrase.)

A phrase differs from a sentence in not containing a predication. Though a phrase may often be used as the equivalent of the subject or of the predicate, it can never take the place of both these necessary parts of a predication.

A clause is a group of words containing both subject and predicate, but used as part of a sentence. Consider the italicized groups of words:

He did not hear *what I said.*
He waited patiently *until the road was cleared.*
That he has made a mistake is obvious.
The man *who owns the farm* lives in town.

The italicized clauses express predications, but these predications are not independent. They cannot stand alone, but depend ("hang from") some independent predication. Each is used to form only part of a sentence, and each is used as the equivalent of a single part of speech.

"What I said" is used as a noun, as object of the verb *hear*. "Until the road was cleared" is used as an adverb to modify the verb *waited*. "That he has made a mistake" is used like a noun, as the subject of the verb *is*. It is modified by the predicate adjective *obvious*. The last clause is used like an adjective, to modify the noun *man*. Each of these groups of words, then, is a *dependent clause*, a group of words containing subject and predicate, but used as a single part of speech to form only part of a sentence. A dependent clause expresses a predication, but the predication is dependent upon other words; it cannot stand alone as an independent assertion. A dependent clause thus differs from a sentence in this fundamental respect: A sentence contains an independent predication, whereas a dependent clause contains a dependent predication.[1]

An *independent* clause is a group of words containing a subject and predicate and capable of standing alone as a sentence.

"The heavens declare the glory of God, and the firmament showeth his handiwork." Each of these clauses is independent, and each could be written alone as a simple sentence:

> The heavens declare the glory of God. The firmament showeth his handiwork.

The use of the comma and the conjunction *and*, however, makes a compound sentence of the two clauses. The thought unit in this sentence, then, is composed of two equal and logically related parts, each of which could stand alone as a complete sentence. Whether such a group of words is a sentence or an independent clause depends en-

[1] Dependent clauses resemble phrases (1) in that the thought expressed by each is incomplete when taken alone, and (2) in that each is used as a single part of speech.

tirely upon the way it is used; it is a matter of rhetorical rather than of grammatical unity. If it begins with a capital and is followed by a period (or question mark, or exclamation point), it is a sentence. But if it is used as a part of a larger unit of thought, it is an independent clause. An independent clause can readily be distinguished if one remembers that every independent clause is potentially a sentence — *could be* a sentence.

Exercise A. Copy each of the following sentences, underscoring the *simple subject* once, the *simple predicate* twice. Be prepared also to point out the *complete subject and the complete predicate.* (For definitions see pp. 148–161.)

1. All summer the trip had been discussed.
2. Not a drop of rain had yet fallen.
3. Have you spoken to him about our plan?
4. Accompanied by a friend, I visited the Exposition grounds.
5. Are you going now?
6. Of the assistants, he alone slept in the house.
7. She took up the pencil without moving the book.
8. What time did he say he would come back?
9. There are many reasons for my answer.
10. The words were interrupted by the sound of groans beyond the door leading to the bedroom.
11. The change from the customary spot and the necessary occasion of such an act — from the dressing hour in a bedroom to a time of traveling out-of-doors — lent a novelty to the idle deed.
12. Through a spur of the ridge, from the Downs to the castle, the old home of the family, ran a dusty and rocky road.
13. The girl on the summit of the load sat motionless, surrounded by tables and chairs with their legs upward, backed by an oak settle, and ornamented in front by pots of geraniums, myrtles, and cactuses, together with a caged canary, — all probably from the windows of the house just vacated.
14. When hope is gone, all has been lost.

15. As soon as we reached the house, we saw our mistake.
16. It seemed to me, as I paced to and fro, that there could be
no other solution.

Exercise B. (1) Point out the phrases, the dependent clauses, and the independent clauses in the sentences below. Explain the function (use in the sentence) of each phrase and dependent clause, and, if the instructor so directs, explain the function of each word.

(2) Point out all the verbal nouns and verbal adjectives in the sentences below.

1. I saw him, but he did not see me.
2. James was there, Jonathan was there, but Henry was not there.
3. When night falls, the lake seems twice as wide.
4. The lake seems twice as wide when night falls.
5. Little men endure little men; but great men aim at a solitary grandeur.
6. The wild goose is more of a cosmopolite than we; he breaks his fast in Canada, takes a luncheon in Ohio, and plumes himself for the night in a Southern bayou.
7. He intended to be gone a year, but returned at the end of two months, harshly criticizing his folly in leaving home.
8. When we try to pick out anything by itself, we find it hitched to everything else in the universe.
9. As he reflected upon the matter now, scowling at the picture on the wall, he remembered his first trip to her home.
10. But some thoughtful person, who had seen him walking across one of his fields, might have regarded him in another light.
11. When the weather is fair and settled, they are clothed in blue and purple, and print their bold outlines on the clear evening sky; but sometimes, when the rest of the landscape is cloudless, they will gather a hood of gray vapors about their summits, which, in the last rays of the setting sun, will glow and light up like a crown of glory.
12. The British worker might or might not be convinced of Henry George's contention that the power of the landlord to

extort rent was the cause of increasing or continuing poverty in the midst of increasing wealth; he was in any case likely to be strongly moved by the contention that poverty increased side by side with wealth, that it increased because the increasing wealth was more and more unequally distributed, and that the evil arose from human law and not from inevitable forces of nature.

Exercise C. (1) Compose three sentences consisting of two or more independent clauses and no dependent clause. Compose three consisting of combinations of one independent and one dependent clause. Compose three consisting of two independent clauses and two or more dependent clauses. (Turn to the **Grammatical Terms,** pp. 148–161, and study the sections on simple, complex, compound, and compound-complex sentences.)

(2) Describe each of the sentences in Exercises B and C as simple, complex, compound, or compound-complex.

2   THE " PERIOD FAULT "

THE confusion of a dependent clause or a phrase with a sentence often reveals itself in the so-called "period fault," or "illiterate period." Because it is symptomatic of a radical misconception of what constitutes a sentence, it is one of the most serious blunders in English composition.

It consists of *the writing of part of a sentence as if it were a sentence* — the use of a period where a comma is required. For example:

> *Wrong:* Milton believed that man should be humble, obedient, and thankful toward God.   Observing and obeying his laws.

Anybody who knows his grammar should recognize "observing and obeying his laws" as a participial phrase — a mere phrase, not a sentence.   Consequently, anybody who writes a phrase like this, or a dependent clause, as if it were a complete sentence, confesses that he does not know what a sentence is. His first task should be to find out, by thoroughly mastering the preceding discussion, pp. 98–103. He will then be in a position to understand why the "sentences" on Milton are really a single sentence:

> *Right:* Milton believed that man should be humble, obedient, and thankful toward God, observing and obeying his laws.

There are four common varieties of the period fault:

a. A phrase consisting of a noun or a pronoun + a verbal in *-ing* is often incorrectly written as a complete sentence.

> *Wrong:* She cared little for society. Her chief interest being the care of her home.
> *Right:* She cared little for society, her chief interest being the care of her home.

Other examples are given on page 5.

b. An appositive phrase is sometimes incorrectly written as a separate sentence. This type of error is most frequently found when the appositive is introduced by such expressions as *namely, that is, for example,* and *such as.*

> *Wrong:* He hated the town very much. As a place of residence especially.
> He was praised by those who knew him best. Namely, his brothers.
> *Right:* He hated the town very much, especially as a place of residence.
> He was praised by those who knew him best, namely, his brothers.

For the punctuation of appositives see pp. 172–173.

c. The second of two *that*-clauses or of two infinitive

phrases is often incorrectly written as a separate sentence.

Wrong: He said that he would certainly help us. That he had no objection to the plan.

Farmer Oak had hardly time to gather these impressions into a thought. To see how strangely the red feather of her hat shone in the light.

Right: He said that he would certainly help us, that he had no objection to the plan.

Farmer Oak had hardly time to gather these impressions into a thought, to see how strangely the red feather of her hat shone in the light.

d. A dependent clause is incorrectly written as a sentence. (See p. 98.)

Exercise. Correct the "period fault" in the following sentences and be prepared to explain your correction.

1. Learning is, in too many cases, but a foil to common sense. Too often a substitute for true knowledge.

2. Some men never reason wrongly. Since they do not reason at all.

3. "You do not know what you are saying," returned my friend. Putting on his hat and turning his back to me.

4. I took no pains to keep my thoughts to myself. And sometimes would smile in his face. Thereby increasing, no doubt, his dislike for me.

5. He stood and watched me fidgeting with my hat. Which I had taken off again.

6. There is one night I shall always remember. Because something memorable happened to me then

7. The citizens have a right to overthrow an unjust form of government and to set up a desirable form. Which will guarantee to them life, liberty, and the pursuit of happiness.

8. He stumbled up the stairs in the dark, singing at the top of his voice. Thereby disturbing the sick man in the room above mine.

9. Emerson says that the priest becomes a form. That the mechanic becomes a machine. And that the sailor becomes a rope of the ship.

10. America is blessed with a democratic government. A government that is a model for the world.

11. More than once an involuntary fear seized me. As I heard above my head the muffled whir of a ringdove's wings hurrying past.

12. He tells about the wolves hunting him as he journeyed through the snow. Especially one big wolf which would pursue everybody who crossed his path.

13. This unknown personage wore an old coat much worn in the folds. And a diamond in the frill of his shirt, and gold earrings in his ears.

14. The quantity of light reflected from the bent needles was so great as to make whole groves appear as if covered with snow. The black shadows beneath the trees greatly enhancing the effect of the silvery splendor.

15. Calhoun and Webster debated the question of States' Rights. Each construing the Constitution in accordance with his own convictions.

16. There is a soul at the center of nature, and over the will of every man. So that none of us can wrong the universe.

17. Do not try to reform everybody. To set the whole town right.

18. The church has reared him amidst rites and pomps. And carries him along with her.

19. We have few readers. Though we have many spectators and hearers.

20. Their mind is not dazzled by its own means. But locked and bolted to results.

3   THE "COMMA FAULT"

THE so-called "comma fault," or "illiterate comma," is one of the most serious errors in the whole of English composition. Like the "period fault" (discussed in the preceding pages) it is an error, not only in punctuation, but also in unity and grammar. Broadly speaking, it consists of *the writing of two sentences as if they were one* — the use of a comma in place of a period. For example, the following "sentence" is wrong:

> I know that he will do it, in all these years he has never broken a definite promise.

One who has any acquaintance with the merest rudiments of grammar will see at once that there are two sentences here, two complete and independent predications. The writer of such a "sentence" publicly reveals that he does not know what a sentence is, that he does not know where one sentence ends and another begins. If the student is in this unhappy condition, he should turn at once to pp. 98–103, and completely master the distinction between sentence, clause, and phrase.

All such double "sentences" may be written with grammatical correctness merely by *the substitution of a period for the comma:*

> *Right:* I know that he will do it. In all these years he has never broken a definite promise.

The student who is seriously troubled with the illiterate comma is urged to rest content with this simple revision.

The more advanced student, however, may aim at a more organic revision. According to the precise relation of his ideas, he may combine the two independent predications in the following ways:

(1) By using a coördinating conjunction — in which case a comma is sufficient (see pp. 167–168):

> I know he will do it, for in all these years he has never broken a definite promise.

(2) By using a semicolon without a conjunction (p. 181):

> I know that he will do it; in all these years he has never broken a definite promise.

(3) By subordinating one of the two independent clauses (see pp. 8–15):

> Since in all these years he has never broken a definite promise, I know he will do it.

These several ways differ in unity, emphasis, rapidity of movement, etc.; which is best in a given case depends, of course, on the thought to be expressed.[1]

Caution: Students who commit the "comma fault" should apply this simple rule. Never use a comma between groups of words capable of standing alone as separate sentences, unless these groups of words are linked together by *and, but, or, nor, yet,* or *for.*

Exercise. In the following "sentences," correct the "comma fault" in the simplest possible manner, that is, by *changing only the punctuation* (and capitalization, where necessary); or, if the instructor so directs, correct it by whatever method seems in each case most appropriate to the thought.

1. I had now come in sight of the house, I decided to wait no longer.
2. In the evening we reached a village, I determined to spend the night there.
3. There is something in the very season of the year that gives a charm to the festivity of Christmas, at other times we derive a portion of our pleasure from the mere beauties of nature.
4. The climax is the crucial point in a narrative, of this the author should have a definite idea before he writes a word of the story.

---

[1] There is one exception to our rule. When a sentence consists of clauses that are (1) short, (2) closely coördinate, and (3) without interior punctuation, commas suffice:

> The wind howled, the rain blew, the thunder roared.

Such a sentence, however, is comparatively so rare that the beginner will do well to disregard this exception.

5. A thought seemed to strike him, the island had been left behind, and the shore lay far off in the hazy sunlight.

6. Kipling wrote "The Man Who Was," this is an excellent story.

7. These orders were sufficient, the rescuers could not return before morning.

8. Furthermore, the people who constitute the National Government also constitute the various states, the people gave to the National Government its powers.

9. "Watch this pitcher," I said, "he isn't going to let the batter touch the ball."

10. Bill lounged lazily in his leather-cushioned chair, his feet were propped up at a comfortable angle.

11. "Well, good-bye," he said, "I'll see you again soon, I hope."

12. "Let's ride through the park," he replied, "it will be cool and pleasant to-day."

13. His gaze strayed slowly from the forest in front of him, it rested intently on the large brick house opposite the hut.

14. "I'll wait ten minutes and then I'll be off," I answered slowly, "you need not wait for me."

15. I hope we shall see a great deal of him in the future, his visits will always be welcome to us.

16. "Sit down," my friend replied cordially, "I do not expect another visitor to-night."

17. "Surely these mills ought to be shut down," he said good-naturedly, "I don't see how the girls live on what they get, a strike's the only chance, there's no use to try reason with the owners."

18. My cousin was an extremely gay and humorous fellow, no matter how dull and blue things were, he could always make the situation pleasant and delightful.

19. "He would come," said Enoch, "he alone is to blame."

20. My lord and I sat one day at the same table upon some tedious business of detail, I have said that he had lost his former interest in such occupations, he was plainly itching to be gone, and he looked fretful, weary, and older than I had ever previously observed, I suppose it was the haggard face that put me suddenly upon my mettle.

4   AGREEMENT

AGREEMENT OF SUBJECT AND VERB

A VERB should agree with its subject in person and number.

a. A singular subject + plural modifier + verb is followed by a singular verb.

> *Right:* A *list* of many things *has* (not *have*) been drawn up.
> The *thought* of the two poems in these volumes *is* different.
> The *ingenuity* of Tom in inducing the other boys to aid him in his tasks about the house of his aunts *is* ably presented to the reader.

b. Singular pronouns, *each, every, either, neither, any one, some one, anybody, nobody, one, no one,* require singular verbs.

> *Right: Each* of the men *was* (not *were*) eager for the fight.

None may be followed by either a singular or a plural verb according to the meaning of the sentence. The singular, however, is more common.

c. The number of the subject is not changed by the addition to it of such words as *including, with, together with, as well as,* or an *and not* phrase. (This rule applies even if the added words are not set off parenthetically.)

> *Right:* I, as well as my brothers, *am* coming.
> He, and not his partners, *was* arrested.

d. Two or more subjects joined by *and* require a plural verb.

> *Right:* The flower and the shrub *were* withered.
> James and I *are* coming.

But when the compound subject consists of two

words of closely related meaning or of two nouns naming the same person or thing, the two subjects form a single unit of thought and require a singular verb.

Right: The tumult and the shouting dies. (The classic example of this idiom.)

His mercy and tenderness is his chief characteristic. The secretary and treasurer was just saying that the whole career and success of his son was suspended upon the decision of the committee.

His son and heir is dead.

e. Two or more singular subjects joined by *or*, *nor*, *and not*, or *but* do not form a plural subject. If the subjects differ in number or person, the verb agrees with the nearer.

Right: Either she or I *am* to be elected.

Neither the man nor his wife *is* at home.

Neither he nor my brothers *are* working this summer. (Such sentences should often be recast: "Either she is to be elected, or I am." "One of us will be elected.")

f. A collective noun, according to the meaning of the sentence, may require either a singular or a plural verb.

Right: The jury *was* to render *its* verdict at noon. (The jury is viewed as a unit.)

The jury *were* requested to take *their* seats. (The individual jurors are viewed separately.)

Note: Treat collectives consistently. Do not regard a collective first as a singular and then as a plural. See **Point of View, 99.**

g. Nouns plural in form but singular in meaning usually govern a singular verb. But usage is not fixed. *Mathematics, athletics, politics, news, means, physics, gallows* are construed as singular; *riches*, *scissors*, and *proceeds* usually as plural; and *pains* and *means* as singular or plural. When in doubt use a singular verb.

h. The expletive *it* always governs a singular verb. The verb after the expletive *there* is singular or plural according to the number of the subject that follows.

> *Wrong:* From Homer to Shakespeare there *stretches* three thousand years.
>
> *Right:* From Homer to Shakespeare there *stretch* three thousand years.

i. A verb agrees with the subject, not with the predicate noun.

> *Wrong:* The reason for my dislike of surf-bathing *are* the large breakers.
> The large breakers *is* the reason for my dislike of surf-bathing.
>
> *Right:* The reason for my dislike of surf-bathing *is* the large breakers.
> The large breakers *are* the reason for my dislike of surf-bathing.

It is often desirable to recast the sentence so as to avoid the awkward difference in number between subject and predicate nominative:

> *Right:* I dislike surf-bathing because of the large breakers.

j. The contracted verb forms demand especial care. Many people who say, "He don't," would never think of saying, "He do not."

k. A relative pronoun referring to a plural antecedent governs a plural verb.

> *Right:* This is one of the most interesting *books* that *have* (not *has*) ever been written.
> It may be one of the little towns that *try* (not *tries*) to appear larger than they really are.

AGREEMENT OF PRONOUN AND ANTECEDENT

A pronoun agrees with its antecedent in gender, number, and person. The case of a pronoun is independent of the case of its antecedent.

l. Singular pronouns should be used to refer only to singular antecedents. Pay special attention to such antecedents as *man, person, each, every, any, either, anybody, kind, sort, everybody.* These words always require singular pronouns.

> *Right:* Every man should be neat in *his* dress (not *their*).
> Everybody in the room raised *his* head and looked at me in surprise.
> Every person raised *his* head, etc.

> *Note:* It is correct to use *he, his, him* to refer to an antecedent of common gender, as in the sentence "Every student should use *his* own book." *His or her, he or she, him or her* should be used only when reference is made to two antecedents of different gender and when it is desirable to emphasize the difference in gender.

> *Permissible:* Each boy and girl in the room must write his or her paper without assistance.

If the antecedents are connected by *or* or *nor*, follow the rule for the agreement of subject and verb. See *e* above.

m. Collective nouns may require a singular or a plural pronoun according to the meaning of the sentence.

> *Right:* The jury rendered *its* decision at noon. (The group acted as a unit.)
> The jury took *their* seats promptly. (The jurors acted individually.)

See note under *f.* above.

Exercise. Revise the following sentences.

1. There is one door and three windows on the front side of the house.
2. An observation of all phases of life together with various experiences help in mastering this subject.
3. All the glamour of feudal days breathe under his touch.
4. There is found shortly after the opening of the chapter many passages of dialogue.
5. In the second class of words comes modifiers.
6. I was surprised to learn that he is one of the few writers who has dealt with this subject.
7. Neither John nor his brother are coming.
8. The best thing about the book were the illustrations.

See also the exercise on p. 70.

See also the exercise on p. 70.

5   CASE

CASE is the classification of nouns or pronouns according to their use in the sentence (as subject, object, indirect object, etc.). Nouns have only two forms to show case, the uninflected, or common, case, and the possessive (genitive): *boy, boy's; boys, boys'.* Some pronouns have as many as three forms to show case: *I, my, me; he, his, him.*

    a. Nominative Case. Note the following cautions for the use of the nominative case:

        1. Do not use the nominative case of a pronoun as the object of a verb or preposition.

            Wrong: Did you know that Mary was married? No; *who* did she marry?
                A crowd of *we* boys went on a hunting trip.
                I want you to keep this a secret between you and *I.*

        2. After the conjunctions *than* and *as* in elliptical clauses of comparison use the nominative case when the expanded clause demands that case.

Right: He is more active than *I* (not *me*).

He is as able to do it as *I* (not *me*).

In such clauses the construction of the pronoun can always be determined by expanding the *than* or *as* clause. *Than* and *as* are conjunctions, not prepositions. For example:

She saw him as well as (she saw) me.

She saw him as well as I (did).

b. Objective Case: Do not substitute the objective for the nominative case. Study the following rules:

1. Do not use the objective case of a pronoun as a predicate complement.

Wrong: It is *me* (*him, her, them*).

Some liberal authorities accept "It is me" as a colloquialism; but the vast majority condemn the expression. No authority has ever defended "It is him," "It is her," etc.

2. Do not substitute the objective *whomever* for the nominative *whoever* in such sentences as these:

Wrong: Show the paper to *whomever* asks about it. (*Whoever* should be used as the subject of *asks*. The object of *to* is the clause "whoever asks about it.") The friend *whom* I thought was coming disappointed me. (The pronoun demanded by this construction is *who*. *Who* is the subject of *was coming*, not the object of *thought*, for the phrase *I thought* may be regarded as parenthetical.)

3. With such prepositional phrases as *as to, in regard to, according to* be careful not to let the subject of the following clause be attracted into the objective case as a sort of pseudo-object of *to*.

Wrong: I want to ask you some questions in regard to *whom* will be elected.

Right: I want to ask you some questions in regard to *who* will be elected. (The whole clause — *who will be elected* — is the object of the prepositional phrase *in regard to*. *Who* is the subject of *will be elected*.)

4. Use the objective case of a pronoun as the subject, the object, or the objective complement of an infinitive.

Right: *Whom* did you take *him* to be?
Did you take *him* to be *me?*

c. Possessive Case. Pronouns form the possessive without an apostrophe.[1] Nouns form the possessive by adding the apostrophe or apostrophe and *s*. (See **Apostrophe, 28.**) Nouns naming inanimate objects form the possessive with an *of*-phrase except in such common expressions of time or space as *a day's work, an hour's journey, a week's vacation* or in phrases where the idea of personification is present, such as "the law's delay," "for mercy's sake," "heart's delight," "Nature's plan."

Right: The roof of the house.
The Mayor of the city.
The cure of the disease.

In the case of relative pronouns, *of which* is used of inanimate objects, *whose* of persons. But where the use of an *of-which* phrase would result in clumsiness, the more colloquial *whose* may be used in reference to inanimate objects:

Awkward: The book the title page *of which* is missing is very rare.
It is a city the builder and maker *of which* is God.

---

[1] The only exceptions are the indefinite pronouns *one, somebody,* etc.

d. Appositives.   An appositive must be in the same case as its antecedent.

> *Right:*   *W*e three are to go, John, you, and *I.*
> He invited *us* three, John, you, and *me.*

Exercise.   Revise the following sentences:

1. He did not say who he saw, but, between you and I, I believe it was her.
2. He wants us — just you and I — to come.
3. I will give the reward to whomever first claims it.
4. Include the names of some friends whom you think might like to communicate with you.
5. Although he is not as old as me, it took three of we boys to hold him.   James and me could not do so.
6. Return the book to Kate or Sarah according to whom calls for it first.
7. I wanted to see if we couldn't hit upon some plan, me and him, for shortening the time.
8. There was nothing to show whom he might have been.
9. I had no suspicion as to whom that man in the gray suit was.

6   POSSESSIVE WITH GERUND

THE substantive modifying a gerund should be in the possessive case:

> *Right:* He slipped away without any one's seeing him.
> I had not heard of his dying so suddenly.

But if the substantive is modified by the verbal, the objective is the proper case:

> *Right:* I cannot imagine him laughing at his unfortunate brother.
> I cannot conceive of him writing such a letter.

The choice between the possessive and the objective case before a verbal in *-ing* depends entirely upon the meaning of the sentence.

Exercise. In some of these sentences the case before the gerund is correct, in others incorrect. Revise the faulty sentences.

1. You can depend on him being on time.
2. I can't imagine him painting such a picture, but I can conceive of him buying it.
3. The king was greatly pleased to hear of him being the famous Robin Hood.
4. He laughed at the idea of Mary's objecting.

7   SUBJUNCTIVE MODE

THE inflected subjunctive has been lost in nearly all English verbs except *be*. The indicative forms have taken the place of the old subjunctive forms, or new phrasal subjunctives have been formed by means of the modal auxiliaries *may, might, should, could, would,* etc. In modern English the older subjunctive forms are used in three cases: to express (1) a wish, (2) a supposition or a very doubtful condition, and (3) an unreal condition. Do not substitute the indicative for the subjunctive in these cases.

a. To express a wish or a regret. The present subjunctive is used to express a wish for the future, or to express a present volition or command. The imperfect subjunctive is used to express a present wish or regret, the past perfect to express a past regret.

> *Right:* I move that the second roll-call be omitted.
> Peace be with thee.
> The devil take thee.
> Oh, that he were here.
> Oh, that he had been here.
> Oh, that he had taken me with him.

b. To indicate that a condition is strongly improbable or to express a pure supposition. The present refers to present or future time.

Right: If he be absent when I arrive, I will give the book to you.   (Condition strongly improbable.)

The phrasal subjunctive with *should* is usually preferred to the inflectional subjunctive in such a sentence.   If the condition is regarded as true or very probably true, the indicative is used:

If he should be absent when I arrive, I will give the book to you.
If he is absent when I arrive, I will give the book to you.

   c. To express a condition contrary to fact.   Use the imperfect to indicate present time, the past perfect to indicate past time.

     Right: If he were only here, all would be well.   (Never "If he was.")
       If he had been here, all would have been well.
       Had I been present, he would not have gone.

Exercise.   Correct the errors in mode in the following sentences.   Some of the sentences are correct.

1. Mr. Brown walks as if he was reading poetry and was expressing the rhythm with his feet.
2. If I was you, I would not go.
3. I wish he was coming.
4. If it was true, it was a horrid fact in one so young.
5. There would be less wonder if there were even a little heard of the second son.
6. I wonder if he dares show himself at such a time as this.
7. To do otherwise than keep silent were to be ungrateful.
8. This principle demands that the author understands his own thought before trying to express it.

8   **TENSE**

Tense is the inflection of a verb to show the time of the action, as present, past, future, etc.   Unlike highly inflected languages, Latin for example, English has very few *tense forms.* But although English has only two inflections for tense, only two real *tense forms*, the language is capable of expressing six or more time relationships, for by means of adverbs or verb phrases a great variety of tenses may be formed. Any discussion of tense should sharply distinguish between *tense form* and *time of action.* In the subjunctive mode especially there is often a seeming conflict between the tense form employed and the time indicated. This conflict is seen, though less often, in the indicative also. Note especially the present indicative.

a. Present. The present tense form generally indicates present action; but it may also be used to indicate future action, past action, and timeless action:

He is leaving now (real present).
He is leaving to-night (future action).
He leaves the shore! He plunges toward the boat! The breakers hurl themselves upon him! (The historical present.)
Ice is cold. Nature abhors a vacuum. (Timeless presents, presents of general truth.) See *Sequence, g* below.

b. Past. The past tense form always refers to an action occurring at some definite time in the past. The time modifier should be supplied if it cannot easily be implied from the context:

Obscure: Time went by in the house, without much change; only they were three instead of four.
Definite: Time went by in the house *after* that, without much change; only they were *now* three instead of four.

When the time modifier refers to past time, never use the present perfect tense:

Wrong: He *has been* sick several times last month.
Right: He *was* sick several times last month.

When a narrative of past events is interrupted by the introduction of a preceding event, use the past perfect, not the past tense:

Obscure: An hour later I made a light again and put on my shoes of felt that I *wore* by my lord's sick-bed, and set forth into the house to call my companions.

It seemed strange that I could have looked upon the ship with so much indifference, for she *brought* death to my brothers.

Definite: It seemed strange that I could have looked upon' the ship with so much indifference, for she *had brought* death to my brothers.

For ordinary narrative, prefer the past tense to the historical present. See pp. 63–64.

c. Future. The future and the perfect tenses are expressed, not by means of single tense forms, but by phrases. The future may be indicated by *am to be, is about to, is going to,* or by *shall* and *will.* (For present for future see *Present* above.)

He is to be shot at sunrise.
He is about to be shot.
He is going to be shot at sunrise.
He will be shot at sunrise.

For *Shall* and *Will,* see **9.**

d. Present Perfect. The present perfect tense indicates an action that is completed at the present. When an adverb of time is used, it must always extend to the time of speaking.

Wrong: He has been sick several times *last week.*
He has *then* come in.

Right: He has been sick several times *this week.*
He has *just* come in.

e. Past Perfect. The past perfect indicates an action that was completed prior to some other past action.

When I called, I found that he had retired an hour before.

See also *Past*, above.

f. Future Perfect. The future perfect indicates an action that will be completed prior to some other future action mentioned or implied.

I shall have gone when he comes to-morrow.

The future perfect tense has almost completely disappeared from ordinary speech.

g. Sequence of Tenses. The tense of a subordinate clause depends on the relation of the action of the subordinate clause to that of the main clause.

Right: I told him to come as soon as he *could* (not *can*).
I explained that I *had called* to see him on Sunday also (not *called*).
He said that he *was going* to New York.
I stated that he *was* wrong.

Note the apparent violation of the sequence of tenses in the gnomic, or timeless, present, a present used to express general truths:

Right: Copernicus *taught* that the earth *revolves* around the sun. (The statement was true in the past and is still true.)
Ptolemy *taught* that the sun *revolved* around the earth. (The past tense is used because the statement is no longer regarded as true.)

h. The Tense of Verbals. Participles and infinitives have no tenses of their own, but depend for their time reference upon that of the governing verb. That is, the present tense of a verbal indicates an action contemporaneous with that of the main verb; the future, an action subsequent to that of the main verb; and the past, an action prior to that of the main verb. The following errors demand especial attention:

1. The improper use of a perfect infinitive instead of a present:

   Wrong: I meant *to have told* you about it.
   Right: I meant *to tell* you about it. (What did I mean then? *To tell.*)

2. The improper use of a present participle to denote an action not contemporaneous with that of the governing verb:

   Wrong: Coming of age on June 5, he was able to enter business for himself in July.
   Walking five miles to the club, he was unable to take part in the game.
   Right: Having come of age on June 5, he was able to enter business for himself in July.
   Having walked five miles to the club, he was unable to take part in the game.

i. Principal Parts of Verbs. Distinguish sharply between the principal parts of such verbs as *come, take, go, eat, drink, begin, run, do.* Confusion of the tenses of such common verbs is a sign of illiteracy. See *Principal Parts* under **Grammatical Terms,** pp. 157–159.

Exercise. Revise the sentences that contain errors in tense:

1. I did not intend to have been late, but my train was delayed thirty minutes.
2. He rode over the ruined mounds, which were used as tombs, but which were abandoned.
3. I hardly wrote the first letter before there came three distinct raps on the door.
4. The column of smoke reminded me of a huge snake that crept here and there in search of something that he may devour.
5. When I arrived, I found that he left town.
6. Coming before six o'clock, he was standing at the head of the line when I arrived two hours later.

7. She would not have let Gerald have done that if she could have helped it.

9   "SHALL" AND "WILL"

To understand surely the proper distinction between *shall* and *will*, one must study the history of these words;[1] for *shall* and *will* have not always been used as future auxiliaries; they were once independent verbs with very clear-cut meanings. In Old English *shall* (infinitive, *sculan*) meant "to owe," "to be under obligation," "to be under necessity," "to be destined"; and *will* (infinitive *willan*) meant "to will," "to intend," "to purpose," "to be determined." In Old English, furthermore, there was no future tense at all; to indicate that an action was yet to take place, that it was to occur in the future, the only device was to use the present tense, often with some adverb implying futurity, as in the modern expression "He comes soon" = "He will come soon" or "He is to come soon." Obviously, this was a very crude device; and the need for a tense that would clearly show future time could be met only by finding or developing some future verb-form or some future auxiliary. As it happened, the English found two verbs whose meaning suited fairly well with the idea of futurity: *shall* = "to be destined," etc., and *will* = "to intend," etc. Accordingly, both these verbs developed a special use as future auxiliaries; that is, they were used sometimes when the speaker was more anxious to put the action unmistakably into the future than he was to emphasize the notion of necessity or intention.

It must not be supposed, however, that the original

---

[1] The present discussion is suggested by and is based in part upon the excellent historical treatment of *shall* and *will* in Fowler's *The King's English*, pp. 133–154 (2d edition, Oxford Univ. Press, 1919).

meanings of these verbs were forgotten when they were thus used as auxiliaries; the idea of necessity, or intention, was suppressed, shoved into the background, but it was still present to consciousness. Now, the first important thing for one to grasp is that this primary, or original, meaning was bound to be more present to consciousness in connection with subjects in some grammatical persons than in the case of others. For example, if one says, "*You* shall go" or "*He* shall go," the idea of necessity or compulsion can hardly be suppressed; the speaker will inevitably seem to be implying that he is authority for the necessity, that he has control over the action. But if one says, "*I* shall go," he may readily be taken to mean no more than that he is destined to go, that he is certainly going; that is, he may seem merely to be predicting a future event without showing his attitude or feeling towards this event. If, on the other hand, one says, "I will go," the idea of intention, purpose, determination, will, is so apparent that, as long as the verb retained clearly its original meaning, that meaning could hardly fail to be noticed. "I will go," therefore, could hardly be felt as a mere future; it shows the speaker's attitude and feeling toward the future act. But if one says, "You will go," or "He will go," the idea of futurity is more prominent than the idea of intention, purpose, or determination, for the speaker cannot be supposed really to know what "you" (or any other person) intend or are determined to do; we cannot courteously make statements about the intention or determination of others.

Therefore it came about quite naturally that the forms "I will go," "you shall go," "he shall go," "they shall go" kept clearly the original strong meaning of *shall* and *will*, and that the forms "I shall go," "you will go," "he will go," "they will go" were so frequently used merely to pre-dict future happenings that the original strong meaning practically vanished, and these forms became future tenses pure and simple. With this explanation before us, we are now ready to understand the reasons underlying the following rules.

a. To express simple futurity use these forms:

I shall go	We shall go
You will go	You will go
He will go	They will go.

Note: The use of "I will" or "we will" to express simple futurity is responsible for four fifths of the mistakes in the use of *shall* and *will*.

Note: "You will go" is used in courteous commands. It is the regular military formula: "You will lead your men one mile forward."

b. To express the speaker's determination, promise, intention, obligation, prophecy, purpose, threat, etc., use these forms:

I will	We will
You shall	You shall
He shall	They shall

Examples: I will go (= "I intend to go").
We will go (= "We intend to go").
You shall go (= "You must go," with the implication that the speaker is determined on your going).
He (they) shall go (= "He (they) must go").

These forms are the reverse of those given in Rule *a*. Properly speaking, they are not future tenses at all. Instead of merely predicting future events, they indicate the speaker's mood or attitude toward these events.

Note: If the idea of willingness or intention is expressed by another word, say "I shall" instead of "I will."

I shall be pleased to come.
I should like to go.

These are the two fundamental rules, and they apply to all plain assertions. The other rules grow logically out of the primary distinction given in *a* and *b*.

c. In questions use the form expected in the answer. In the case of questions, the same reasons hold good. One never has occasion to ask some one else about one's own intention; therefore, one never says, "Will I go?" (unless to echo a preceding question). When one asks, "Shall I go?" one may be inquiring about a necessity or may be asking for information about a destined future act; it makes no difference; for "Shall I?" and "Shall we?" are the only possible forms in questions of the first person. But one may ask either, "Will you go?" or "Shall you go?" The former quite clearly expects the answer "I will," i.e., "I intend," and so is not a pure future; the latter expects the answer "I shall," and is a pure future. Similarly, one may ask, "Will he go?" expecting the answer "He will," a pure future, or "Shall he go?" expecting the answer "He shall," which implies necessity and so is not a pure future. Study the following paradigm:

Pure Future	*Necessity or Intention*
[Will I go? An absurd question, never used except to repeat a question: Will I come? I will do my best to come.]	Shall I go? Answer: You shall (= must).
[Will we go? Absurd question.]	Shall we go? Answer: You shall.
Shall you go? Answer: I shall.	Will you go? Answer: I will (= intend).
Will he go? Answer: He will.	Shall he go? Answer: He shall (= must).

*d. In indirect discourse use the auxiliary that was used in
the direct discourse.* In the case of indirect quotations,
the same reasons still hold good. But change *shall* to
should, *will* to *would,* if the sequence of tenses demands
the change. As the question is modeled on the answer
expected, so the indirect quotation is modeled on the
exact original words which are quoted indirectly.

> *Examples:* I think that I shall go.   (Original thought: "I
> shall go," pure future.)
> I promise that I will go.   (Original thought: "I
> will go," intention, promise.)
> You say that you will be there.   (Original
> thought: "I will be there," intention, promise.)
> You said that you would be there.   (Original
> thought: "I will be there.")
> He said he should go.   (Original thought: "I
> shall go," pure future.)
> He said he would go.   (Original thought: "I will
> go," intention, promise.)
> I said that he shall come.   (Original thought:
> "You shall come," determination.)
> I said he will go.   (Original thought: "You will
> go," pure future.)

It is clear from these examples that, whenever the
subject of the indirect quotation is the same as that in
the main clause, the original statement or thought was
an "I-thought," and that *shall* is the correct auxiliary
in all persons for the pure future, and *will* for the future
of intention or determination. When the subjects of the
two clauses are different in person, one must still consider what were the original words spoken or thought.
Simply change the words of the indirect quotation into
the words of the original thought or statement.

e. Use **should** *and* **would** *in accordance with the rules
for* **shall** *and* **will,** *except when Rule f applies.*

Examples: I should accept if I could.   (Simple futurity.)

I would accept if I could.   (Promise, determination.)

I said that I should accept.   (Original statement: "I shall accept," pure future.)

I said that I would accept.   (Original statement: "I will accept," promise.)

Should you accept if you could?   (Answer expected: "I should," simple futurity.)

Would you accept if you could?   (Answer expected: "I would," willingness, determination.)

f. Use **should** *for all persons in subordinate conditional clauses, or in a main clause that expresses a promise that would have been fulfilled had the condition stated in the subordinate clause been met.*

Examples: If he (you, they, she) *should* choose to go with me, I should be glad to pay all expenses. (Subordinate conditional clauses.)

If I could grant your request, he (they, we, I, you) *should* be set free.

Note: Should and *would* are also used in all persons as independent verbs, *should* meaning "ought," and *would* expressing a wish, a willingness, or a customary action.

I (you, he, they, we) *should* pay better attention.

I (you, he, they, we) *would* always take the short cut to the lake.

I *would* that he were here now.

This method of hardening steel *would* often cause trouble.

Should is used for all persons to form the future subjunctive, *would* to form the future optative.

Examples: If you (I, we, he, they) *should* return now, you could see the man you have been looking for. (Simple future act or possibility, future subjunctive. See also the first example under Rule *f.)*

If you (I, we, he, they) would return now, you
could see the man you have been looking for.
(Willingness, future optative.)

Exercise. Supply *shall, will, should,* or *would* in the blanks
below:

1. If we ...... know science, we must learn to observe.
2. He said that he ...... go (futurity).
3. He said that he ...... go (promise).
4. I fear that I ...... not be able to come since I ...... not be
   in town this week; but if I ...... return in time, I ...... be
   very glad to accept your invitation. ...... you have to
   know in advance or ...... I be welcome if I come without
   warning?   Mother insists that I ...... not return until
   next week, but I ...... try to persuade her that your invitation is worth a sacrifice.
5. Great things were expected for the future when he ......
   have become more experienced.
6. I am the younger and I ...... go first.
7. We ...... live to repent this choice.
8. If you loved me as well as I love you, you ...... have
   stayed with me.
9. If I could get the book, you ...... have it.
10. If you ...... only think, you could recall the name.
11. I am sure I ...... be very thankful to have fallen into such
    good hands.
12. I ...... do that for fifty dollars.
13. What ...... we do if we were left with the old gentleman
    on our hands?   I ...... take care of him.
14. But you ...... pardon an old man's grumbling.

10   ESSENTIAL AND NON-ESSENTIAL MODIFIERS

ONE of the most important grammatical distinctions is that
between essential and non-essential modifiers.[1]   Every

---

[1] Essential modifiers are sometimes called *restrictive* or *determinative,*
and non-essential modifiers *descriptive, additive,* or *non-restrictive.*

student should understand the difference between them in meaning and in punctuation.

a. *Definition.* Modifiers of any kind (whether word, phrase, or subordinate clause) may be used: (1) merely to *describe* an antecedent — *to give additional information* about an antecedent already identified and defined. Such modifiers are known as *non-essential* because they are not necessary to the identification of the antecedent; (2) to *identify* or *define* an antecedent — to show exactly what particular person or thing or what particular class of persons or things is meant. Such modifiers are known as *essential* because they are necessary to the definition or identification of the antecedent. For example:

Non-essential, merely descriptive and additive: We had been sailing on Carr Lake and were now returning home. The water, *which was cool and clear*, gently lapped the sides of our boat.

Essential, necessary for the identification of the antecedent: Water *that is stagnant* is unwholesome.

Observe that the modifier "which was cool and clear" gives a further description of the water of Carr Lake. It describes an antecedent that has already been identified. It could be omitted without serious loss to the thought. Observe, on the other hand, that the modifier "that is stagnant" is an integral part of the thought, limiting "water" to a particular kind of water — stagnant water. The subject is not merely *water* but "water that is stagnant." The omission of the identifying modifier would radically change the meaning of the sentence — "Water is unwholesome"!

b. *Tests.* There are, accordingly, two leading tests to determine whether a given modifier is essential or non-essential:

Test I: Does the modifier *merely give additional information* about a person or thing already identified? If so, it is non-essential. Or does it *identify* the person or thing it modifies? If so, it is essential. In applying this test, ask *what* water was "cool"? *what* water is "unwholesome"? If the answer is, "The water we have been talking about" or "Any water," the modifier is non-essential. But if the answer repeats the words of the modifier in question — if you answer, "The water that is stagnant" — the modifier is essential.

Test II: What would be the effect on the thought of the sentence if the modifier were omitted? Experimentally bracket the modifier in question; thus: "Water [that is stagnant] is unwholesome." If the bracketed matter could be omitted without serious loss to the thought of the sentence, the modifier is non-essential. If the omitted matter is absolutely essential to the meaning, if its omission distorts the meaning of the sentence or leaves the meaning "obviously or painfully indefinite," [1] the modifier is essential.

c. Punctuation. Non-essential modifiers should always be set off by commas. Essential modifiers should always be left unpunctuated. (See pages 171–174.)

Exercise. Determine which of the following modifiers are restrictive, which are non-restrictive, and which may be either. (All punctuation marks within the sentence have been omitted.)

[1] Summey, *op. cit.*, p. 86.

1. The four birds which were sitting on one limb afforded an easy target.
2. Sorely troubled in his mind he left the place dreary now and untenanted and walked as fast as possible towards the village.
3. A system of espionage was established of which he was the victim.
4. No poem ever makes me respect its author which does not convey a truth of philosophy.
5. Bunyan who was an ignorant man was imprisoned in Bedford Jail where he wrote several of his books.
6. The man who would not respond to such an appeal is heartless.
7. The time will come when you cannot do as you choose.
8. We lit our meerschaums filled with fine Turkish tobacco and smoked in silence whenever we could afford the time.
9. We encountered a shattered wreck with no life visible floating listlessly on the river.
10. Short and stout with a square face sunburned into a preternatural redness he was certainly not an imposing figure.
11. Then years ago when he was a famous athlete he had won many medals but now if one looked at him casually one would never guess his past.
12. I began to think of myself in the condition of the good man that had a wife who took a dislike to his gray hairs.

11   ADJECTIVE AND ADVERB

Do not use an adjective where the construction calls for an adverb. See **Grammatical Terms** for the difference in function between these parts of speech. See also *Copula*, and *Predicate Complement*.

Wrong: I think he talks too rapid.
Right: I think he talks too rapidly.

After copulas — verbs like *is, was, seems, feels, tastes, smells, sounds, becomes* used merely to link the subject with a predicate adjective — use an adjective if the word modifies or identifies the subject, an adverb if it describes or limits the action of the verb.[1]

> *Right:*   I feel bad.
>   He looks sick.
>   You seem comfortable.
>   The fruit tastes sour.
>   He stood quiet and motionless.

In a few cases the meaning of the sentence is the same whether adjective or adverb is used:

> The sun shines bright.
> The sun shines brightly.

But in most cases there is a difference in meaning:

> He nailed it firm (describing the condition of the object).
> He nailed it firmly (describing the action).
> He held it tight.
> He held it tightly.

Exercise. Detect and correct the misuse of adjectives or adverbs in the following sentences. (Some of the sentences are correct.)

1. He certainly looks badly.
2. We should take the little things, which count so much toward the making of a strong character, serious, as well as the big things.
3. He remained silent and looked at me steady for a few moments.
4. The waves were rolling high; the sun shone bright.
5. He came as quick as he could.
6. He is feeling some better to-day.
7. We should have more laboratories and class rooms, but these are not needed so bad as many other things.

---

[1] The word in question should be an adjective if *is*, *was*, or *seems* could be substituted for the copula without a change in the meaning of the sentence. Compare the following sentences:
He looked solemn.
He talked solemnly.

12 CONJUNCTIONS

In order to write with grammatical correctness, one should be thoroughly familiar with the difference between the various kinds of conjunctions. An ignorance of this grammatical difference is a serious handicap to correct writing and leads to obscure, weak, and awkward expression. The various classes of conjunctions should be carefully distinguished from each other and from other parts of speech.

A *conjunction* is a word used to connect words, phrases, clauses, or sentences.

a. Coördinating Conjunctions. A conjunction used to connect expressions of equal rank is a *coördinating conjunction.* The expressions joined by coördinating conjunctions in the following sentences are of equal rank, are grammatically parallel:

> He was tall *and* slim.
> I looked for him all day, *but* he was not to be found.
> To be *or* not to be — that is the question.

The coördinating conjunctions are *and, or, nor* (= *and not*), *but,* and sometimes *yet,* and *for* (when it has the meaning "and the reason is that"). *While* should not be used as a coördinating conjunction. Take especial pains to use coördinating conjunctions only between coördinate sentence elements.

> John *and* I looked for him all day, *but* he was not to be found.
> Or
> John *and* I looked for him all day. *But* he was not to be found.

b. Subordinating Conjunctions. A conjunction that connects a dependent clause with a main clause is a *subor-*

dinating conjunction. Subordinating conjunctions join sentence elements which are not of equal rank, which are not grammatically parallel. In the following sentences each of the subordinating conjunctions introduces an expression that is unequal in value with the expression to which it is joined:

When I asked for him, I was informed that he had left the city.

Although the weather was extremely disagreeable, we decided to start on our journey.

Some of the most common subordinating conjunctions are *although, as, because, if, than, that, while,* and *unless.* (See the list on pp. 13–15.) Some common conjunction groups are *as if, as long as, in order that, so that.* Relative adverbs — *where, when, whence, while, since, whither, how, why, before, after, till* — and relative pronouns, *who, which, that, what, as* — may also be classed as subordinating conjunctions since they often have the same function.

c. *Conjunctive Adverbs.* Certain words usually employed as adverbs are sometimes used to connect independent clauses and so to form compound sentences. When such adverbs, in addition to their regular adverbial function of indicating relations of time, place, manner, cause, degree, etc., thus assume the function of conjunctions, they serve a double function. When used to connect independent clauses, such adverbs are called *conjunctive adverbs.* Since they are at the same time adverbs and conjunctions, they form a special class of conjunction.

It is imperative that the student distinguish sharply between simple conjunctions and conjunctive adverbs. The common conjunctive adverbs are *so, therefore, hence, moreover, also, thus, then, still, accordingly, how-ever, consequently, furthermore, likewise, nevertheless, be-sides,* and *otherwise.* Although the beginner has great trouble with the punctuation of clauses connected by conjunctive adverbs, he can avoid this difficulty if he remembers (1) that these words all retain an adverbial function, a function which no simple conjunction possesses; and (2) that they are used to join only *coördi-nate independent* clauses and thus have the function of *coördinating*—never of subordinating—conjunctions.[1] If these reminders do not enable you to use these words correctly, then learn the list given above and re-member always to use a semicolon—*never a comma*—between independent clauses which are joined merely by these conjunctive adverbs. See the Semicolon, **Use I,** p. 182.

The difference between a pure adverb, a conjunctive adverb, and a simple coördinating conjunction may be seen in the following sentences:

Pure adverb: He was *so* weary with the day's work that he left at once.
He departed *hence.*
Conjunctive adverb: He was weary with the day's work; *so* he left at once.

---

[1] When *so, however, still,* etc., are not used to connect two independent clauses, they are better regarded as pure adverbs, not conjunctive ad-verbs. These adverbs become conjunctive only when they are used as coördinating conjunctions — with which they are classed in most gram-mars. If a subordinate conjunction is used to connect the main clause and the dependent clause or if a coördinating conjunction joins two in-dependent clauses, the adverbs *so, however, still,* etc., are relieved of their function as conjunctions and remain pure adverbs.

Examples: Though he was convicted of the crime, *still* the people be-lieved in his innocence.
He was convinced of his innocence and *so* persuaded others to believe in him.

He departed; *hence* we could not ask him to help us.

Simple coördinating conjunction: He was weary with the day's work *and* so left at once.

He departed, *and* so we could not ask him to help us.

Exercise A. Compose five sentences in which some of the conjunctive adverbs are used as pure adverbs. Compose five sentences in which the same words are used as conjunctive adverbs. Then reconstruct the second group of sentences in such a way as to change the compound sentences into complex sentences.

> d. *Correlative Conjunctions:* Coördinating conjunctions are often used in pairs to connect sentence elements of equal rank or value. When so used, these conjunctions are called *correlative conjunctions.* The most common correlatives are *both — and, not only — but also, either — or (else), neither (no, not, never) — nor, so — as, as — as,* and *whether — or.* Correlatives should be used only to connect expressions that are grammatically parallel. See **Parallelism, 88.**
>
> *When — then, where — there* are similar pairs — subordinating conjunction and correlative adverb.
>
> For Exercise, see p. 30.
>
> e. *Conjunctions and Other Parts of Speech.* Many of the words we have been discussing are not always used as conjunctions. They are often employed as nouns, prepositions, adverbs, or other parts of speech. *For, since, notwithstanding,* for example, may be used either as prepositions or as conjunctions.
>
> He went home *for* his father (preposition).
> He went home, *for* his father had sent for him (conjunction).

By analogy to these words, which are employed sometimes as one part of speech and sometimes as another, the careless writer extends the use of other words into functions that have not been sanctioned. For instance, *like*, which should be followed by a noun or pronoun without a verb, is sometimes used (instead of *as* or *as if*) to connect clauses. Remember that *like* should be followed by a noun or pronoun *without a verb*, and that *as* or *as if* should be followed by a noun or pronoun *with a verb*.

Wrong: He pitches ball like a professional does.
　　　　I want you to do like I do.
Right:　He pitches ball like a professional.
　　　　I want you to do as I do.

Exercise B. Copy the following sentences and insert *like*, *as*, or *as if* in the proper place.

1. He does it just ...... his brother does.
2. It looks ...... it might rain.
3. ...... all his brothers, he is a good athlete.
4. I wish I could sing ...... Scotti.
5. I don't think ...... you do about this matter.
6. Buy Liberty Bonds over here ...... they fight over there.
7. Chaucer ...... many other writers of his time, attacked the flagrant abuses in the medieval church.
8. Chaucer attacked the flagrant abuses in the medieval church ...... many other writers before him had done.
9. He talked ...... we had never heard of this subject before.

13　　　　USES OF *SO*

So and the other conjunctive adverbs give the beginner much trouble. To learn the correct use of these words the student should study carefully pages 137–140 and should bear in mind the following reminders:

　a. Remember that conjunctive adverbs differ from simple adverbs only in the fact that conjunctive adverbs are used to connect independent clauses.

b. Remember that when *so* is used as a connective between clauses of a compound sentence it should be preceded by a semicolon, not a comma.

c. Remember that in comparisons with *as . . . so* and in clauses of purpose introduced by *so that*, *so* is not a conjunctive adverb and should not be preceded by a semicolon. Distinguish between *so* and *so that*.

> *Right:* As we judge others, so others judge us.
> He came early, so that he might get a good seat. (Purpose.)
> He came early; so he got a good seat. (Result.)

d. Remember that the use of a conjunctive adverb for forming a compound sentence is at best an awkward device and that a smoother and more emphatic sentence may be constructed by subordinating one of the independent clauses.

> *Weak:* The rain was falling in torrents; *so* we decided to stay at home.
> *Better:* *Since* the rain was falling in torrents, we decided to stay at home.

e. Remember that the use of the adverb *so* as a loose equivalent of *very*, *exceedingly*, etc., is weak and childish, since it leaves the comparison vague and obscure.

> *Vague:* I am *so* tired to-day.
> *Clear:* I am very tired to-day.
> I am *so* tired to-day *that* I cannot work. (The proper conjunction in such comparisons is *so* . . . . . . *that* = *to such a degree that.*)

Note: The same rule applies to *such*. See **Incomplete Comparisons, 74.**

In negative comparisons use *so — as:*

Right: He is not so dissipated as he used to be.

Exercise.   Revise the following sentences in such a way as to correct any errors in the use of *so.*

1. He is so irritable.
2. He bought a new motor so he could take a longer trip.
3. The wind had subsided; so we went toward the house and were aware of a strange noise about us in the night; so when we came out of the forest we lit a lantern — it was so dark — and began to investigate.
4. We hid our guns so we could climb better.
5. There were no footprints in the dust, so we knew the campers had not followed this road.

14   CLASSES OF PRONOUNS

A *pronoun* is a word used instead of a noun.   The noun for which the pronoun stands is called its *antecedent.*   A pronoun agrees with its antecedent in gender, number, and person, but the case of the pronoun is independent of the case of the antecedent.   See **Reference, 95, Apostrophe, 28, Case, 5,** and **Agreement, 4.**

a. Classes.   Pronouns are classified as

1. Personal (I, you, he, she, they, etc.).
2. Compound personal, used either as reflexives — to refer to the same person as the subject — or as intensives — to emphasize a preceding substantive.   "He cut *himself*" (reflexive); "I *myself* saw it" (intensive).
3. Relative, used both to refer to an antecedent and to connect a dependent clause with a main clause: *who, which, that, what, as, whoever, whatever,* etc.
4. Interrogative, used to ask questions: *who, which, what.*
5. Demonstrative, used to designate a definite or specific person or thing: *this, that, these, those.*

6. Indefinite, used to refer to a person or thing less definitely than a demonstrative does: *some, some one, each, either, all, few, several, many,* etc.

7. Reciprocal, used to express mutual action or relationship: *each other, one another.*

b. Syntactical Uses. Any pronoun may be used as a noun: as subject, direct object, indirect object, appositive, etc. Demonstratives, indefinites, possessives, interrogatives, and relatives may be used as adjectives. They are often called pronominal adjectives. Relatives and, sometimes, interrogatives often have the function of subordinating conjunctions.

c. Common Errors in the Use of Pronouns. The following are the most common errors in the use of pronouns.

1. A disagreement in number or person between the pronoun and its antecedent.

   Wrong: Every man should be neat in *their* dress.
   Right: Every man should be neat in *his* dress.

   See also **Agreement, 4.**

2. Vague or obscure reference. See **Reference, 95.**

3. The use of a compound personal pronoun instead of a personal pronoun:

   Wrong: He asked me to keep this a secret between *himself* and *myself.* [Say "him and me."]
   John and *myself* can prepare the plans by tomorrow.

4. The use of *he, his,* or *him* to refer to the indefinite pronoun *one.* In formal well-considered speech or writing use *one* or *one's* to refer to the indefinite pronoun *one:*

   In this state of affairs *one* should govern *oneself*

as best *one* can. (*He, his, him* may be used to refer to *one* in less formal and precise writing.)

5. The use of *you* or *they* as an indefinite pronoun.

Objectionable: *You* should hold your head high in swimming.

Unobjectionable: *One* should hold the head high in swimming.

Objectionable: *They* are giving away souvenirs at Wrightson's.

               They had a terrible automobile accident on Pine Street last night.

Unobjectionable: Wrightson's is giving away souvenirs.

               There was a terrible automobile accident on Pine Street last night.

6. The use of *these, those,* and *it* in a loose, indefinite way.

Vague: It was one of *those* warm summer days.

       In my history book *it* says the battle was fought on Monday.

Clear: It was a typical warm summer afternoon.

     My history book states that the battle was fought on Monday.

7. The confusion of the relatives *who, which,* and *that.* *That* refers to persons or things, *who* only to persons, *which,* only to things — except in such a sentence as

The jury, *which* had just reached a decision, now entered the room.

Here *which* is properly used to refer to a group of persons regarded as an impersonal unit.

Who and *that* are usually employed as essential relatives, *which* as a non-essential relative.

As a rule, do not use *whose* to refer to inanimate objects; prefer *of which*. But see **Case, 5.**

Exercise. Correct the misuse of pronouns in the following sentences:

1. The doctor and myself found the lost automobile.
2. They manufacture much furniture at Grand Rapids.
3. In my dictionary it says that the word has two syllables.
4. When you first enter the room, you have a strange feeling.
5. It was on one of those cold December mornings that my uncle and·myself set out on our journey.

15 CLAUSES

a. Definitions. Perhaps the most serious errors in composition are due to an ignorance of the difference between main clauses and subordinate clauses. A *subordinate clause* is always used as a single part of speech. It always performs the function of a noun, an adjective, or an adverb. A main clause is a clause containing or modified by a subordinate clause. See pp. 101–103 for examples.

b. Common Misuses.

1. The use of a subordinate clause as a sentence. See **Period Fault, 2,** and **Sentence Defined, 1.**
2. The use of a sentence as a subordinate noun clause.

Wrong: The greatest benefit I received from him was he showed me how to learn a foreign language. (Insert *that* after *was.*)
We learn, as a man expresses himself in what he writes, so a nation expresses itself in its literature. (Insert *that* after *learn.*)

Note: A quoted sentence may be used as a noun clause:

"Every beginning is hard" is the translation of a German proverb.

3. The writing of two sentences as one. See **Comma Fault, 3.**

4. The use of an adverbial clause in a construction that calls for a noun clause.

> *Wrong:* The reason I was late was *because* I was sick. ("The reason was" must be completed by a substantive or a clause used as a substantive.)

> *Wrong:* I see in to-day's paper *where* the Senate has approved the new treaty. (Use *that.*)

5. Overlapping dependent clauses. See **Overlapping Dependence, 70.**

6. Dangling Elliptical Clauses. See **Dangling Modifiers, 94.**

7. Misplaced Clauses. See **Position of Modifiers, 93,** and **Coherence, 92.**

Exercise A. Revise the following sentences in such a way as to correct the misuse of clauses:

1. The reason we didn't go is because it rained.
2. "Slicing" is when the ball is hit with a sweeping cross stroke.
3. The result was he was put out of the room.
4. He has no reason for refusing except he is sick.
5. "I say this," he replied, "when very obstinate people are met, there are only two ways of dealing with them."
6. He then rode away to the North. Which caused sorrow to all he left behind.
7. It was the absolute certainty nobody in the world could have seen him do it explained his calmness.

Exercise B. Compose sentences to illustrate dependent clauses used as nouns (subject of verb, object of verb, object of prepositions, predicate complement, appositive), as adjectives, and as adverbs (to modify a verb, an adjective, or another adverb).

16   DOUBLE NEGATIVE

FEW students are guilty of such gross double negatives as

> I didn't want to say nothing.
> They don't never come on time.

But even careful writers fall into the error of expressing the negative idea twice with such words as *hardly, scarcely, only, but* (= *only*), and *nor*. (See Correlatives, p. 140.)

Wrong: I can't *hardly* come to the meeting to-night.
     He *cannot* watch *but* one ball at a time.
     I do not think that I shall play tennis *nor* go swimming.

Right: I can hardly come to the meeting to-night.
     He can watch but one ball at a time.
     I do not think that I shall play tennis or go swimming.
     (*Or* is used if the subject of the sentence or the main verb is modified by a negative.)

Exercise.

1. He is not beaten until all the votes are counted and, so his friends say, not then neither.
2. I don't think that I can hardly come to-morrow nor stay very long if I do.
3. He never misses a stroke, not even on the roughest ground.
4. Assistance from you is not expected or desired.
5. He did not have any friends nor any house to live in.
6. The etymology of words was not noted in this dictionary nor in any previous dictionary.
7. There was no doubt but that he was lying.

17   GRAMMATICAL TERMS

Absolute. A word or phrase with no syntactical relation to any word in the sentence. Absolute phrases consist of a substantive and a participle: " *The day being chilly,* we put on our coats." *Day* is called a *nominative absolute.*

148

Adjective. A word used to modify a substantive. See **Adjective and Adverb, 11.**[1]

Adjective Clause. A subordinate clause introduced by a relative pronoun or adverb and used like an adjective: "The house, *which was old and deserted,* stood near the road."

Adverb. A word used to modify a verb, an adjective, or another adverb. Relative and interrogative adverbs are like subordinating conjunctions in that they serve to join a main clause and a subordinate clause: "I do not see the place *where* he put the box." "I do not know *why* he came." See **Conjunctions, 12,** and **Adjective and Adverb, 11.**

Adverbial Clause. A subordinate clause used as an adverb. Adverbial clauses express ideas of time, place, purpose, result, etc. (See the list of connectives on pp. 13–15.)

Agreement. See **Agreement, 4.**

Antecedent. The substantive to which a pronoun refers. "The man introduced me to *his* brother." *Man* is the antecedent of *his.*

Appositive. A substantive used to limit or explain another substantive and referring to the same person or thing. "Mr. Smith, *my uncle,* wrote the editorial." (*Uncle* is in apposition with *Smith.*) Phrases and clauses may also be used as appositives. See page 173.

Article. *The* is the definite article; *a* and *an* are indefinite articles. *A* is used before words beginning with a consonant sound, *an* before words beginning with a vowel sound.

---

[1] The references in bold-face type are to the numbered sections of Book II; the references *in italics* are to entries in this list of grammatical terms.

Auxiliary. A verb used in forming a verb phrase indicating voice, mood, tense, etc. *Have, may, can, be, shall, will, must, go,* and *do* are common auxiliaries. "I *have* lost my purse." Auxiliaries are also often used as independent verbs: "I *have* no brothers."

Case. See Case, 5.[1]

Clause. See Clauses, 15.

Collective Noun. See *Noun* below.

Comparison. The change in the form of an adjective or adverb to indicate the degree of quality, quantity, or manner. The three degrees are *positive, comparative,* and *superlative: good, better, best; high, higher, highest; quickly, more quickly, most quickly.*

Complement. See *Object,* and *Predicate Complement,* below.

Complex Sentence. A sentence containing one main clause and one or more dependent clauses: "When we reached the summit, we saw the village far away in the valley."

Compound Sentence. A sentence containing two or more main clauses. "The heavens declare the glory of God, and the firmament showeth his handiwork."

Compound-Complex Sentence. A sentence containing two or more main clauses and one or more dependent clauses: "When Burns plowed up the daisy, he was impressed with the analogy to his own fate, and he wrote a poem to give vent to his feelings."

Conjugation. The inflections of a verb.

Conjunction. See Conjunctions, 12.

Conjunctive Adverb. See Conjunctions, 12.

Construction. The grammatical use of a word in a sentence.

---

[1] The references in bold-face type are to the numbered sections of Book II; the references in italics are to entries in this list of grammatical terms.

In the sentence "He walks rapidly," *he* is the *subject* of the verb and *rapidly* is the *modifier* of the verb.

Coördinate. A term applied to sentence elements of the same logical importance and having the same grammatical construction.

Copula, Copulative Verb. A verb used to link the subject with the predicate complement and expressing the relation between subject and complement. *Is, was, seems, becomes, looks, smells, tastes, sounds,* and *feels* are common copulas. "The man was my brother." "I feel bad."

Correlative Conjunctions. See **Conjunctions, 12.**

Declension. . The inflections of a substantive to show relation of case, number, etc.

Demonstrative. See **Pronouns, 14.**

Dependent Clause. See **Clauses,** p. 102.

Direct Address. See *Vocative* below.

Ellipsis. The omission of a word or words easily implied from the context, but necessary to the grammatical completeness of the sentence. "These are the books [that] I bought." "He is taller than I [am]."

Essential Modifier. See **Essential and Non-Essential Modifiers, 10.**

Expletive. *It* or *there* when used to introduce a verb that precedes the subject. "*There* are many men present." "*It* is true that he is not coming."

Finite, or Predicative, Verb. A verb that changes in form to agree with the subject in person and number; a verb form that is capable of making an independent assertion concerning the subject. The non-finite forms of the verb — infinitive, gerund, and participle — are incapable of making an independent assertion. See pp. 99–100.

Gender. The classification of nouns and some pronouns

as masculine, feminine, common, and neuter: *man, woman, child, book, I, you, he, who, that.*

Gerund. A noun in *-ing* derived from a verb and sharing the nature of both verb and noun. The gerund resembles a verb in taking an object and in being modified by an adverb. It resembles a noun in that it can perform the chief functions of a noun and can be modified by an adjective. "*Walking* a mile every day is good exercise." The present participle has the same form as the gerund. See *Participle* below. See also **Possessive with Gerund, 6,** and **Sentence Defined, 1.**

Government. A verb or a preposition is said to "govern" its object; that is, the verb or preposition requires the substantive object to assume a form showing its relation to the governing word. Likewise, a clause on which another clause depends is said to "govern" the dependent clause.

Idiom. See page 246.

Independent Clause. See **Clauses, 15.**

Independent Element. A word or a group of words not having any grammatical connection with the sentence in which it stands. Vocatives, interjections, absolute phrases, and parenthetical expressions are independent elements.

Infinitive. The first principal part of a verb (often preceded by *to*) used as a noun. The infinitive resembles a verb in that it may have an adverbial modifier and can take an object or predicate complement; it resembles a noun in that it can perform the chief functions of a noun. It may be used as subject of the verb, as direct object, as complement, as appositive, etc.

Inflection. The change in the form of a word to show a change in meaning. See *Declension, Conjugation,* and *Comparison* in this list.

Interjection. An exclamatory word or phrase used independently in a sentence.

Intransitive, Transitive. According to its use in a sentence, a verb is transitive or intransitive. A *transitive* verb is a verb followed by a substantive showing the person or thing directly affected by the action of the verb (direct object, object of verb) or stating the result produced by the action. Every transitive verb takes an object. An *intransitive* verb is a verb that does not require the addition of a direct object to complete its meaning. An intransitive verb is either complete in itself or can be completed by the addition of a predicate complement (used with copulative verbs). An intransitive verb does not take an object. The same verb, *walk*, for example, may often be used transitively or intransitively.

> *Examples:* I called him. (*Him* is the direct object of the transitive verb *called*.)
> He manufactures paper. (*Manufactures* is a transitive verb; *paper* shows the result of the action of the verb. It is the direct object.)
> He slept soundly. (Intransitive verb, complete in itself.)
> The day seemed clear. (*Seemed* is a copula; *clear* is a predicate complement.)
> He walked slowly. (Intransitive.)
> He walked his horse. (Transitive.)

Limit. See *Modification* below.

Main Clause. See **Clauses, 15.**

Modal Auxiliary. An auxiliary verb used to form a verb phrase indicating mode. "He *may* come." "I *should* have come sooner." See **Subjunctive, 7,** and **Shall and Will, 9.**

Mode. A change in the inflections of a verb to indicate

the manner in which the speaker views the action of the verb. The *indicative* mode states or questions a fact: "He came." "Did he come?" The *subjunctive* mode views the action as doubtful, desired, supposed, or unreal. "If he *were* here, we could go on with the program." The *imperative* mode is used to give a command or an entreaty. "*Listen* carefully." Other modes, such as the potential, the conditional, the optative and the obligative, are usually formed by verb-phrases. See also *Infinitive, Participle,* and *Gerund* in this list, **Shall and Will, 9,** and **Subjunctive, 7.**

Modification. Limiting or restricting the meaning of a word or a group of words. "Stagnant water is unwholesome." *Stagnant* modifies the noun *water* and gives it a meaning not possessed by the unmodified noun.

Modifier. A word or group of words used to modify other words.

Mood. See *Mode* above.

Nominative Absolute. See *Absolute* above.

Nominative of Address. See *Vocative* below.

Non-Essential Modifier. See **Essential and Non-Essential Modifiers, 10.**

Non-Finite. See *Finite* above.

Non-Predicative. See *Finite* above.

Non-Restrictive. See **Essential and Non-Essential Modifiers, 10.**

Noun. A word used to name a person, place, or thing. A *proper* noun names a particular person, place, or thing: *John, Mount Pleasant, Austria, Chicago.* A *common noun* names any one of the members of a class of persons, places, or things: *man, apple, river, mountain, street.* A *collective* noun names a group or a class, not a single person or object: *jury, choir, party, company, flock,* *swarm.* An *abstract* noun names a quality or an idea: *whiteness, government, love, truth.* A *compound* noun is a noun formed by uniting two or more words: *port-hole, father-in-law.*

Noun Clause. See *Substantive Clause* below.

Number. The change in the form of a noun, a pronoun, or a verb to show whether it designates one (*singular*) or more than one (*plural*).

Object. A word, phrase, or subordinate clause used to indicate the person or thing affected by the action of a transitive verb; or the substantive following a preposition. The person or thing directly affected by the action of a verb is called the *direct object:* "I saw *him.*" "He grows *wheat.*" (See also *Intransitive* above.) The person or thing indirectly affected by the action of the verb is called the *indirect object:* "He gave *me* the book." The noun or adjective referring to the same person or thing as the direct object is called the *predicate objective,* or *objective accusative:* "The men elected Harry [direct object] captain [predicate objective]."

Parenthetical. Any expression inserted in a sentence that would be grammatically complete without it. See *Independent Element* above and pages 167–170. For the punctuation of parentheses, see pages 170–175.

Parse. To analyze the form and use of a part of speech.

Participle. An adjective derived from a verb and sharing the nature of both adjective and verb. A participle differs from a verb in not being able to make an assertion. It resembles a verb in that it may be modified by an adverb and may take an object. It resembles an adjective in that it may modify a substantive. The participle has two forms, present and past: *walking, walked; beginning, begun.* See also **Sentence Defined, 1.**

Parts of Speech. The classification of words according to their use in sentences. The eight parts of speech are *noun, pronoun, adjective, adverb, verb, preposition, conjunction,* and *interjection.* These are all discussed in their proper alphabetical order in this section. To determine what part of speech a word is, ask yourself how it is used in the sentence. Disregard the form of the word, since the same form may be used as more than one part of speech.

Person. The change in the form of a pronoun or a verb to indicate whether a person is speaking, is spoken to, or is spoken about: "I come, you come, he comes."

Phrase. A group of related words not containing both subject and predicate. See also **Sentence Defined, 1.**

Predicate. That part of a sentence containing what is said about the subject. The predicate may be either a single word or a group of words: "He *slept.*" "He *has been sleeping.*" The *simple predicate* is the predicate verb or verb-phrase. The *complete* predicate is the predicate verb or verb-phrase together with all its modifiers.

Predicate Adjective. See *Predicate Complement* below.

Predicate Complement. The word or words used to complete the meaning of a copulative verb and to describe or identify the subject of the verb. The predicate complement may be a noun, a noun clause, an infinitive, a gerund, a pronoun, an adjective, or an adjective phrase. These kinds of predicate complements are illustrated in the following sentences:

> John is my *brother.*
> My suggestion is *that we leave at noon.*
> To see is *to believe.*
> Seeing is *believing.*
> It is *he.*

I am *tired*.

He is *out of sight*.

Predicate complements are also called *subject complements* and *predicate nominatives*. Predicate complements must be sharply distinguished from direct objects. A predicate complement always refers to the same person or thing as the subject and is used only after intransitive verbs. See *Object* and *Intransitive*, above, and **Adjective and Adverb, 11.**

Predicate Noun. See *Predicate Complement* above.

Predicate Objective. See *Object* above.

Predicative. See *Finite* above.

Predication. A combination of subject + verb; an assertion expressed or clearly implied: "You are going." "(You) go now." See also page 99.

Preposition. A word joined to a substantive to form a phrase. A preposition shows the relation of the substantive to the other words in the sentence. "He rode *over* the hill." Distinguish carefully between prepositions and conjunctions.

Principal Parts of a Verb. The principal parts of a verb are the three forms from which the complete conjugation of the verb is derived. The principal parts are the present infinitive, the past tense first person singular, and the past participle. Learn the principal parts of the following verbs:

arise	arose	arisen
begin	began	begun
bid	bid	bid (offer money)
bid	bade	bidden (command)
bite	bit	bitten, bit
blow	blew	blown
break	broke	broken
burst	burst	burst

choose	chose	chosen
cleave	clove, cleaved, cleft	cloven, cleaved, cleft (split)
come	came	come
dig	dug	dug
do	did	done
drink	drank	drunk (adjective, drunken)
eat	ate	eaten
fall	fell	fallen
find	found	found
fly	flew	flown
freeze	froze	frozen
get	got	got
give	gave	given
go	went	gone
grow	grew	grown
hang	hung, hanged	hung, hanged
know	knew	known
lay	laid	laid
let	let	let
lie	lay	lain
ride	rode	ridden
ring	rang	rung
run	ran	run
see	saw	seen
set	set	set
shine	shone	shone
sing	sang	sung
sit	sat	sat
slay	slew	slain
slide	slid	slid
smite	smote	smitten
sow	sowed	sown, sowed
speak	spoke	spoken
spring	sprang	sprung
stand	stood	stood
steal	stole	stolen
strike	struck	struck, stricken
strive	strove	striven
swim	swam	swum

take	took	taken
tear	tore	torn
thrive	throve	thriven
throw	threw	thrown
tread	trod	trodden
wake	woke, waked	woke, waked
wear	wore	worn
weave	wove	woven
win	won	won
wind	wound	wound
write	wrote	written

Note that the second principal part of a verb is always used alone as a past tense and the third principal part is never used alone, but always forms part of a verb phrase: *I saw, I have seen.* See **Tense, 8.**

Pronominal Adjective. See **Pronouns, 14.**

Pronoun. See **Pronouns, 14.**

Restrictive Modifier. See **Essential and Non-Essential Modifiers, 10.**

Sentence. See **Sentence Defined, 1,** and *Simple, Complex, Compound,* and *Compound-Complex* in this list.

Sentence Element. Subject, predicate, complement, or modifier, one of the separable parts into which a sentence may be analyzed.

Shall. See **Shall and Will, 9.**

Simple Predicate. See *Predicate.*

Simple Sentence. A sentence containing a single predication. Either the subject or the predicate, or both, may be compound, but there must be but one predication, but one clause. "John has come." (Simple subject and simple predicate.) "John and his brother have come." (Compound subject and simple predicate.) "John has come and will stay several days." (Simple subject and compound predicate.) "John and his brother have come and will stay several days." (Simple sentence with compound subject *and* compound predicate.) Distinguish between a simple sentence with compound predicate and a compound sentence. Compare the sentences given above with this compound sentence: "John has come, and his brother came with him."

Simple Subject. See *Subject* below.

Strong Verb. A verb that forms its principal parts by a change of vowel and without the addition of *-ed*, *-d*, or *-t: sing, sang, sung.*

Subject. A substantive naming the person or thing about which an assertion is made. The *simple subject* is a noun or its equivalent. The *complete subject* is the simple subject with all its modifiers. See also **Agreement, 4.**

Subordinate Clause. See **Sentence Defined, 1.**

Substantive. An inclusive term for noun and pronoun, a naming word.

Substantive Clause. A dependent clause used like a noun, as subject, direct object, appositive, etc. "*That he will come* is certain." (The dependent clause is used as the subject of *is.*)

Syntax. That part of grammar which deals with the relation of words in a sentence; sentence architecture or structure.

Tense. See **Tense, 8.**

Transitive. See *Intransitive* above.

Verb. A word capable of making an assertion concerning a person or thing. See **Sentence Defined, 1.**

Verb Phrase. A verbal used with an auxiliary verb.

Verbal. A word derived from a verb, but used as a noun or an adjective. The verbals are *infinitive*, *gerund*, and *participle*. See these terms above. For the distinction between verb and verbal see page 100.

Voice. The change in the form of a verb to indicate whether the subject acts (*active voice*) or is acted upon (*passive voice*).

Weak Verb. A verb that forms its principal parts by adding *-ed*, *-d*, or *-t* to the infinitive: *walk, walked, walked; step, stept, stept.*

Will. See **Shall and Will, 9.**

CHAPTER II

PUNCTUATION

The writer who neglects punctuation, or mis-punctuates, is liable to be misunderstood. . . . Even where the sense is perfectly clear, a sentence may be deprived of half its force — its spirit — its point — by improper punctuation. — POE

INTRODUCTION: THE PURPOSE OF PUNCTUATION

PUNCTUATION is not mechanical in nature, but organic. Punctuation marks, like words, are a means of expressing our thoughts, as in these sentences: "He is gone." "He is gone?" "He is gone!" We must use them, as we use words, in the same way in which men conventionally use them, since if we adopted a private system of punctuation, our readers could not understand us. In order to be understood, we must first of all understand ourselves — master the thought we are trying to express — and then write a sentence in which the relations of the constituent parts are indicated by punctuation as men have agreed to employ it. The standard system of punctuation depends mainly upon grammatical elements; consequently, the study of punctuation presupposes a knowledge of grammar. No writer should expect to attain correct punctuation before he has acquired an easy familiarity with the rudiments of grammar.

18   COMMA

OF the various symbols used to show the relation of thoughts within the sentence, the comma is by far the most troublesome, because of its variety of uses. These many uses we shall learn more easily if we learn first the general principles underlying them.

The most important principle is the distinction between one comma and two commas, between the use of *one comma* to *separate* parts of the sentence and the use of *two commas* to *group*. One comma divides words that are connected, but not closely interwoven; two commas enclose, or set apart, a group of words added to the skeleton of the sentence by way of comment, explanation, or parenthesis. These two uses of the comma we may call the *separative* and the *grouping*.

Study the three sections that follow (**19, 20, 21**).

19   ONE COMMA TO SEPARATE

I. The Separative Comma

ONE comma is used to separate parts of the sentence that are not arranged in their normal order or that are not closely welded together. One comma has the effect of momentarily checking the progress of the thought from subject to predicate and of marking a separation between parts of the sentence which are not fused into an unbroken unit. It prevents the reader from reading together groups of words that are loosely connected, groups that the writer does not wish to have regarded as single groups. The separative comma is used in two cases: (A) to prevent misreading, and (B) to separate coördinate words, phrases, and clauses.

A. To Prevent Misreading.

A comma is used to prevent the reader from connecting words that do not properly belong together. It is a common experience to begin reading a sentence and to find, when we are in the middle of it, that we have started on the wrong track and that we shall have to begin all over again.

This experience is due to the fact that the eye does not see the words of a sentence singly, but takes them up in groups. Hence we must be careful to punctuate in such a manner as to indicate the natural groups, particularly when we use words that are sometimes one part of speech and sometimes another. Note the effect of the absence of punctuation in the following sentences:

As I munched and munched a half-naked boy ran by and disturbed my noon meal.

Ever since he has been afraid of water and has not since taken a boat trip. [What part of speech is the first "since"?]

To Paul Williams announced the good news that their candidate had been elected by a majority of 20000 votes. [Is "Paul Williams" one person or two? Would a comma after 20 clarify the figures?]

The problem is is he going to help us? That he is is my firm conviction. [Would commas help to indicate the word groups?]

In the window stood a small vase and a large table reposed in the center of the room. [Does *and* connect two nouns or two clauses?]

Comma after Preceding Dependent Clause. Notice particularly the first sentence above. To guard myself against all suspicion of cannibalism, I must place a comma after "As I munched and munched." Otherwise, the reader may regard *boy*, the subject of the main clause, as the object of the verb in the preceding dependent clause. Often, it is true, an introductory dependent clause similar to our "As I munched and munched" clause is in no serious danger of being misread, and yet would be more immediately clear if followed by a comma. For example:

As I stood there and watched the door of the house, a man who looked like my friend came out.

Although the last sentence would be clear without the comma, cases where misreading may occur are so common that the unskilled writer will find it safe to employ the comma habitually after a dependent clause preceding the main clause. If exceptions are made at all they should be confined to those cases where the dependent clause is short and contains the same subject as the main clause.[1]

Comma before **for.** The same principle — prevention of misreading — explains the use of the comma before the conjunction *for* to distinguish it from the preposition *for:*

> As soon as he received the letter, he went home, *for* his brother was dangerously ill.

If the comma were omitted before *for*, the eye would grasp as one unit "He went home for his brother." (See also **Use I,** B, *c.*)

B. To Separate Coördinate Words, Phrases, and Clauses.

a. Comma between members in a series. When consecutive adjectives, adverbs, nouns, verbs, or dependent clauses used in the same construction — *coördinate* sentence-elements — are *not joined* by a conjunction, the members of the series should be separated by commas:

> He was a tall, sallow, gaunt man.
> He spoke with energy, with gusto, with charm.
> Steadily, steadily, steadily we trudged along the path.

When the last two members of the series *are joined* by a conjunction, the comma should be used before *and:*

> The cool, white fog drifted in from the sea, obliter-

---

[1] When the dependent clause *follows* the main clause, the comma is necessary only when the dependent clause is non-essential. See **Essential and Non-Essential Modifiers, 10.** Dependent noun clauses are set off by a comma only if they are appositives.

ated the lighthouse and the islands, and lost itself in the trees, spires, and towers of the city.

He was out before eight o'clock, a thin, upright figure in hard straw hat and gray flannel clothes, walking with the loose poise of a soldier, smoothing his drooping gray moustache, and considering what best should be done for his niece.

Note: In the last sentence no comma is used between *hard* and *straw*, between *gray* and *flannel,* or between *drooping* and *gray* because these pairs of adjectives are not coördinate, but blend to form a single adjective idea. Or we may say that *hard* modifies the group *straw hat, gray* the group *flannel clothes.* The adjectives should be separated only when they are coördinate, only when each modifies the noun separately.

To determine whether a series of modifiers are coördinate, change the order of the members of the series or insert *and, or,* etc., between them. If there is no change in the meaning of the sentence, the members of the series are coördinate. See also the sentence from Dickens below.

But when the last two members form a separate unit, no comma is used before *and:*

We made a fire and cooked bread, potatoes, ham and eggs.

He handled the advertising for the following firms: Paul W. Smith, James Buchanan, John Wanamaker, Sears and Roebuck.

When all of the members are joined by conjunctions, the comma is not necessary. If it is used, it gives separate emphasis to each member of the series as in this sentence from Dickens:

Right: Therefore she has come away from the place in Lincolnshire and has left it to the rain, and the crows, and the rabbits, and the deer, and the partridges and pheasants.

Right: He was a tall and sallow and gaunt man.

With Separate Emphasis: He was a tall, and sallow, and gaunt man.

Note: A comma is always used before *etc.*, but the comma is omitted before *and* in the name of a business firm: Thompson, Brown and Company.

b. To separate the coördinate parts of a compound predicate. The comma is necessary only with long or involved compound predicates or when there is a shift in subject, mood, or tense:

Jackson had gathered his men behind a high hill near the village of Dawkins, and had kept them in hiding there until the moment for the attack had come.

But:

Come and see for yourself.

We need the money and are going to have it.

Note: A comma is often used before *but* or *or* when it introduces the second verb of a compound predicate. The comma is used for emphasis.

Right: We need the money but cannot get it.

More Emphatic: We need the money, but cannot get it.

c. To separate independent clauses that are connected [1] *by a simple coördinating conjunction:*

The rains descended, and the floods came.

Mariners detect the flowery perfume of land-winds far at sea, and sea-winds carry the fragrance of jungle and tangle far inland.

---

[1] Use a semicolon, not a comma, if the clauses are *not* connected by a coördinating conjunction. See **Comma Fault, 3.**

If the clauses are short and closely coördinate or if the style is colloquial, no comma is needed:

> He came and he went at his leisure.
> He played and I sang.

The comma is usually employed before *but, not,* or *and not* to emphasize the contrast and before *or* to emphasize the alternative:

> No one is earning more than two dollars a day, but all are able to live on what they earn.
> I called John, not you.
> He was sick, and not really able to see visitors.

(The comma is always used before the conjunction *for.* See p. 165.)

In such a contracted compound sentence as

> Grammars are useful as stepping stones, but not as a final resting place,

the comma is used because the group of words introduced by *but* may be regarded as an elliptical clause:

> Grammars are useful as stepping stones, but [they are] not [useful] as a final resting place.

The following sentences are also correctly punctuated:

> Classics live for all time, but best sellers for only a limited period.
> It was not hatred, but pity that stirred him. (The comma heightens the contrast. The use of the comma in such a case is determined by considerations of emphasis.)
> It was not hatred but pity that stirred him. (*But pity* may also be set off as a parenthesis. See II, D, *d.*)

d. Comma with idiomatic question. In such idiomatic questions as

> He is here, isn't he?
> You are coming, aren't you?

a comma is used between the declarative statement and the question following it.

20 TWO COMMAS TO GROUP

II. Grouping, or Enclosing, Commas

COMMAS are used *in pairs* to set apart a group of words which is to be regarded as explanatory, non-essential, transitional, incidental, or in any other way loosely connected to the skeleton of the sentence. Remember that these commas are always used in pairs, except, of course, where the element to be set off stands at the beginning or end of the sentence, or where for any reason there is another mark at the point where one of the required commas would stand. The same expression may sometimes be set off by commas and sometimes written without commas:

> Then, too, much power was given to the President.
> Then, too much power was given to the President.
> Then too much power was given to the President.

But *both commas should be used or both omitted;* one comma, it should be remembered, is always separative.

All of the following cases may be classed, more or less roughly, as varieties of parenthetical expressions. Parenthetical matter is matter inserted in a sentence by way of comment, explanation, or transition in such a way as to interrupt momentarily the forward movement of the thought. Commas should be used to enclose all such parenthetical groups. Note the cases in which the commas are necessary and the cases in which the commas are optional. In general, it may be said that commas are necessary to indicate clearly that the inserted matter is not an organic or essential part of the predication.

A. **Independent Parentheses, Elements Having No Grammatical Construction in the Sentence:**

    a. Parenthetical sentence. Comma necessary.

> He was not pleased, I suppose, with my plan.
> I am, you must know it, growing weary of the work.

    b. Nominative absolute. Comma necessary.

> Everything being ready, we started at once.
> The car being out of repair, we had to walk.

Note that these expressions modify the whole sentence, whereas participial phrases, which sometimes resemble them in form, modify some single word in the sentence. See C, *a* below. Nominative absolutes are always set off; other participial phrases are set off only if they are non-essential. Introductory participles are nearly always non-essential.

    c. Direct address.

> You know, John, how I feel about this matter.

    d. Interjection. Comma necessary if an exclamation point is not used.

> Alas, I can no longer make a choice.
> Alas! I can no longer make a choice.

See also **Exclamation Point, 25.**

    e. Yes, no, well, surely, etc. modifying the sentence as a whole. Comma necessary. (See also B, *a, b, c.*)

> Yes, I shall be glad to come.
> No, I had no idea he was here.
> Well, I must be going soon.

If greater separation or independence of predication is desired, a semicolon or a period may follow such sentence words as *yes* and *no*.

B. Adverbial Modifiers:

a. Introductory adverbial modifier of the whole predication — indeed, certainly, possibly, perhaps, etc. Comma usual with a long or with an emphatic transitional modifier.

> In order to keep my appointment, I returned home by the first boat.
> Accordingly, I returned at once.
> Now, just what do you mean by that remark?
> For some strange reason, I was unable to speak.

b. Emphatic or summarizing adverb or adverbial phrase. Comma usual.

> There were, then, four reasons for his action.
> We should, therefore, take our time in this business.
> We shall, to summarize our case, make four points.

c. Non-essential adverbial modifier, whether word, phrase, or dependent clause. Comma necessary.

> The soldiers, in a sudden panic of fear, dropped their guns and fled.
> He was, as my friend said, a man to attract attention anywhere.
> On Monday he sailed for France, where he intends to live for two years.
> There was something sinister about the way she repeated his question, as if the word "home" were strange to her.
> Really, that is too much to expect.
> He is, certainly, not altogether wrong.

C. Adjective Modifiers:

   a. Non-essential adjective modifiers, whether word, phrase, or relative clause. Comma necessary.

> The house, old and deserted, stood at the intersection of the roads.
> Blake, not seeing the obstacle, ran into it.
> The house of my friend, which was situated in the country, was filled with Eastern curios.

Note: Remember that all non-essential modifiers should always be set off by commas and that essential modifiers are never set off. (For the distinction between these two kinds of modifiers see **10**.) This distinction in punctuation is essential to clearness, for a given group of words may be essential in one sentence, non-essential in another. The difference in punctuation, therefore, is due to a difference in the meaning of the sentences.

Note that participles that modify a noun in the manner of an appositive are non-essential, whereas participles used as predicate adjectives or objective predicates are essential.

> Being out of his pale, he is in the highest state of wonderment and inaptitude.
> Think of him in a multitude, forced to travel and wondering what it is that drives him.
> Perhaps he would not say much at first, being oppressed with the greatness of his success.
> The horse came galloping down the street.
> I saw him driving along the beach.
> He heard the noise of horses pawing in the street below.

   b. Appositive. Comma nearly always necessary. An appositive, with or without *or, such as, namely,* or other introductory words should be enclosed by commas:

Any baggage, such as trunks, must be left at home.

Jackson, a man of ability, was in charge. (Note that the appositive and its modifier constitute an appositive phrase.)

My friend, Captain Aiden, called this morning.

Professor Browning, of Cowles College, delivered the address.

The solving of a plot, or the *dénouement*, requires careful handling.

His first statement, that he was sick, is obviously untrue. The *that*-clause is appositive.

(See also **Colon, 23,** and **Dash, 27.**)

But (1) when the appositive is part of a proper name,

(2) when it is quoted or italicized, or

(3) when it is used to identify its antecedent, no comma should be used. In such cases the appositive is an essential modifier.

William the Conqueror was the first Norman king of England. (Here *the Conqueror* is part of the title of William of Normandy.)

The word *burgle* and the expression "He gets my goat" are not accepted in standard English.

The dramatist Pinero wrote many interesting plays. (Here *Pinero* is closely connected with its antecedent *dramatist;* it limits an antecedent of general reference. This appositive may be called the limiting or identifying appositive.)

He himself told me.

My son James is very fond of Hawthorne's story "The Minister's Black Veil."

The statement that all men are dishonest is not true. (The *that*-clause is used as an appositive.)

Note: 1. *Namely, that is, viz, i.e.* When introducing an appositive, these words are always preceded by a comma, a colon, or a dash, and are always followed by a comma. But when these words introduce the second clause in a sentence, they should be preceded by a semicolon and followed by a comma. (See **Colon, 23,** and **Dash, 27.**)

2. *Such as, as, e.g.,* and *for example.* When these words are used to introduce an example or a series of examples they should be preceded by a comma:

I have many things to do to-day, such as writing letters, settling my accounts, packing my trunk, and buying my ticket.

If these words introduce independent clauses, they are preceded by a semicolon.

D. Other Sentence Elements.

a. Title after a proper name. Comma necessary. Titles may be regarded as a variety of appositives.

James Cole, D. D., spoke to the graduating classes.

b. Explanatory dates and geographical names. Comma necessary.

Portland, Oregon, derived its name from Portland, Maine.
He lives at No. 367 West Avenue, Chicago, Ill.
June 21, 1888, is the date I referred to.
December, 1872.
Tuesday, June 20.

But note that there is no comma in such expressions as

May 12.
In the year 1776.

c. Suspended sentence elements.   Comma optional.
Commas may be used with suspended sentence
elements to give additional emphasis to the suspended element or to suspend the attention of the
reader:

> It is charming, not only for the story it contains,
> but also for the purpose behind the story.   (See also
> I, B, *c.*)
> He has shown me how literature can create in me,
> and keep before me, the vision of the ideal.
> Literature will give one a broader view of, and a
> deeper sympathy with, mankind. (This type of sen-
> tence, however, is awkward and should be improved
> by rewriting, not by punctuation. (See **Awkward
> Word Order, 85.**)

d. Strongly contrasted or transposed sentence elements.
Comma necessary for emphasis.

> Mercy, not justice, is what he asked for.   (See also
> I, B, *c.*)
> When I awoke at seven, I heard, barking furiously
> near my window, the dog I had locked up the night
> before.

The use of the commas in such sentences is
determined by considerations of emphasis or clearness.   The comma further emphasizes the transposed words.   A comma may also be necessary for
clearness.   (See p. 163.)
The following sentences are all correctly punctuated:

> **Beyond,** the horizon stretched in a broken semi-
> circle.

Without, the rain was falling fast. (In these two sentences the comma is used to prevent misreading, not because the words followed by the comma are transposed.)

To schools with high standard, the new laws mean little.

To schools with high standards the new laws mean little.

Without the slightest hesitation, he replied to my question.

Without the slightest hesitation he replied to my question.

21 UNNECESSARY COMMAS

Avoid the use of unnecessary commas. Be prepared to justify every comma you use. When in doubt, remember that it is a far more serious error to use a comma that cannot be justified than to omit a comma where it is needed. A good rule to remember is that ordinarily no comma should be used between such closely related sentence elements as subject and verb, verb and direct object, substantive and essential modifier, preposition and object, and verb and predicate complement. Although it is usually wrong to use one comma in such cases, it is permissible to use two commas to set off parenthetical matter.

The following are the most common types of unnecessary commas:

a. A comma between subject and verb or between verb and direct object. This rule applies to noun clauses used as subject or as object.

Wrong: The vase on the table in the center of the room, was imported.

He said, that he would come.

I do not see, how he does it.

How he does it, is not clear.

b. A comma with introductory phrases that are not parenthetical.

Wrong: On the desk, is a rare book.

For the punctuation of introductory phrases see II, B, above.

c. A comma before the first member of a series.

> *Wrong:* I finished without interruption, the fifth, the sixth, and the seventh chapters. ¯(Two commas may be used in this sentence to set off "without interruption" as a parenthetical phrase.)

d. A comma after the last member of a series of adjectives, adverbs, etc.

> *Wrong:* There rose in front of us a high, bare, rocky, hill. (*Rocky*, an essential modifier, should not be separated from *hill*. See **10** above.)

e. A comma between an intensive pronoun and its antecedent.

> *Wrong:* We are made to feel as if we are in the city, itself. (A comma is permissible only in the rare cases where separate and strong emphasis upon the intensive is desired.)

f. A comma with an essential modifier. (See **10** above.)

g. A comma before an indirect quotation or before quoted titles. (See **Dialogue and Quotations, 30,** and study section *a* above.)

h. A comma between correlatives or between the elements of compound conjunctions *so . . . that, so . . . as, as . . . as,* or before *than* in comparisons.

> *Wrong:* He was hit so hard, that he did not know what had happened.
> It is better to know in advance by what mo-

tives men are guided, than to learn too late.

He is neither my brother, nor my friend.

Note: The error of misplaced modifiers often leads to the use of unnecessary commas. The writer feels vaguely that something is wrong in his sentence and instead of revising it makes matters worse by using unnecessary commas:

Wrong: They find that each has sacrificed, what he him-self prized most, for the other.

Right, with modifier correctly placed: They find that each has sacrificed to the other what he himself prized most.

Exercise A. Supply commas *where they are needed* in the following sentences and explain the use of each comma you employ (whether **Use I,** A, **Use II,** A, etc., and if you can, specify the exact subhead, as **Use I,** B, *a*, **Use II,** A, *c*, etc.).

1. I am not altogether without musical feeling (**Use I,** B, *c*), but I could never appreciate the operas of Wagner.
2. He was a faithful though not on the whole a very capable workman.
3. As a result of his hasty decision the plan failed at the first trial.
4. The most interesting character is Macbeth the tyrannical king.
5. You see now James that I was right.
6. Considering the structure of the play we see that it is divided into five acts each of which has three or more scenes.
7. I stepped forth asking my friend not to wait for my return.
8. Alas I have no home.
9. Augusta Maine is a smaller city than Augusta Georgia.
10. I shall not wait longer for the train has not been reported.
11. The work was begun on July 18 1912.
12. We came to the foot of the mountain rested our horses for an hour and then began the toilsome climb to the summit.

13. I voted for John Jones for William.
14. When he began to walk his horse slowly followed him.
15. True since we had no longer the domination of the lord to contend with there was less occasion to be strict.
16. These ships fitted out with the detecting device were not in much danger.
17. Hamlet who was the son of the former king regarded Horatio his best friend with much admiration.
18. Everything being prepared we began to pull the boat down to the shore.
19. The men carried axes shovels and picks.
20. Psychology is a science that deals with consciousness and human behavior.
21. There were many generals in the last war who showed superb military ability.
22. The student of character knows that he judges men and especially himself not by abstractions but by concrete actions.
23. In order to bring Dorothea's traits into full relief George Eliot hastens to introduce a characterizing situation.
24. The paragon of common sense pictured by most people as being somehow unliable to human frailties could not yet screw himself up to the point of ringing a dentist's door-bell.
25. Having taken Mrs. Baines' chair he bent his face down to the fire seeking comfort from its warmth.
26. It is for this reason that though these books were written long ago their characters will stand the test of time.
27. He was so all his constituents thought the ideal man for the office.
28. There were then four important reasons for his action.
29. The boat being fitted out we set sail the following morning.
30. The peasants examined the cows went off came back always in great perplexity and fear of being cheated never quite daring to decide spying the eye of the seller trying ceaselessly to discover the tricks of the man and the defect of the beast.
31. The sea should come if not up to the cliffs at least very near to them and then above all things the water below them

should be blue and not of that dead leaden color which is so familiar to us in England.

32. I passed down a staircase long and winding requesting him to be cautious as he followed me.

33. I had told them that I should not return until morning and had given them explicit orders not to stir from the house.

34. These orders were sufficient I well knew to insure their immediate disappearance one and all as soon as my back was turned.

35. Pearson have you noticed that Professor James C. Robinson F. R. S. is going to deliver an address to-night?

36. Poetry is the product of and a stimulus to activity of the imagination.

37. These people you could see from their forms had seen hard work.

38. Several seconds after its horn could be faintly heard in the distance.

39. Classics live for all time but best sellers for only a day.

40. These things accomplished there seemed little need for my continued presence in the town and a great desire to get away seized me.

41. A sentence should read as if the author had he held a plough instead of a pen could have drawn a furrow deep and straight to the end.

42. The salary in any business under heaven is not the only nor indeed the first question. It must not be supposed however that monetary considerations are entirely wrong.

43. As a matter of fact we can go little further back in the analysis of culture than these primitive people.
The address is 943 Main Street Huntersville Mo.

44. These characteristics dwell in they belong to literature.

45. Here and there on the shining beach was a fishing boat and beyond them brown nets and in among the mending nets an old hut before the door of which sat my old seafaring friend.

46. The flying squirrel was one of the most interesting of the little animals we found in the woods a beautiful brown creature with fine eyes and smooth soft fur like that of a mole or field mouse. He is about half as long as the gray squirrel

but his wide-spread tail and the folds of skin along his sides that form the wings make him look broad and flat something like a cat. In the evenings our cat often brought them to her kittens at the shanty and later we saw them fly during the day from the trees we were chopping. They jumped and glided off smoothly and apparently without effort like birds as soon as they heard and felt the breaking shock of the strained fibers at the stump when the trees they were in began to totter and groan.

Exercise B. Turn to the exercise under **Essential and Non-essential Modifiers, 10,** and insert commas where they are needed.

22   SEMICOLON

THE semicolon indicates a wider break in thought or in construction than does the comma. It may therefore be substituted sometimes for the comma and sometimes for the period, but never indiscriminately. Remember that the semicolon has well-defined uses of its own and should not be regarded as a loose substitute for the comma or period.

There are two distinctly different uses of the semicolon: (1) there are cases when the semicolon *must* be used, and (2) there are cases when the semicolon *may be* used.

Use I. Between Independent Clauses not Joined by a Simple Conjunction

The semicolon *must be* used between independent clauses of a compound sentence whenever these clauses are *not* joined by one of the simple coördinating conjunctions. This principle explains the use of the semicolon in the following types of compound sentences:

a. When no connective of any sort is used between the independent clauses:

We must not rely on appearances; we must get at the facts in the case.[1]

b. When no conjunction is used, but an explanatory expression introduces the second clause:

Before I can answer your questions I shall have to know several facts; *for example,* I shall have to know whether your friend has had any experience in this kind of work.

In such a case the punctuation is just the same as it would be if the explanatory expression — *namely, for example, that is, i.e., viz.* — were omitted entirely.

Note that in neither of the two cases above is a conjunction used to connect the clauses.

c. When the clauses are connected by a conjunctive adverb (see the list on pp. 138–139).

The thunder clouds were rapidly gathering; *so* we made haste to get our boat under cover.

She turned her head to see if the storm had abated; *then* she looked attentively downward.

A mastery of the foregoing use of the semicolon is a sure remedy for the "comma fault."

Use II.   Between Other Sentence Elements

The semicolon *may be* used between the independent clauses of a compound sentence even if the clauses *are* joined by a coördinating conjunction.   In such a case the choice between comma and semicolon depends upon considerations of rapidity of movement, emphasis, or clearness of word grouping.

a. Rapidity of movement.   Clauses joined by a simple

---

[1] The semicolon in such a sentence is a mark of coördination (here equivalent to a comma + *but* or *for*).   A colon may be used if the second clause explains or amplifies the first.   (See **Colon, 23.**)

coördinating conjunction and separated by a comma move more rapidly than clauses separated by a semi-colon. Note the retarding effect of the semicolon in the following sentence:

Nearly all his time had been spent in Paris; but of this sojourn he had brought back but two souvenirs.

b. *Emphasis.* Since the semicolon marks a greater degree of separation than does the comma, it gives greater emphasis and independence of meaning to each of the two clauses. The semicolon is also used to balance or contrast two clauses more sharply than can be done by a comma:

Presley was easy-going; but Anniston was the acme of alertness.

c. *Clearness of word-grouping.* (1) *Compound sentences.* When the clauses of a compound sentence are complicated in structure, especially when they contain interior punctuation, it is often advisable to employ a semicolon in order to indicate clearly the chief divisions in the sentence. In the following sentence the comma would not indicate the chief divisions so clearly as does the semicolon:

Dorothea immediately took up the necklace and fastened it round her sister's neck, where it fitted almost as closely as a bracelet; but the circle suited the Henrietta-Maria style of Celia's head and neck, and she could see that it did, in the pier-glass opposite.

The use of a semicolon shows that the clauses are grammatically independent but too closely connected in thought to be put in separate sentences. The use of a period gives the greatest possible emphasis and independence to each of the clauses.

(2) *Complex sentences.* Considerations of emphasis or ease of reading justify the semicolon even between *subordinate* sentence elements. Note carefully the use of semicolons in the following sentence:

A true classic, as I should like to hear it defined, is an author who has enriched the human mind, increased its treasure, and caused it to advance a step; who has discovered some moral and not equivocal truth, or revealed some eternal passion in that heart where all seemed known and discovered; who has expressed his thought, observation, or invention, in no matter what form, only provided it be broad and great, refined and sensible, sane and beautiful in itself; who has spoken to all in his own peculiar style, a style which is found to be also that of the whole world, a style new without neologism, new and old, easily contemporary with all time.

In this sentence the semicolon shows clearly the chief divisions between the series of parallel *who-*clauses — subordinate clauses in common dependence. Note also the interior punctuation in most of these clauses. This use of the semicolon should be reserved, however, for only highly complicated sentences, and the novice should not experiment with it. The cases in which the semicolon is used to separate sentence elements other than dependent clauses in a series are so rare as to demand no consideration.

Misuse of the Semicolon

Never use the semicolon without good reason. Although an indispensable mark of punctuation, it is used far less than the comma, especially in the present age. When it seems to you that either the comma or the semicolon would be correct, the safer course is to use the comma. The incorrect use of the semicolon is commonest in the following cases:

(1) When it is used as a substitute for the comma between a dependent clause and a main clause.

> *Wrong:* If it does not rain; we shall leave at four o'clock.
> We shall leave at four o'clock; if it does not rain.

(2) When it is used as a substitute for the comma or colon after the salutation in letters or before a direct quotation.

Exercise. Punctuate the following sentences and explain the use of each semicolon you employ. Some of the sentences may be written without semicolons.

1. I didn't like school very much; [**Use I,** *c*] so I was late about three times a week.
2. The people have made progress in many ways for example they have better schools and churches.
3. You are standing on a sort of shelf down below you the river flows silently along.
4. The corner cupboard was already old in service it had held the medicine of generations.
5. First come the men with the axes they go ahead and cut down the small trees.
6. It was ten o'clock when they mounted the steps it was about midnight when I saw them coming back.
7. I could think of no good reason for going therefore I remained at home.
8. We should not look on with idle hands we should do our part.
9. They had seen the French colors flying on Fort St. George they had seen the chiefs of the English factory led in triumph through the streets.
10. When manners have changed when the clergy the moral leaders of the country have ceased to lead when the whole order of society has undergone a complete revolution al-

though a bloodless and peaceful revolution we must see that the time is ripe for reform.

11. It was indeed Cromwell as we have seen who more than any other man had reared this fabric of king-worship but he had hardly reared it before it began to give way.

12. His works may sell for a time he may get a name in his day but this will be all his readers will in the long run grow tired of his books and then his popularity will drop as suddenly as it rose.

13. The tongue of King Alfred is the very tongue we speak but in spite of its actual identity with modern English it has to be learned like the tongue of a stranger.

14. Edmund Spenser himself stands first in this field that of lyric poetry and next to him is probably Sir Philip Sidney. In the relations of actual life Spenser was but one of the satellites of his noble and distinguished friend but in poetry he is the central sun and even Sidney is but one of his humble followers.

15. Henry the VIII's quarrel with Rome soon resulted in the advancement of many Protestant leaders. Shaxton a favorer of the new changes was raised to the see of Salisbury Barlow a yet more extreme partisan to that of St. David's Latimer himself became Bishop of Worcester and in a vehement address to the clergy in convocation taunted them with their greed and superstition in the past and with their inactivity when the King and his Parliament were laboring for the revival of religion.

16. Those who roused the people to resistance who directed their measures through a long series of eventful years who formed out of the most unpromising material the finest army that Europe had ever seen who trampled down king Church and aristocracy who in the short intervals of domestic sedition and rebellion made the name of England terrible to every nation on the face of the earth were not vulgar fanatics.

23 COLON

THE colon is a mark of anticipation. It is used most frequently in the following cases:

a. The colon is used as a formal mark of introduction, usually after an expression serving as an introduction to a list, a series of examples, a formal appositive, or a formal or extended quotation.

> There was one word he used constantly and with great effect, namely: *home.*
> There were three reasons for his dismissal: [1] laziness, lack of ability, and dishonesty.
> After a pause, the speaker began as follows: "I have often looked forward to the opportunity of speaking in this hall."

See also **Dialogue and Quotations, 30.**

b. The colon may be used between two independent clauses if the second clause gives a concrete illustration or an amplification of a preceding general statement and is anticipated by the first clause:

> Everything was favorable to our plan: the weather was good, our equipment was in excellent condition, and we had all the necessary men.
> When grammars and rhetorics blunt our desire to go beyond, they are worse than useless: they are positively harmful.

In such sentences as these the semicolon — the mark of balance or sharp contrast — may be used instead of the colon. Or the colon may be replaced by a period. Considerations of unity determine the choice of the proper mark of punctuation. But in no case is a comma to be used. (See the **Comma Fault, 3.**)

c. The colon is used to separate the introductory words

---

[1] When a list is introduced informally no punctuation is necessary:
The three causes for his dismissal were laziness, lack of ability, and dishonesty.

from a quoted speech when no verb of saying introduces the speech.

> She hesitated a moment: "I really don't know how to answer such a strange query."

d. The colon is used in references to separate the title of a book from the subtitle, the chapter from the verse, the act from the scene of a play, the name of the publisher from the place of publication. A colon is also used after the formal salutation of a letter and between the hour and the minute figures.

Examples:
The Essentials of Writing: A Textbook in Composition.
Putnam: New York.
John 6: 8–12.
Macbeth, I: 1, 30–40.
Dear Sir:
At 4:30 P.M.

Note: Capitalize the first word after a colon only when it begins an independent sentence or a completely distinct passage.

Exercise. Punctuate the following sentences:

1. As a student of philosophy he had read widely in the philosophies of many men Plato Aristotle Hume Kant Hegel and Nietzsche.
2. Lincoln had many qualities which made him easily accessible to all men good-nature humor affability kindness and fair-mindedness.
3. The important thing is this that under such a government as ours the broad path of opportunity is open equally to all men.
4. Friday has been a remarkable day in his life he was born on Friday he entered college on Friday he married on Friday and he was elected to the United States Senate on Friday.

5. There were two steps in the process first he cut thin strips of bark then he placed them in an oven for two days.

6. When we judge too hastily we do more than injure the person we judge we injure our own reputations.

7. Presently he resumed and spoke for ten minutes without interruption "The young girl watched her cousin as he cut his sippets with as much pleasure as a grisette takes in a melodrama where innocence and virtue triumph. Charles brought up by a charming mother improved and trained by a woman of fashion had the elegant dainty foppish movements of a coxcomb."

8. Three persons descended from the automobile the host a thin man very quick in movement with a nervous habit of twitching his mouth his wife a pretty woman with a tinge of auburn in her abundant hair and eyes that were bluer than common but inclined to wander inattentively and the guest an inconspicuous perhaps shy man in the thirties revealing when he removed his hat little bald salients extending from a broad not too full forehead.

[See **Use II,** *c*, of the semicolon.]

24 PERIOD

a. Use a period after every declarative sentence. The slovenly omission of end punctuation — period, question mark, or exclamation point — is inexcusable.

Use a period — or other end punctuation — after a fragment of a sentence that stands for a complete sentence.

"Are you going?" he asked.
"Yes."
"When?"
"To-morrow."

The beginner should carefully distinguish between such elliptical sentences as the foregoing and sentence fragments incorrectly written as separate sentences. In the case of the former, a complete predication can easily be supplied by the reader; "Yes" and "To-morrow" are really sentence words. In the latter, a complete predication is not implied; the group of words is not grammatically complete (see **Period Fault**, 2).

b. Use a period after every abbreviation:

Mass., *i.e.*, Mr., Col., LL.D.

Within a sentence the abbreviation period may be followed by any mark that would be used if there were no abbreviation period. But at the end of a sentence one period serves to mark the abbreviation and to end the sentence.

Note: No period should be used after Roman numerals, after headings, after words in a column, after contractions (don't, isn't, 12th, 2nd), or after Miss and per cent.

GENERAL EXERCISES IN PUNCTUATION

Exercise A. Punctuate the following sentences, omitting all unnecessary punctuation:

1. The first thing you see is a log cabin if you look closely you will see that it has been repaired many times.
2. I lived a happy life until one memorable day. When Mr. Smith my father's partner came into the house to speak to me.
3. Men should not choose their professions before entering college such a choice would be harmful to them.
4. He goes out early to kill birds. After he has killed all they will need for dinner. He stops hunting and goes home in the evening when his work has been finished he will take a good book for an hour's reading.
5. They have opened up one big new plant. A flour mill which turns out the best flour in the State.
6. They rushed wildly after the new lands some of them did it for love of freedom and others for love of property.

7. If business is carried on in this way it is a great benefit otherwise it is a great loss to the nation.

8. Whitman believed in an individualistic democracy. A democracy that gives every man the opportunity to express himself.

9. When they were ordered to enter the house they imagined that the man was joking and being in a jovial humor they laughed at the absurdity of the idea.

10. To conclude the whole business is a farce as I said before we began it.

11. Thus idling and wandering stretching themselves now and then among the grass and now getting up to look at some specially fertile place which another called them to see and which they thought might be turned to trading purposes they came upon a mound covered with trees which looked into a flat wide lawn of rank grass with a house at the end of it.

12. As he was plowing the field his plow struck something hard he picked it up and strange to say it was an old iron chest.

13. Dress as neatly as you can but not too expensively in other words let your dress be good but not extravagant.

14. And now the stupor of despair fell upon him he saw the approach of the horse and rider but as in a dream.

15. They then gazed at the result of their work but with mingled awe and pleasure.

16. In eight months he had done the work of two years and then after a short rest he had completed the rest of the course.

17. For George Spenser professed a great admiration.

18. At length allowing his attention to wander from the road he soon fell into a reverie from which he was awakened by the sound of a cart rumbling over the bridge.

19. I had several reasons for refusing to go first I did not have the time secondly I did not need the trip and thirdly I preferred to spend my vacation nearer home.

20. However as Annixter stepped from the porch of the ranch house he was surprised to notice a gray haze over all the sky the sunlight was gone there was a sense of coolness in the air the weather-vane on the barn a fine golden trotting horse with flamboyant mane and tail was veering in a southwest wind.

21. The main of life is indeed composed of small incidents and

petty occurrences of wishes for objects not remote and grief for disappointments of no fatal consequence of insect vexations which sting us and fly away impertinences which buzz awhile about us and are heard no more of meteorous pleasures which dance before us and are dissipated of compliments which glide off the soul like other music and are forgotten by him that gave and him that received them.

Such is the general heap out of which every man is to cull his condition for as the chemists tell us all bodies are resolvable into the same elements and the boundless variety of things arises from the different proportions of very few ingredients so a few pains and a few pleasures are all the materials of human life and of these the proportions are partly allotted by Providence and partly left to the arrangement of reason and of choice.

Exercise B. Copy a paragraph from some good book or magazine, omitting all sentence divisions and marks of punctuation. Put your copy aside for several days and then punctuate it. Compare your copy with the original paragraph and explain any differences in sentence division and punctuation.

25 EXCLAMATION POINT

THE exclamation point is used to show strong feeling or surprise. Do not overwork it.

The exclamation point may be used at the end of an exclamatory sentence or, more rarely, after an exclamation within the sentence. In the latter case the comma is used for all except very strong exclamations. See **Two Commas to Group, 20 (Use II**, A, *d*).

Examples: Ha! you have not given your gold for nothing? Come, speak the truth!
What! here, in my own home, under my very eyes, somebody has taken your gold! — the only gold we have! — and I'm not to know who has got it!
You hear me — go!

26 QUESTION MARK

THE question mark is used:

a. At the end of every *direct* question, whether original or quoted.

Examples: Are you going?
"Are you going?" he asked.

Caution: Do not use the question mark after an *indirect* question.

Right: I do not know whether he is coming.

b. At the end of each interrogative element in a compound question, if separate emphasis is to be given to each of the elements.

Right: What do you think now of his boasted honor? his integrity? his upright character?
(Here separate emphasis is given to each interrogative element.)
What do you think now of his boasted honor, his integrity, his upright character?
(Without separate emphasis on each interrogative element.)

Note: This use is very rare, in fact, almost obsolete.

c. Within parentheses to show that the writer is uncertain or doubtful as to the correctness of the preceding word or fact.

Example: "Chaucer was born in 1328 (?) in the city of London."

Caution: Do not use the question mark to label your own irony or humor.

Exercise. Use the question mark and the exclamation point correctly in the following sentences:

1. "No, no," cried he.   "You will break your neck."
2. "Are they calling us," she quietly asked.
3. She asked me whether I wanted to play tennis.
4. Did he ask you whether I had given you the watch.
5. Look they are coming now.

27   DASH

a. The dash is used most frequently to indicate a decided interruption, a sudden shift in construction, or
uncertainty or suspense on the part of a speaker.

> "She had behaved like" — and then he refused to go
> further in his condemnation.   (Interruption.)
> "Ah! Mr. Sheppard, how — you up from the country?
> How's your friend — the — er — painter?"   (Sudden
> shift of construction, and hesitation.)

b. Dashes may also be used instead of commas or marks
of parenthesis to set off an emphatic parenthesis
loosely connected with the sentence in which it stands,
a long parenthesis, or a parenthesis containing commas within itself.

> Society — she knew, she must know — cared little for
> the forms, the outside of things.

See **29**.

c. The dash gives the effect of heightened suspense
before an expression added as an after-thought or as a
summary of a preceding statement or of a series of parallel dependent clauses, or before an emphatic appositive or one containing commas within itself.

> She felt the turmoil of sudden fear, wondering whether
> she was showing it, lost it in unnatural alertness — all in
> the second before she answered.   (Summary.)

I then found out what had long puzzled me — the house was not deserted.   (Emphatic appositive.)

d. The dash is used to give any expression greater emphasis through greater separation and heightened suspense.

> Nice position for one to be in — that.
> It can't — it mustn't be.

e. In connected writing, the dash is only rarely combined with other marks of punctuation.   When a sentence ends with a dash, the period is always omitted, but an exclamation point or a question mark should be used if the meaning of the sentence demands it.

f. Misuse of the dash.   A too frequent use of this mark of punctuation results in a jerky, incoherent, even hysterical style.   E. A. Poe summed up the function of the dash by saying that it "represents *a second thought — an emendation.*"   Second thoughts, or afterthoughts, are obviously more appropriate in informal correspondence and in familiar essays than in the more deliberate forms of discourse.   Use the dash sparingly in formal writing.

Exercise. Use dashes where they are needed in the following sentences:

1. What was it I paused to think what was it that so unnerved me?
2. They are to be buried in the ocean that wide and nameless sepulcher.
3. I can hold the the Thing but a short while longer.
4. At that moment I became what I am now an outlaw.
5. I'd just as soon as I'd rather my name should not be mentioned.   And yet and yet I know I should be willing to take my share of the responsibility.
6. He was abashed I had almost said distressed to find his wickedness made public.

28 APOSTROPHE

THE apostrophe has three common uses:

   a. To form the possessive case of nouns. The possessive case of nouns is formed either by adding an apostrophe and *s* (*'s*) or an apostrophe alone (*'*).

     1. Add *'s* to form the possessive of a noun, whether singular or plural, not ending in a sibilant sound (*s, x, z*).

       Examples: boy's, man's, John's, children's, men's, deer's, Le Roux's (silent *x*).

     2. Add the apostrophe alone to form the possessive of plural nouns ending in *-s*.

       Examples: boys', girls', brothers'.

     3. Add either the apostrophe alone or apostrophe and *s* to form the possessive of proper nouns ending in a sibilant sound (*s, x, z*). Add apostrophe and *s* if the noun is a monosyllable. Add the apostrophe alone if the noun is not a monosyllable:

       Examples: Monosyllables: *Keats's, James's, Mills's, Burns's.*

           Dissyllables: *Moses', Cambyses', Jesus', Dickens'.*

   Note: Before *sake* or another word beginning with a sibilant sound use the apostrophe alone: *for goodness' sake, for conscience', kindness', Jesus' sake.* Always omit the *s* after the apostrophe if the possessive form is difficult to pronounce.

   b. To show that letters or figures have been omitted:

       Examples: Its, the possessive of *it,* should not be confused with *it's,* the contraction of *it is.*

       The class of '09 held a reunion last week.

c. To form the plural of letters, figures, signs, or words:

> *Examples:* There are two *a*'s in *separate.*
> Don't write your *3*'s and *5*'s alike.
> A beginner uses too many *so*'s in his writing.

Cautions: Never use the apostrophe to form the plural of nouns or the possessive of any pronouns except the indefinite pronouns *one, somebody,* etc.

Never put the apostrophe before final *s.* Write *Keats's,* not *Keat's.*

Place the apostrophe at the point where the letters are omitted: *ass'n* [not *as'sn*], *don't, didn't, ne'er.* Clipped forms — shortened forms without omitted letters — do not require an apostrophe: *Amer., Eng.* These are really abbreviations, not contractions.

Exercise A. Revise the following sentences. Pay close attention to the use of the apostrophe.

1. Don't make your 3s and 5s alike. Make them like Beatrices; her's are made properly.
2. Three boy's robbed Jones' chest of it's contents
3. Its now six o'clock, but theyre not here yet.

Exercise B. Form the possessive of *girl, girls, oxen, sheep, William, Williams, Jones, Ulysses, Saint Kitts, Alexius, Faunce,* and *Brahms.*

29   PARENTHESES AND BRACKETS

Parentheses

a. With Loosely Attached Parenthetical Expressions. Matter connected very loosely with the main predication of the sentence should be enclosed within parentheses.

In consequence of the many stories that were told about

the lady (really, I should never end if I related them all!) I expected to find her a fascinating coquette.

Parenthetical matter may be separated from the rest of the sentence by means of commas, parentheses, brackets, or dashes.[1] Commas are used to indicate only a slight degree of separation between the matter set off and the rest of the sentence. Parentheses indicate a more decided break in the continuity of the thought; they enclose somewhat foreign or irrelevant, or purely explanatory, matter. Brackets are used only for matter interpolated by the writer in a quotation or citation. Dashes indicate a parenthesis which is less formal, but more emphatic and more necessary to the thought of the sentence than that indicated by parentheses (curves). When the parenthetic expression contains commas, dashes are preferred to other marks of parenthesis. (See **Dash, 27** *b*.)

b. In cases *where accuracy is essential*, explanatory words, signs, or figures are enclosed in parentheses.

I enclose a check for twenty dollars ($20).

c. Figures put into the body of a sentence to mark the divisions of an enumeration are enclosed within parentheses.

The speaker referred to two important tendencies: (1) the tendency towards decentralization in government, and (2) the tendency towards a better understanding between the different social classes.

d. Punctuation of Parentheses. If the parenthesis is not a complete sentence, punctuation marks follow the parenthesis only if these marks would be required in

---

[1] "The most frequent parenthetical points are commas, with dashes second and curves a distant third." (Summey, *Modern Punctuation*, p. 107.)

case the sentence contained no parenthesis. When punctuation marks are used, they should be placed *after* the second parenthesis. (No mark ever precedes the first parenthesis.)

If you enter the front room (the old music hall), you will at once notice the antique furniture.

If the parenthesis is a complete sentence, there are two ways of punctuating:

1. If the complete sentence is inserted between two other sentences, write it precisely as you would if it were not enclosed within parentheses.

    He was sent for one evening just as he was going to bed. (He was then living alone.) His friend, Madame de Merret, had sent for him.

2. If the complete sentence is inserted in the body of another sentence, the first word of the inserted sentence is not capitalized and the inserted sentence is not followed by a period. A question mark or exclamation point, however, must not be omitted.

    He was sent for one evening (he was then living alone) just as he was going to bed. His friend, Madame de Merret (you have heard me speak of her before, haven't you?) had sent for him.

Note: When the parenthesis is a complete sentence, prefer curves to other marks of parenthesis.
Parentheses are never used to cancel a word.
Do not use parentheses indiscriminately, for they retard the smooth movement of the sentence.

Brackets

e. Uses of Brackets. Brackets are used to mark an interpolation added by the writer to material he is quoting or citing. This interpolation may be an explanation, a comment, or a correction.

> This poem [*Piers Plowman*] is thoroughly characteristic of the age [second half of the fourteenth century], in which it was written. The author [or authors, as some scholars would have us believe] was widely imitated by other writers.

f. Brackets are used to enclose a parenthesis within a parenthesis.

> This book was printed in New York (Smith and Rowe [now Smith and Wilson]) some time between 1845 and 1850.

Exercise. In the following sentences use brackets and parentheses wherever they are needed.

1. I enclose my check for fifty dollars $50.
2. We had ten (10) rifles and twenty (20) revolvers.
3. This poem which I may say I have never been able to read with any pleasure was published in New York in 1843 Hamilton and Wright now Hamilton and Powers and is the author's most famous work.
4. The old gentleman he died shortly after the publication of this famous book had always indulged his favorite hobby.
5. In that same village and in one of these very houses which to tell the precise truth was sadly worn and weather-beaten there lived a simple old peasant Gaston by name.

30 DIALOGUE AND QUOTED MATTER

a. Use of Quotation Marks. (1) Quotation marks are used before and after every direct quotation, regardless of its length.

> He said, "Will you come?"
> I replied, "Yes."

If the quotation is interrupted by words that are not

quoted, each portion of the interrupted quotation is enclosed within quotation marks:

Wrong: "My father wants to meet you, he said. Will you call to-night?"

Right: "My father wants to meet you," he said. "Will you call to-night?"

A single uninterrupted quotation consisting of several sentences, however, contains only one set of quotation marks:

Right: He said, "My father wants to meet you. Will you call to-night?"

Cautions: Do not use quotation marks with indirect quotations:

Wrong: He said that "he would be happy to meet us."

Right: He said that he would be happy to meet us.

Do not change the wording of the original unless you explain your changes in brackets.

Do not use quotation marks for common, well-known phrases which any reader can recognize as quoted.

Do not put the second quotation marks until you come to the end of the speech:

Wrong: "If this is true, I cannot go." "I shall have to wait until another day."

Right: "If this is true, I cannot go. I shall have to wait until another day."

(2) If a quotation consists of several paragraphs, put quotation marks at the *beginning* of each paragraph, but at the end of the last paragraph only.

(3) A quotation within a quotation should be enclosed within single quotation marks:

The witness testified: "I heard the defendant say, 'I had no idea that my uncle was in the city that day.'"

b. Punctuation. (1) The words introducing the direct quotation are always separated from the quotation itself. The comma is used unless the quotation is long or formal, in which cases a colon is preferred to the comma.

> He said, "I see you have an engagement."
> "I see you have an engagement," he said.
> "I see," he said, "that you have an engagement."
> Very slowly he replied, "I'll do it," and then walked slowly toward the cabin.

Note: No comma is used if the quoted expression is short and is a grammatically necessary and integral part of the sentence in which it stands; that is, if it is less than a complete sentence:

> He said that he would be "happy to come."
> Twice he answered "No."
> His response was "Yes."

No comma is used before quoted titles.

(2) If two statements in the same speech are independent clauses, punctuate them as independent clauses. Do not separate them by a comma. The use of a comma in such a case is one of the most common varieties of the "comma fault."

> *Wrong:* "I see you have an engagement," he said, "I'll call again."
> *Right:* "I see you have an engagement," he said. "I'll call again."
> "I see you have an engagement," he said; "I'll call again."

(3) Whenever a word is followed by both quotation marks and some other marks of punctuation, note: (1) That the apostrophe, the comma, the period, and ellipsis periods are always placed *within* the quotation marks

and that the semicolon and colon are always placed *outside* the quotation marks unless they are a part of the quotation itself. Study the examples given above. (2) That a question mark or an exclamation point is placed outside the quotation marks if the whole sentence in which the quotation stands is a question or an exclamation, but that it is placed inside the quotation marks when it applies only to the quoted part of the sentence: "Have you an engagement?" he said. Did he say, "I have an engagement?" (3) That a question mark or an exclamation point should not be followed by a comma or other mark of punctuation:

Wrong: "What are we waiting for?," said the priest.
Right: "What are we waiting for?" said the priest.
He said, "If any intelligent people were asked the question: 'What can literature do for you?' they would give very different answers."

c. Paragraphing. In writing dialogue make a separate paragraph for every change of speaker. Each speech, no matter how short, demands a separate paragraph. The explanatory words of introduction or comment accompanying the direct quotation may be put in the paragraph with the speech.

"You must marry," observed the parson, replacing the pipe in his mouth.

"Is that the right thing to do, think you?" demanded Will.

"It is indispensable," said the parson.

"Very well," replied the wooer.

When the verb of saying precedes the quoted speech, the quotation may be paragraphed separately:

To this the pastor remained silent, but after a while he asked:

"What is your errand this evening?"

See **Colon, 23.**

For capitalization, see **35.**

For the quoting of verse, see **Manuscript Form, 38.**

Exercise. Punctuate and paragraph the following passages correctly, paying special attention to the writing of the dialogue.[1]

1. Miss kinzer heres a lady wants to learn shrilled the high nasal voice miss kinzer wheres miss kinzer oh here you are as a young woman emerged from behind a pile of pasteboard boxes ive a learner for you miss kinzer shes a green girl but she looks likely and i want you to give her a good chance better put her on table work to begin with and with that injunction the little old maid hopped away leaving me to the scrutiny and the cross questioning of a rather pretty woman of twenty-eight or thirty ever worked in a factory before she began with lofty indifference as if it didnt matter whether i had or had not no where did you work i never worked any place before oh-h there was a world of meaning as i afterward discovered in miss kinzers long drawn out oh-h in this instance she looked up quickly with an obvious display of interest as if she had just unearthed a remarkable specimen in one who had never worked at anything before youre not used to work then she remarked insinuatingly straightening up from the rude desk where she sat like the judge of a police-court she was now all attention well not exactly that i replied nettled by her manner and above all by her way of putting things i have worked before but never at factory work then why didnt you say so she now opened her book and inscribed my name therein where do you live over in east fourteenth street i replied mechanically forgetting for the moment the catastrophe that had rendered me more homeless than ever home no i room then reading only too quickly an unpleasant interpretation in the uplifted eyebrows a disagreeable curiosity mirrored in the brown eyes

[1] From Margaret Richardson's *The Long Day*, The Century Company. Reprinted by permission.

beneath i added hastily i have no home my folks are all dead what impression this bit of information made i was unable to determine as i followed her slender slightly bowed figure across the busy roaring workroom.

2. did you ever read daphne vernon or a coronet of shame phoebe asked no i havent read them either i replied oh mama carry me out and let me die groaned mrs smith throwing down her paste brush and falling forward in mock agony upon the smeared table water water gasped phoebe clutching wildly at her throat im going to faint whats the matter what did i say that wasnt right i cried the nature of their antics showing only too plainly that i had put my foot in it in some unaccountable manner . . . what was it you was asking phoebe inquired presently with the most innocent air possible i said i hadnt read the books you mentioned i replied trying to hide the chagrin and mortification i felt at being so ignominiously laughed at eyether of them chirped mrs smith with a vicious wink eyether of them warbled phoebe in her mocking bird soprano it was my turn to drop the paste brush now eye-ther it must have slipped from my tongue unconsciously i could not remember having ever pronounced the word like that before i didnt feel equal then and there to offering them any explanation or apologies for the offense so i simply answered no are they as good as little rosebuds lovers no it aint said mrs smith decisively and a little contemptuously and it aint two books eye-ther its all in one daphne vernon or a coronet of shame.

CHAPTER III

MECHANICS

Habit is the succour God sends in aid of Perseverance; that is, he decrees that what you have done laboriously you shall do easily. — EMERSON

Habit simplifies the movements required to achieve a given result, makes them more accurate and diminishes fatigue. — WILLIAM JAMES

31   ITALICS AND QUOTATION MARKS

Italics.   Underscore once to indicate italics.   Italics are used most frequently in the following cases:

a. To mark foreign words or abbreviations of foreign words:

> This is an example of the argument *ad hominem.*
> *Op. cit., ibid., idem., sic., q.v., loc. cit.*

> *Note:* Such common abbreviations as i.e., e.g., cf., A.M., etc., vs., and viz. are often written without italics.   Such foreign words as have been naturalized need not be italicized: a priori, café, début, ennui, alibi, etc.

b. To refer to a word or a letter as such:

> Care should be taken to distinguish between *accept* and *except*, between *ac* and *ex*.
> There are two *a's* in *separate.*

c. To emphasize a word.   This use is comparatively rare. (See pp. 31–32.)

d. To mark the word *Resolved* in formal resolutions.

e. To indicate quoted titles of books, dramas, newspapers, magazines, and the names of ships:

I have been reading the *Outlook*, Miss Cather's *One of Ours*, and the Springfield *Republican*.

The name of the author or the name of the city in the title of a newspaper should not be italicized. (See **Quoted Titles, 32.**)

Quotation Marks. Quotation marks, like italics, are used to call special attention to a word or an expression as such. Note the following common uses:

f. To mark a technical word, a slang word, or a word used in a special ironical or humorous way:

> The pilot gave orders to "luff round."
> Oscar Wilde speaks of his hero's going "Bunburying."

But if such a word is repeated, there is no necessity for repeating the quotation marks.

g. To define or translate a word which needs explanation.

> *Except* means "to exclude." *Sprachgefühl* means "speech consciousness."

h. To enclose titles of short poems, short stories, essays, articles, pictures, and subdivisions of books. (See **Quoted Titles, 32.**)

> *Examples:* "I Have a Rendezvous with Death," "The American Scholar," "The Man Who Would Be King," "The Angelus," "What is Poetry?"

i. To mark off a quotation from another author.

> *Examples:* Emerson says that "Travel is a fool's paradise."
> "Travel," says Emerson, "is a fool's paradise."

Caution: Be sure, on the one hand, that you include within the quotation marks all the author's words, and on the other hand, that you do not include any of your own.

j. For the use of quotation marks in dialogue, see **Dialogue and Quotations, 30.**

Caution: A too frequent use of quotation marks gives the impression of undue self-consciousness, or gives too much emphasis. Never employ quotation marks without good reason.

Caution: Do not insult your reader's intelligence by labeling your humor or irony. When slang or technical expressions are used in a slang or technical context, they should not be quoted.

Exercise. Use quotation marks and italics correctly in the following sentences:

1. He said that "he would be glad to come."
2. "I think I shall go now, he said. Will you go with me?"
3. "No." "I can't leave just now, I replied."
4. Poetry, he says in his famous essay What is Poetry? is always concrete.
5. He deliberated a moment and then said, The result of Wordsworth's observation is then flashed upon the inward eye.
6. Chesterton remarks in one of his essays that we hear too much of prejudice and not enough of postjudice.
7. This "adorable" child then began to howl.
8. For Greek poetry, where quantity depends upon length of syllable the term metre is appropriate. In classical poetry, of course, accent was also recognized.
9. He recalled the time when *Martin Luther* defied the Pope.
10. Herrick's Hesperides was published in 1648.
11. Non vi sed saepe cadendo was a favorite expression of his.
12. The sound of a in hat is not really the short sound of a in fate; i.e., the two sounds differ in quality as well as in quantity.
13. Our ship, the Imperial, had become so unmanageable that it was high time for us to make for our port de carrénage.
14. This word is discussed at length in Webster's New International Dictionary, s.v. liable.

32 QUOTED TITLES

a. Capitalize the first, the last, and all important words in the titles of books, poems, plays, stories, chapters, newspapers, magazines, and pictures. Articles, prepositions, auxiliary verbs, and conjunctions are not capitalized unless, of course, they stand first in the title. If an article stands first in the title of a newspaper or magazine, however, it should not be capitalized:

> He read the *Saturday Evening Post*, the New York *Times*, the *Century Magazine* and the *Nation*.

b. Use quotation marks for the titles of short poems, stories, pictures, essays, articles, and parts or sections of books. (See **Italics and Quotation Marks, 31.**)

c. Italicize the titles of books, newspapers, magazines, or other separate publications. (See **Italics and Quotation Marks, 31.**)

d. Take pains not to omit an article which forms part of a title. The article should be capitalized and either quoted or italicized — except in the titles of newspapers and magazines. (See *a* and *c* above.) But in the case of familiar titles the article may be omitted if a possessive precedes the title:

Correct: "The Piece of String" is one of De Maupassant's best-known stories.
"The Eve of Saint Agnes," one of Keats's poems, deals with an ancient superstition.

Also correct: Keats's "Eve of Saint Agnes."
In his "Piece of String" De Maupassant deals with the tragic results of a trivial act.

Exercise. Use italics and quotation marks and capitals correctly in the following sentences:

1. I have subscribed for The Century Magazine, the New York Times, Reedy's Mirror, and the Chicago Tribune.
2. My reading list comprised the House of seven Gables, Kipling's Man who Would be King, and O. Henry's story the Handbook of Hymen in the volume entitled the Heart of the west.
3. Shakespeare's Hamlet is my favorite character. Hamlet is one of my favorite plays.

33   HYPHEN

THE hyphen has two uses:

    a. To indicate the division of a word at the end of a line, but never at the beginning. (See **Syllabication, 34.**)

    b. To join the members of compound words: *twenty-four, father-in-law, so-called.* There are no fixed rules for the writing of compounds. When in doubt, consult a good dictionary. (But see **Compounds, 50.**)

34   SYLLABICATION

THERE are no hard-and-fast rules for dividing words into syllables. When in doubt, consult a good dictionary or observe the practice of a reputable publishing house. Wherever possible, avoid dividing a word. When you divide a word, separate the two parts by a hyphen at the end of the line (never at the beginning), and remember that the division always comes between syllables since it is based on pronunciation, not on spelling. The following general rules will cover most cases:

    a. Always place the hyphen at the end of the line.

    b. Avoid dividing monosyllables or digraphs (*th, ph, gh, sh, ch,* etc.) *through, though, fifth.* Divide only between syllables.

    c. Do not divide a word so that a single letter stands alone as a syllable; and, except for prefixes and suffixes, rarely write two letters as a separate syllable: *many* (not *man-y*), *across, bring, only, ever.*

d. Never divide a word so that any syllable is unpronounceable.

e. A single consonant or a digraph standing between two vowels is put in the following syllable, except after a preceding short stressed vowel: *te-di-um, sa-ted, fa-ther;* but *sat-in, tra-gic,* etc., are exceptions.

f. Two consonants or double consonants are usually divided except in such words as *call-ing,* where the simple word ends in a double consonant: *com-mit, per-mit;* but *tell-ing, spell-ing, spell-er.*

g. Three consonants are divided so that the consonants that are pronounced together stand in the same syllable: *demon-strate, mael-strom, per-spec-tive.*

h. Compound words are divided between their component parts: *black-board, over-take, battle-ground.*

i. Prefixes and suffixes are usually written separately except that *-ed* stands alone only when it is pronounced as a separate syllable, and except where the rule for doubling a single final consonant gives two consonants (as in *oc-cur-red*) *man-ly, re-duce, ante-date,* but *gnarled, walked.*

Exercise. Divide the following words into syllables if they can be properly divided:

Fail, mystery, unpretentious, bounded, learned, forcible, potted, cowardly, dialogue, tough, baker, across, pursue, cordial, teacher, general, cabin, disenchant, older, raisin, superintendent, suspicion, graphically, destruction, define, longest, blubber, permission, catch, single, thimble, bracken, length.

35 CAPITALS

THE present tendency is to avoid capitals wherever possible.

A good rule, therefore, is: *Never capitalize a word unless you have good reason for doing so.* When in doubt, consult a good dictionary or observe the practice of a reputable printing house. Since these authorities differ in the use of capitals, you will avoid confusion by following one authority consistently.

The two fundamental uses of capitals are (1) to mark a new unit of thought and (2) to designate a word as proper and not common. On the basis of these principles certain definite rules may be formulated.

Capitals to Mark a New Unit of Thought or a Line of Poetry

a. Capitalize the first word of every sentence, of every *direct* quotation if it is a complete sentence (see **30**), of every formal resolution or salutation, of every query, and of every question or answer that is formally introduced and that forms a unit of thought.

> *Examples:* He said, "I cannot come."
> The rule is: Never begin a task unless you know you can complete it.
> The question is, Will he come if we ask him?

b. Capitalize the first word of every line of poetry.

Capitals to Designate Proper Nouns or Adjectives

a. Capitalize all proper nouns or adjectives. Names of persons or the equivalents of such names; names of races, languages, religious, political, social, legislative, educational, or military organizations; of wars, historical epochs or movements; of the days of the week, of the months, of holidays — are capitalized because they refer to specific, individual persons or things.

Examples: Mr. Smith, Spaniards, "Greasers," English, the Puritan Revolution, the Broad River (but the river Broad), Magna Carta, Cowden College.

Note: It is often difficult to determine whether a given noun is proper or common. But the context will, in most cases, enable one to determine whether the reference is to a *particular* person or thing or to *any one* of a class of persons or things. Note the use of capitals in the following sentences:

I do not belong to any club or society.
He belongs to the Geological Club.
Are you going to the Club?
He is only a junior in high school and so is not ready to enter college.
He has not been graduated from a high school yet.
He is attending the Jonesboro High School.
When I go to college, I shall go to Holley College. I intend to study Latin, English, physics, mathematics, and chemistry. I intend to do most of my work in the Department of Chemistry.
Are you going with us, Sister?
How many sisters have you?
He sailed west.
The West has grown rapidly in population.

b. Capitalize all words — except relative pronouns — referring to God, Christ, the Trinity, or the Bible. If the antecedent is expressed, personal pronouns referring to God or Christ need not be capitalized.

c. Capitalize titles of honor preceding a proper name and all degrees following a name. But if a title is used alone, only titles of great respect should be capitalized. (Capitals, of course, are never used when the reference is not to a *particular* person.)

Examples: President Monroe; J. C. Powell, President (or president) of Holley College. The Crown Prince called on ex-President Taft. We are going to elect a president and a secretary this afternoon.

    d. Capitalize the first and all important words in quoted titles. (See **Quoted Titles, 32.**)

Miscellaneous Uses of Capitals

    a. Capitalize *I, O* (not *oh*), *B.C., A.D.,* and *Esq.* (*A.M., P.M., Jr.,* and *Sr.* may be written without capitals.)

    b. Capitalize personified abstractions.

    c. Capitalize the words *Whereas* and *Resolved* in formal resolutions and the first word following either of these words.

Misuses of Capitals

    a. Do not capitalize for emphasis.

    b. Do not capitalize the names of the seasons unless they are personified.

    c. Do not capitalize *north, east, south,* and *west* when these words merely indicate direction.

    d. Do not capitalize the names of studies in the curriculum unless they are proper nouns or adjectives or unless they form part of the name of a specific course, such as *Physics I, Mathematics II.*

    e. Do not capitalize the first word of a direct quotation that is less than a sentence.

    f. Do not capitalize the first word after a semicolon. After a colon capitalize the first word only when it begins a complete and independent sentence.

    g. Do not capitalize proper nouns that have become common nouns: *chinaware, canton cloth, hector, mentor, babel, boycott, stoical, quixotic, india rubber.*

Exercise. Supply capitals in the exercise on pp. **204–205.**

36 ABBREVIATIONS

a. Except in footnotes, bibliographies, technical matter, and citations, where condensation is desirable, avoid abbreviations. Only the following classes of abbreviations are permissible in formal or literary discourse.

   1. Such common abbreviations of titles as *Mr., Mrs., Rev., Esq., Jr., Dr., D.D., Ph.D. used with proper names,* and the abbreviations No., A.D., A.M., P.M., *used with other words.*

   2. Such common abbreviations as i.e., etc., e.g., cf., viz., vs., but not & for *and.* In formal writing it is better to spell out even these words and to write *namely, that is, for example.*

b. A period should be used after all abbreviations. (But see **Period, 24.**)

c. Avoid the abbreviation of titles not followed by a proper name, of names of months, states, countries, and of the words *street, avenue, railroad, mountain, company,* etc.

d. In formal writing avoid contractions — words written with an apostrophe to indicate the omission of a letter from the body of the word. No period is required after a contraction.

Exercise. Revise the use of abbreviations in the following sentences:

   1. I called the Dr. twice this p.m.
   2. The accident occurred in Oct. on Peters St. just where the R.R. passes in front of the main offices of John Dewitt & Bros. My Math Prof. has some stock in this Co.

3.   Albany, N Y
                                                      11/14/'22
James Forster, M D.
        Peterboro, Col,
   Dear Dr:
     Yours of Oct 12th at hand.   I beg leave to state that the
   col. is not in Cal.
                          Yrs. truly,
                                        Jas. J Thompsen
4. Ten per cent. of the errors have been left unchanged.   These
   have already been pointed out and the James Mfg. Co. has
   been notified.

37   REPRESENTATION OF NUMBERS

a. Do not spell out the numbers in dates, hours (when
     A.M. or P.M. is used), pages or sections of books,
     room or street numbers, or cardinal numbers preceded
     by a word of enumeration.

     Right: July 27, 1888.   1788 Jackson Avenue.   Pages 9, 12,
          and 15.   Part II, Section 4.

b. For other numbers use figures for all numbers which
     cannot be written in one or two words.   But never use
     figures and words for numbers in the same sentence or
     paragraph.

     Right: He is seventeen years old.   Nineteen hundred men.
          1,562 infantry.

     This rule applies also to sums of money.   The dollar
     sign should not be used for sums less than a dollar.

c. Do not begin a sentence with a figure.   Spell the
     number out, or recast the sentence.

d. Do not write "two thousand forty-six" for "two
     thousand and forty-six."

e. Except in cases where extreme accuracy is desired, do
     not repeat a number in parenthetical figures.

Undesirable: We killed ten (10) birds.
Right: We killed ten birds.

f. Except in dates and street numbers use commas to set off figures in groups of three.

Right: 1,586; 1,789,678.

g. Use a hyphen in compound numerals for sums less than a hundred.

Right: twenty-four, eighty-six, ninety-nine.

Exercise. Revise the following sentences and represent the numbers correctly:

1. He sold nine thousand eight hundred and forty bushels of wheat and after deducting all expenses cleared nine hundred and forty eight dollars and twentyfive cents.
2. John Gower was born in one thousand four hundred and eight. His *Confessio Amantis* is a work of 30,000 lines.
3. 787 men engaged in the battle, but only twentyfour were killed. About 1/4 were wounded. The battle was fought at 3 o'clock on Saturday, November twentythird, eighteen hundred ninety six.

38   MANUSCRIPT FORM

A WRITER should, out of consideration for his readers, remove every mechanical obstacle to the easy and comfortable reading of his manuscript. His writing will then be clearer, more easily intelligible, and more effective. In speaking, people with good speech manners do not mumble, swallow syllables, or talk in a high or nasal tone. Common politeness demands that we make the task of our hearers or readers as agreeable and as easy as possible. In writing, we should pay special attention to these matters of manuscript form:

a. Legibility. Do not run letters or words together or leave a space between letters of the same word. Write with a good pen, use clear ink, and write distinctly. Do not let the loops of letters overlap between the lines. Take care to avoid the omission of end punctuation, of the dot over an *i* or *j*, and of the cross of a *t*. Take especial pains to write proper names correctly and to distinguish in form and size between capitals and small letters.

b. Paging. Number and arrange the pages of your manuscript in proper order. Use arabic numbers in the upper right-hand corner of the page. Use white paper of a standard size and write on one side only.

c. Spacing. Leave a margin of one inch on both sides of the page. Do not crowd your writing on the bottom of the page; leave the last line blank. Do not leave part of a line blank except at the end of a paragraph or before a quotation placed below the words introducing it.

d. Indention. Indent each new paragraph at least one-half an inch to the right of the ruled margin of the paper. Take care to indent quotations and verse correctly.

e. Erasures and Corrections. Do not leave unsightly erasures or blots on your paper. To cancel a word draw a single straight line through it. Do not use brackets or parentheses to cancel.

To insert an omitted expression use a caret $(_\wedge)$ below the line at the point of omission and write the inserted words either between the lines above the caret or in the margin opposite the caret. Rewrite a page rather than leave it full of unsightly blots, blurs, or corrections.

f. Footnotes. Numbers referring to footnotes should be

inserted immediately after and above the words to which they refer. (See pp. 5, 204, 224 for examples.) The footnotes may be numbered serially throughout the page or separately for each manuscript page. A straight line should separate the body of the text from the footnotes.

g. *Endorsement of Theme.* Unless the instructor otherwise directs, the endorsement should be written on the side of the paper which is uppermost when the fold is at the left of the reader, and should conform to the following model.

> John Thomas
> English A, Section 2
> June 1, 1923
> The Best Short Story I Have Read
> Paper No. 10

h. *Correct Form for the Title of a Theme.*

1. Capitalize the first and every important word in the title of the theme. Ordinarily articles, prepositions, conjunctions, and auxiliary verbs are not capitalized unless they stand first in the title.

2. Do not use quotation marks or italics with the title unless these marks are called for by the rules given in sections **31** and **32**.

3. Write the title on the first line, or lines, of the page. Center it so as to leave equal spaces between the title and the marginal lines. For titles longer than one line, fill up the first line and center the last line.

4. No period is needed after the title. But if the title is a question or an exclamation, use a question mark or an exclamation point.

5. Leave a space of at least one inch (or two lines) between the title and the first line of the body of the theme.

6. Make the first sentence of the theme independent of the title. The opening sentence should be clear without reference to the title. Do not begin your theme with such a sentence as "This subject is a very important one." State what the subject is.

7. Do not omit important words in the title of your theme. Indicate the subject clearly and explicitly.

8. Make the title of the theme specific, apt, and accurate. Do not use such general titles as "William Shakspere," "Les Miserables," "Modern Democracy," "Prohibition" — unless you are writing a book or an extended essay.

i. Verse.

1. Begin each line of verse with a capital. If the complete line cannot be written on one line of the paper, indent to the right the portion carried over, as below:

> The moon went down and nothing now was
>   seen
> Save where the lamp of a Madonna shone
> Faintly — or heard, but when he spoke, who
>   stood
> Over the lantern.

2. Follow exactly the line divisions of the original.

3. If a quotation of verse is inserted in a prose passage, the first line of verse should begin on a new line and should be centered, or indented from both margins, as below. The prose follow-

ing the inserted verse quotation should not be indented unless it begins a new paragraph.

Examples: The lines which Lowell wrote concerning heroic deeds:

> "When a deed is done for Freedom, through
> the broad earth's aching breast
> Runs a thrill of joy prophetic, trembling
> on from east to west,"

are true for all ages and all nations.

If less than a complete line of verse is quoted, it need not be written on a separate line:

> Tennyson speaks of Ulysses' purpose "to sail beyond the sunset."

39   PUNCTUATION MARKS AT THE BEGINNING OF THE LINE

NEVER put a comma, a semicolon, a colon, a period, a question mark, an exclamation point, or a hyphen at the beginning of a line.

40   PARAGRAPHING

PARAGRAPH divisions, always indicated by indentation, are mechanical, but not arbitrary. Do not indent from mere whim, as the writer of "scrappy paragraphs" usually does, nor from a feeling that your page should look well to the eye. Remember that the paragraph is a unit of thought. (See pp. 80–83.)

For the paragraphing of dialogue, see **Dialogue and Quotations, 30.**

41   OUTLINING

SEE pp. 83–86. Note also the following detail: Do not employ the *form* of subdivision unless your *matter* is susceptible of division, since of course subdivision involves division into at least two parts.

Wrong: A. Among recent writers, I prefer:
        1. Joseph Conrad.
      B. . . . .

Right: A. Among recent writers, I prefer Joseph **Conrad.**
      B. . . . .

Right: A. Among recent writers, I prefer:
        1. Joseph Conrad, and
        2. Arnold Bennett.
      B. Among ancient writers . . .

CHAPTER IV

SPELLING

Attention and accuracy ... are the two things in which all mankind are more deficient than in any other mental quality whatever. — HUXLEY

"I *will* see her," said Arthur. "I'll ask her to marry me, once more. I will. No one shall prevent me."

"What, a woman who spells affection with one *f?*" — THACKERAY, *Pendennis*

INTRODUCTION: RECORDING ERRORS

REMEMBER that the world deals harshly with misspellers. Acquire at once the habit of guarding yourself in this matter by (1) consulting a dictionary whenever you are in the least doubt as to the correct spelling of a word, and (2) collecting a list of words that *you* misspell, in order to discover and thoroughly master the words that constantly mar your work. In concentrating your attention on these words try to learn their exact *look* and *sound*. Note the arrangement of the letters of the word and pronounce each word slowly and deliberately even if you exaggerate the syllable division and the sound of the unaccented vowels. Copy each word several times and notice the arrangement and formation of the letters as you write them. You will be agreeably surprised to find that the list of words you habitually misspell is much shorter than you expected — from twenty-five to a hundred words, unless you are a notoriously bad speller.

You will find it valuable to prepare a list of all the words you have misspelled and to indicate how often you have

misspelled each. How many of your words are in the list
of 400 words on pages 237–242?

42 PRONUNCIATION AND SPELLING

POOR spellers should remember that mispronunciation is
responsible for over ten per cent [1] of misspelled words. If
one mishears or mispronounces a word, one is almost certain
to misspell it. Following are examples:

athlete	necessary
athletics	perform (not pre)
boundary	perhaps
candidate	prevalent
cavalry	probably
curiosity	quantity
definite	recommend
despair	referee
disease	separate
every	similar
February	sophomore
generally	surprise
government	tragedy
height (no th sound)	translate
hundred	usually
laboratory	whether
library	whither

Exercise. Pronounce the following words slowly and carefully. Then copy them, and mark the division into syllables. (See **Syllabication, 34.**)

*Athlete, brilliant, chocolate, dormitory, eighth, element, govern-
ment, mischievous, nominative, persistence, particularly, positive,
salary, unanimous, graphically, business, cruelty, threshold,
wicked, grammar, cavalry, Calvary, every, February, height.*

---

[1] Lester, *op. cit.*, p. 14.

43   CONFUSION OF SIMILAR FORMS OR SOUNDS

AVOID the confusion of words similar in form, or similar or identical in sound.[1] The following groups are often confused by careless students:

accept, except
advice, advise
affect, effect
all right, almost
all ready, already
all together, altogether
berth, birth
born, borne
capital, capitol
coarse, course
conscious, conscience
choose, chose
complement, compliment
council, counsel, consul
desert, dessert
decent, descent
dining, dinning
forth, fourth
guard, regard
hear, here
holy, wholly
its, it's
knew, new
know, no

lead, led
loose, lose
mind, mine
of, off
past, passed
peace, piece
plain, plane
practice, practise
precede, proceed
principal, principle
quiet, quite
respectfully, respectively
rite, right, write
sense, consent
sight, cite, site
stationary, stationery
staid, stayed
straight, strait
their, there, they're
till, until
to, too, two
weather, whether
which, witch

Exercise. Choose ten of the groups given in the preceding section and compose sentences to illustrate the correct spelling and meaning of the words in each group. Write a separate sentence for each word in the group.

[1] According to Professor John A. Lester thirteen per cent of misspellings are due to such confusion. See note on p. 236.

44 ETYMOLOGICAL KINSHIP

A KNOWLEDGE of the etymology of a word will often help one to recall the spelling. If you have studied a foreign language, use your knowledge of etymology to guide you in spelling. For instance, one who knows that *definite* is derived from Latin *finis* will not spell the word *definate*.

Learn to associate derivatives from the same root words: *prepare, apparent, preparation, preparatory, compare; satisfaction, dissatisfaction; four, fourth; villa, villain; cease, decease; point, appoint, disappoint; govern, government; court, courtier, courtesy, courteous; opera, operate, operation; grade, degrade, degradation; sociable, associate.*

Distinguish carefully the following pairs of prefixes:

ante, "before": *antedate*	*anti,* "against": *anticlimax*
dis, "not": *disappear*	*de,* "from," "down": *decease, degrade*
for, "from" or "greatly": *forbid, forlorn, forspent*	*fore,* "in front," "before": *foreground, foretell.*
mis, "wrong": *misarrange, misappropriate*	
per, "through," "thoroughly": *pervert, perchance*	*pre,* "before": *precede, prevent.*
un, "not": *unfriendly*	*un,* "reverse action": *unfurl, unfold*

Note the three words ending in *-ceed: proceed, exceed, succeed.* Except for *supersede,* most other words of this class are spelled *-cede.*

Exercise A. Write several derivatives of each of the Latin stems listed below. Use a hyphen between the stem and the prefix or suffix:

-fine (de-fine, de-finite-ness). -cede, -form, -cred (believe),

cur- (care), *curr-* (run), *-vent, -vide, port-, -volv* (roll, turn), *dict-, liber* (free), *migr-* (move), *anim-* (mind), *ann-* (year), *aud-* (hear), *mult-* (many), *pell-, puls-* (drive), *ple-, plete-* (fill, full).

    Supply: cede, ceed, ced, or *sede:* pre...., re...., con...., inter ...., pro...., ex....., suc.... super...., pro...., ure.

Exercise B. Make a list of as many words as possible formed with the prefixes listed in the second paragraph of this section.

Exercise C. Write derivatives of the following words. Separate the stem from the suffix or prefix.

    Sure, glad, govern, grammar, battle, case, busy, labor, scribe, appoint, appear, ease, conceive, four, satisfy, dress, appear, mischief, victory, total.

45   *Ei* AND *Ie*

THE following guides may help one to remember whether to write *ie* or *ei:*

   (1) Where *l* or *c* precedes the digraph, note that *i* usually follows *l* and *e* follows *c,* as in *lice,* or *Celia.*

   (2) Write *i* before *e*
        When sounded as *ee*
        Except after *c.*

   (3) Write *i* before *e*
        Except after *c,*
        Or when sounded as *a*
        As in *neighbor* and *weigh.*

The following are the more common words in this class:

Spelled *ei*	Spelled *ie*
receive	relief
deceive	relieve
conceive	belief
receipt	believe

Spelled *ei*	Spelled *ie*
perceive	chief
weird	grief
leisure	thief
seize	piece
either	series
neither	friend
foreign	fiend
height	fiery
their	mischief
heir	handkerchief

When the sound is *a* write *ei*: veil, weigh, neighbor, freight, neigh, eight, vein, rein, reign, deign.

Exercise. Make a list of words spelled with *ei* or *ie* and add them to the two columns above.

46 DOUBLING A FINAL CONSONANT

BEFORE a suffix beginning with a vowel, a single final consonant is doubled (1) if it is preceded by a single vowel and (2) if the consonant stands either in a monosyllable or in a word accented on the last syllable. If both of these conditions are not fulfilled, the consonant is not doubled.

Monosyllables

drag	dragging
run	running
stop	stopping
get	getting
hot	hottest
din	dinning
sin	sinning
rob	robbing
drop	dropping
whip	whipping
fit	fitting

228

Monosyllables

bid	bidding
quiz	quizzes
man	mannish
quit	quitting

Note the following monosyllables that contain a **digraph** (two vowels) before the final consonant, or that end in a double consonant:

read	reading
brief	briefer
stiff	stiffer
act	actor

Note these dissyllables accented on the last syllable:

begin	beginning
omit	omitted
occur	occurred
refer	referred, but reference
confer	conferred, but conference
transfer	transferred, but transference
compel	compelled
permit	permitted
commit	committee

Exercise A. Write the present participle and the past tense of each of the following verbs:

Drag (dragging, dragged), sin, rob, quit, din, compel, occur, act, daub, fill, stay, admit, excel, dine, refer, permit, transfer, fix, pass, desert, war.

Exercise B. Write the third person singular present indicative of each of the words listed above.

47   DROPPING FINAL -E

WORDS ending in unpronounced final *e* usually drop the *e* before a suffix beginning with a vowel, but retain the *e* before a suffix beginning with a consonant:

arrive	arriving, arrival
believe	believing
change	changing
choose	choosing
come	coming
fleece	fleecy
force	forcing, forcibly
guide	guidance
have	having
hope	hoping, but hopeless
imagine	imaginary, imaginable
like	liking, but likely
lose	losing
love	loving, lovable
move	moving
please	pleasure
shake	shaking
shape	shaping
true	truism, but truly
use	usable, usage
write	writing
arrange	arranging, but arrangement
mistake	mistakable

Exceptions:

1. *Dyeing, singeing, tingeing* retain the *e* to distinguish these words from *dying, singing,* and *tinging* (="*tinkling*"). *Shoeing, hoeing, eyeing, acreage,* and *mileage* also retain the *e*.

2. Since *c* and *g* followed by the back vowels *a*, *o*, or *u* generally have the hard sound, the *e* is retained after *c* or *g* before the suffixed *-able* or *-ous* in order to preserve the soft sound of *c* or *g*: *changeable, courageous, advantageous, serviceable, noticeable, peaceable.*

Exercise. Write the present participle of each of the following words:

Love, come, hope, prove, sing, singe, use, dine, din, shoe, hoe, eye, dye, die, take, please, lose, write, use, argue.

Change each of the following words into an adjective by adding *-able*, *-ible*, or *-ous:*

Service, change, love, break, accept, sense, prefer, rely, admire, religion, peace, remark, notice, courage, humor, grieve, outrage, trouble.

Form derivatives of the following words by adding *-ment*, *-ly*, or *-ty:*

Like, love, commence, arrange, safe, god, develop, amaze, ripple, partial, special, able, jangle, subtle, sick, general, entire, sure, great, nine.

48   FINAL -Y

WORDS ending in *-y* preceded by a consonant change the *y* to *i* before any suffix except one beginning with *i:*

mercy	merciful
embody	embodied, but embodying
rely	reliance
happy	happiness
beauty	beautiful
busy	business
study	studious, but studying
hurry	hurried, but hurrying
easy	easily

When the final *-y* is preceded by a vowel it is not changed:

stay	stayed
valley	valleys
employ	employed

But note the exceptions *pay, paid; lay, laid; say, said.*

Exercise. Write the third person singular present indicative and the past tense of each of the following words:

Try (tries, tried), die, deny, carry, cry, study, spy, marry, tarry, supply, envy, say, lay, pay, hurry, rely.

49 PLURALS

(a) *Plurals in -s or -es.* Most nouns form the plural by adding *s* to the singular: *boys, trees, seas, bells, cups.*

But nouns ending in a sibilant sound: (*s, se, ce, x, z*) add *es* to form the plural: *kisses, horses, fences, axes, quizzes.*

(b) *Plural of Words in -y.* Nouns ending in -*y* preceded by a consonant change the *y* to *i* and add *es* to form the plural: *flies, cries, skies, studies, ladies, mercies, armies, pities.* Nouns ending in -*y* preceded by a vowel, usually retain the *y* and add *s* for the plural: *days, keys, plays, joys, quays, monkeys.*

(c) *Plural of Words in -o.* Nouns ending in *o preceded by a vowel* add *s* to form the plural: *cameos, folios.*

Nouns ending in *o preceded by a consonant* add *s* or *es.* The following form the plural by adding *es: echo, hero, no, potato, tomato, cargo, mosquito, negro, hero.* Most other words of this class add *s: canto, dynamo, halo, memento, quarto, piano, solo.*

(d) *Irregular Plurals.* Traces of the Old English irregular declensions survive in the irregular plurals *oxen, children, brethren, geese, feet, mice, men, women, sheep, deer, swine, trout.*

(e) *Plurals of Foreign Words.* Many words derived from foreign languages retain the plural of the language from which they were borrowed. Many words of this class have been partly naturalized and have a second, anglicized plural. The present tendency is to anglicize the plural of foreign nouns.

alumnus: alumni
radius: radii or radiuses
focus: foci, or focuse?

cherub: cherubim or cherubs
seraph: seraphim or seraphs
basis: bases

phenomenon: phenomena
crisis: crises
index: indices or indexes
beau: beaux or beaus
tableau: tableaux or tableaus
alumna: alumnæ
formula: formulæ, or formulas

hypothesis: hypotheses
analysis: analyses
datum: data
stratum: strata or stratums
medium: media or mediums
memorandum: memoranda or memorandums.

(*f*) *Plural of Compounds.* Compound nouns usually form the plural by adding *s* or *es* to the important word in the compound: *sons-in-law, courts-martial, bystanders, passers-by.* But if the component elements are so closely joined as to be felt as a simple word, the suffix is added to the end of the word: *cupfuls, handfuls.* In a few words both elements are pluralized: *men-servants, women-servants.*

(*g*) *The Plural of Letters, Figures, Signs, etc.* (See **Apostrophe, 28.**)

Exercise A. Write the plural of each of the following words:

Fish, lily, brother, beau, index, radius, canto, banjo, fly, tree, negro, glass, crash, ox, sky, valley, pity, key, horse, quiz, joy, day, solo, deer, echo, piano, hero, potato, mouse, stratum, trout, mercy, valley, beauty.

Exercise B. Write the singular of:

Alumni, alumnæ, radii, criteria, data, dicta, phenomena, cherubim, seraphim, theses, bases, crises, banditti, tableaux, memoranda.

50 COMPOUND WORDS

THE hyphen is used between the parts of compound words in which the elements of the compound are still felt as separate words. The first stage of a compound is the writing of two words side by side, such as *volley ball, railway engineer.* When a closer unity is felt, a hyphen is used to join the two words into a loose compound, such as *bull's-eye*, *absent-minded.* The final stage is the writing of the two words as one. The last stage represents a real compound word, for the new word is accented as if it were a single word and, in some cases, has a meaning different from the sum of the meaning of its elements. Note the difference in accent and meaning between *black board*, *blackboard*, *black berry* and *blackberry.*

There are no hard and fast rules for the use of the hyphen, for, in many cases, usage is not fixed. The majority of the errors, however, are due to an excessive use of the hyphen. *When in doubt, write the word without division.*

The following rules cover ninety per cent of the common words. Use the hyphen in the following cases:

a. *Self, fellow, half, quarter,* followed by another word: *self-esteem, self-praise, fellow-citizen.*

b. Prepositional phrases forming a compound noun: *father-in-law, man-of-war.*

c. Two or more words *preceding the noun* and used as a single adjective: *up-to-date, salmon-pink, pearl-gray, first-class, ten-foot, well-known, so-called, soft-spoken.* But "He was well known." "The house was well lighted."

d. Compound numerals less than a hundred, when the numeral precedes the noun: *sixty-three, forty-eight, ninety-nine, one-third.*

Fractions used as adjectives are written without the hyphen: *He spent one third of his income for supplies.*

e. Words that may be misread: *re-creation, recreation; co-respondent, correspondent; twenty five-dollar bills, twenty-five dollar bills; common school teacher, common-school teacher, a black lead pencil, a black-lead pencil.*

f. All + another word: *all-pervading, all-inclusive;* but *all right.*

Write the following classes of words solid:

a. A compound noun composed of two other nouns: *baseball, football, handbook, workman, battleship, textbook, footstep, classmate.* But if the first noun is used as an adjective modifying the second noun, that is, if the two words express separate and distinct ideas, write the nouns separate: *iron age, air pump, fellow citizen, mother tongue, human being, drug store.*

b. A compound consisting of *any, every, no, some* + *-body, -thing,* or *-where: anybody, anything, anywhere.*

c. Compound personal pronouns: *myself, himself, itself, yourself.*

d. Words consisting of a root + a prefix or suffix: *ahead, beside, outdoor, overtake, upward, goodness, kingdom,* but *ex-President.*

e. Derivative prepositions: *into, within, upon, furthermore, towards, without, into, unto.* But *on to.*

    Write separate all words which have separate grammatical constructions, all words which express distinct, even though closely related, ideas. Compare *a black bird, a good deal, a good man, good will: a blackbird, goodman.*

    Write separate the following common words:

all right	et cetera
any one	inasmuch as
every one	near by
no one	in spite of
some one	

The following words have two accepted forms:

to-night	tonight
to-day	today
to-morrow	tomorrow
per cent	percent

Exercise. Classify the following words in three groups: (1) those written solid, (2) those written with a hyphen, and (3) those written as separate words:

Fatherinlaw, teacup, manofwar, porthole, blackbird, baseball, volleyball, football, handball, passerby, backbone, bookkeeper, anybody, sometimes, classmate, eyesight, fireplace, workshop, oneself, northeast, myself, eightysix, onethird, ninetynine, onehalf, salmonpink, rosebud, twentyfour, selfconfidence, firstclass, grayhaired, allright, anyone, hardhearted, battleground, groundfloor, groundwork, eyebrow, alltogether, altogether, already, today, inasmuch as, nevertheless, etcetera, without, onto, inspite of, despite.

51 SPELLING LIST

THIS list contains the 400 words most commonly misspelled. Almost sixty per cent of errors in spelling are due to the misspelling of these 400 words. Every student should master the list at once, for by doing so he can eliminate the greater part of his errors. Check the words you misspell and review them every day until you are sure you have mastered the correct forms. The fifty most important words — which are responsible for 19.2 per cent of the spelling errors — are printed in italic type.[1]

[1] The writers are indebted to Professor John A. Lester for permission to incorporate the results of his excellent study and classification of errors in spelling. These results are published in *The Journal of Educational Psychology*, February and March, 1922, and in *A Spelling Review*, by John A. Lester, The Hill School, Pottstown, Pa. This speller, based on the exhaustive analysis of 14,000 errors of 2,414 candidates for the College Board Entrance Examinations in English, 1913–1919, is one of the most scientific and practical ever prepared, and is indispensable to every teacher of English.

Some of these words, it will be observed, illustrate the use of the apostrophe, which is treated separately. (See pp. 196–197.)

absolutely
accommodate.
accomplish
accusative
achievement
acknowledge
acquaintance
across
adjectival
adverbially
advice
aeroplane
affairs
affect
all right
allowed
almost
already (different from all ready)
although
altogether
always
amateur
ammunition
among
amount
angle
another
anything
anywhere
apartment
apparent
appearance
arctic
argument
around

arouse
artillery
association
athlete
athletics
attempt
attractive
authorities
automobile
auxiliary
awkward
balloon
baseball
battalion
because
before
beginning
believe
beneficial
benefit
border
borne
break
breathe
business
busy
can't
capital
carburetor
cemetery
characteristic
chauffeur
chocolate
choose
chosen

clause
cliff
climb
clothes
colloquial
coming
commission
committed
committee
companies
comparatively
competent
competitive
complement
completely
compulsory
conceive
conjunction
conscientious
control
convenient
corner
corps
course
cozy
cries
criticism
criticize
curriculum
custom
deceive
decide
decision
declarative
deficient
democracy
dependent
describe
description

despair
destructive
develop
development
difference
disappear
disappoint
discipline
discussion
disease
divided
doctor
doesn't
don't
dormitories
dropped
drunkenness
effect
efficiency
efficient
employee
enemy
engineer
enthusiastic
entirely
equipped
equivalent
erroneous
especially
etc. (= et cetera)
every
everybody
everything
everywhere
excel
excellent
exercise
existence
expected

expense
experience
extension
extensive
extremely
financial
finally
football
foreign
foremost
foresee
forest
formerly
forward
fought
four
friend
frightened
fulfill or fulfil
further
gaiety, gayety
generally
genitive
genius
glorious
good-bye or good-by
government
grammar
guard
harass
haven't
height
heroes
hoping
horde
hypocrisy
imagine
immediately
incident

independent
indefinitely
indispensable
inevitable
influential
innocent
interest
interested
involve
irresistible
isn't
its
it's
knew
knowledge
known
laboratory
laid
lavender
led
lightning
likely
loath, loth
loneliness
loose
lose
losing
magnificent
maneuver
manual
manufacture
mathematics
meant
medicine
militarism
miniature
minute
modifier
modifies

modifying
morale
mosquitoes
motor
muscle
naturally
necessary
necessity
nervous
nevertheless
nominative
no one
northeast
noticeable
noun
obedience
occasion
occasionally
o'clock
occurred
occurrence
off
omitted
opinion
opportunity
ordered
organization
original
ought
ourselves
outdoor
outside
paid
parallel
participial
participle
particularly
passed
perceive

perform
perhaps
phrase
physical
physically
piece
plain
pleasant
possess
possession
possessive
potato
practically
practice
precede
preceding
prefer
preferred
prepositional
prevalent
principal
principle
privilege
probably
proceed
profession
propaganda
propeller
prophecy
prophesy
proudest
pursue
pursuing
putting
quarter
quite
raised
realize
really

receive
receiving
referring
religious
remembrance
rendezvous
scarcely
scene
schoolboy
scrape
secretary
seized
sense
sentence
sentinel
separate
sergeant
service
severely
shipyard
significant
similar
slight
socks
something
sometimes
source
southwest
speed
straight
strength
strengthen
stretch
struggle
studying
subordinate
succeed
success
successful

sunrise
superintendent
surprise
suspense
swimming
tasting
tenant
tendency
than
their
themselves
there
thereabout
therefore
therefor
thorough
thought
threw
through
throughout
tired
to
together
too
tournament
toward
tragedy
tries
truly
two
tyranny
unanimous
undoubtedly
unnecessary
until
use
useful
using
usually

vegetation
vengeance
victorious
village
villain
volunteer
warrant
warring
weird
welfare

whether
where
wherever
whom
without
woman
wonderful
won't
you're

EFFECTIVENESS: Diction, Unity, Emphasis, Clearness

CHAPTER V

DICTION

They be not wise, therefore, that say, 'What care I for a man's words and utterance, if his matter and reasons be good?' . . . For good and choice meats be no more requisite for healthy bodies than proper and apt words be for good matters. — ROGER ASCHAM

I conceive that words are like money, not the worse for being common, but that it is the stamp of custom alone that gives them circulation or value. I am fastidious in this respect, and would almost as soon coin the currency of the realm as counterfeit the King's English. — HAZLITT

In composing, one hardly knows what one meant to say, until one has said it. The word, in fact, is what completes the thought and gives it existence. By the word it springs into light — *in lucem prodit.* — JOUBERT

INTRODUCTION: IMPORTANCE OF DICTION

DICTION is the choice of words for the expression of thought and feeling. A man's choice of words is not accidental, but proceeds organically from his own nature: such as he is, such will his choice of words be. Listen to him for five minutes, or read a letter he has written, and you will know what manner of man he is — his breeding, his character, his outlook on life will be expressed by the particular words that he uses. The fiction writer, knowing this, makes each of his characters use words that are, as we say, "in character," words befitting the personality and social standing of the character. He makes one habitually say, "I ain't," another "I'm not," and another, "I am not"; one says "good eats," another "good meals," and another, "savory repasts."

There is thus a kind of fatalism in our diction: it depends

upon what we are. Yet this is, fortunately, not the whole of the matter; since, in turn, what we are depends partly upon our choice of words. Resolve nevermore to say "I ain't," and you are already, in some measure, a new man; you have made both a social and a literary advance. A man who avoids all vulgar expressions cannot well remain a vulgar man. Similarly, a man whose diction is growing more and more exact and expressive is at the same time growing mentally; he is learning to think.

Diction must be viewed with respect to both Correctness and Effectiveness. Whereas grammar, punctuation, mechanics, and spelling deal with a right and a wrong way, an approved and a disapproved way, diction deals partly with the right and the wrong, the approved and the disapproved, and partly, also, with the effective and the ineffective, the best and the inferior. Our words must, first of all, be used correctly; this is the minimal requirement, the negative virtue of words. In addition, they should be used as effectively as possible, for they may have a positive as well as a negative virtue.

Since effective diction has been discussed in Book I (pp. 32–33, 55–56, 66–69), most of the present section is concerned with correct diction.

CORRECT ENGLISH: GOOD USE

Correct English, or Good Use, is the English sanctioned by the use of the best writers and speakers of English. As Ben Jonson observed long ago, "Custom is the most certain mistress of language. . . . When I name custom, I understand not the vulgar custom . . . but that I call custom which is the consent of the learned." It is not the usage of people in general — vulgar custom — but of cultivated people. It is not the usage of a single cultivated person, but of cultivated persons as a class. Correctness in language, like correctness in social manners, is not determined "democratically" by the majority, but "aristocratically" by a select class.

In a sense all English is good — good for those who use it. A section hand's English passes muster among section hands; a shopgirl's English invites no criticism in her society. But the question is, Do you wish your English to be section-hand English, or shopgirl English? What sort of English are you trying to use? That of the indiscriminating masses or of the more fastidious classes? There is no law, no compulsion. You merely place yourself in one class or another by the language you use. Do you wish your English to seem queer in another section of the country or among the more discriminating classes? Are you content that it seem right only in your own neighborhood?

Correct English, to put the matter more exactly, must be "present," "national," and "reputable."

PRESENT USE

52   ARCHAIC AND OBSOLETE WORDS

WE must use words that are intelligible to the present generation. Old words are constantly dropping out of the language or changing their meanings; and new words are constantly being added to express new ideas. Our vocabulary, to be intelligible, must exclude

Archaic words, words that are antiquated, such as *whilom* for *formerly, thou* for *you,* etc.

Obsolete words, words or meanings that have totally passed out of present use, such as *dole* meaning "grief," *prevent* in the sense of "to precede," and *cuisse* (a part of the armor).

NATIONAL USE

OUR words must also have national currency, must be intelligible throughout the nation. The two most common classes of words violating this test of good use are *unidiomatic* expressions and *provincialisms* or other dialect words or phrases.[1]

53   IDIOM

AN idiom is an expression that is peculiar to a particular language. Using the wrong preposition with certain verbs, nouns, or adjectives is the most common form of unidiomatic English. For example, "I cannot comply *to* this request" violates the established idiom "comply with." Similarly "to home," "angry at," and "independent from" are violations of long-established idioms. (Additional examples may be found in the **Glossary, 59.**) The student can collect many other examples for himself by watching the speech of foreigners or of children, by studying literal translations from a foreign language, or by reading stories written in such dialects as Pidgin-English, German-English, or French-English.

54 PROVINCIALISMS AND TECHNICAL WORDS

OTHER violations of the test of national use are provincialisms or technical words — dialect words. *Provincialisms,*

---

[1] Other, less common, violations of the test of national use are *foreign* words and *Anglicisms. Foreign words* that have not yet been fully naturalized, such as *raison d'etre, affair de cœur, éclat, quid pro quo,* should rarely be used if there is an English equivalent for the same idea. The use of such foreign tags smacks of pedantry. Likewise, where there is a difference between American and English usage, prefer the usage of your own country. Prefer *elevator, baggage, common laborer, store,* and *engineer* to the Anglicisms *lift, luggage, navvy, shop,* and *driver.*

or *localisms,* are words confined to a limited section of a country. Every region has words widely current among its speakers but rarely or never used in other regions. These words — which one perhaps has used from childhood without thinking of them as incorrect — are the most common violation of national use and are, without question, the most difficult to detect and correct. Although provincialisms may sometimes be used in conversation and in familiar writing, one should refrain from using them in formal speech or writing, since they stamp one as provincial. Examples of provincialisms are *calculate, allow,* or *reckon* for *think, wait on* for *wait for, chunk* for *throw, scotch* for *block* or *prop, tote* or *pack* for *carry,* and *out it* for *put it out.*

Technical words, such words as *volplaning, bungo, camouflage, luff round, bagasse,* words confined to a particular sport, trade, or profession, constitute another class of dialect words. Technical words should ordinarily be used only in technical writing: they are usually unintelligible to all except specialists.

REPUTABLE USE

"Ain't" and "I haven't got no books" and many other incorrect expressions satisfy the first two tests of good use; but they fail to meet the third and most important test: they are not in reputable use. To be reputable, a word must have the sanction of the best writers. It must not be a vulgarism, an impropriety, a colloquialism, or slang.[1]

---

[1] Vulgarisms and improprieties are undisputed violations of correctness. Unlike colloquialisms and slang, they are never permissible, either in familiar or in well-considered, formal language.

55 VULGARISMS, OR BARBARISMS

WORDS used only by the vulgar, by people of bad speech-manners, should always be rigorously excluded from one's speech. Some examples are *used to could, unbeknownst, remember of, where at, ain't, them books, pants, belong to go, anywheres, hisself,* and *as how.* Many vulgarisms are illiterate coinages from existing words: *enthuse, complected, burgle, tobacconist, uptodately, to butch, to suicide.* Others are humorous coinages, such as *shootlery,* a *revusical* comedy, and *jazzhemia.* Still others are clipped words: *bike, pep, phone, ad,* and *prof.*

56 IMPROPRIETIES

VULGARISMS, as we have seen, are words never found in standard English. An impropriety is the incorrect use of a standard English word, either (a) in an incorrect meaning or (b) in an incorrect function.

a. *Improprieties in Meaning. Can* for *may, mad* for *angry, aggravate* for *irritate, expect* for *suspect,* and *learn* for *teach* are examples of improprieties in meaning. Many improprieties in meaning are due to the confusion of words of similar sound, such as *affect, effect; accept, except; council, counsel, consul; later, latter.* (For further examples see the **Glossary, 59,** and the spelling list on pages 237–242.)

b. *Improprieties in Function.* In careless speech one often transfers a word from one function to another not yet sanctioned by good use. Thus, *like* and *without* are often improperly used as conjunctions. (See **Conjunctions, 12.**) Similarly, the nouns *loan, suspicion, wireless, suicide, wire, housekeeping* are incorrectly used as verbs; and verbs like *combine, invite, eat,* and *raise* are incorrectly employed as nouns. (See also the **Glossary, 59**.)

57 COLLOQUIALISMS

A COLLOQUIALISM,[1] as the name suggests, is an expression permissible in an informal, intimate style, either spoken or written, but not permissible in a more formal literary style. Every one should distinguish sharply between these two styles and should exclude from his formal, well-considered style any word or expression that has a colloquial flavor. Some typical colloquialisms are *funny* for *queer* or *strange*, *fix* for *mend*, *shape* for *condition*, and contractions, such as *don't*, *isn't*, and *won't*.

It is sometimes difficult to draw the line between colloquialisms and improprieties. To one person *mad* in the sense of *angry* is an impropriety, and is never to be permitted; to another it is a colloquialism, to be excluded only from formal, well-considered language. Some writers on language classify this expression — and hosts of others similar to it — as a colloquialism, others as an impropriety. This difference of opinion is explained by the fact that there is no objective test of correctness. In these border-line cases, each of us must form his own opinion. If all educated men should agree in such matters, no impropriety or vulgarism or slang would ever be elevated to the rank of standard English. But such expressions have been elevated and others undoubtedly will be. Colloquialisms probably represent the intermediate stage through which vulgarisms, improprieties, and slang pass into standard English.

[1] Unlike vulgarisms and improprieties, colloquialisms and slang are permissible when used on the proper occasions.

58   SLANG

THE term *slang* is too often used to include all objectionable words; and many objections to slang are not objections to slang as such, but to *vulgar, trite, affected, vague,* or *undignified* slang. This vague attack upon slang is doubtless due to the difficulty of exactly defining just what slang is, a difficulty arising from the fact that it is often a matter of individual feeling as to whether a given word is slang or a colloquialism. Slang is thus easy to illustrate, but hard to define.[1]

Greenough and Kittredge define slang as "a peculiar kind of vagabond language always hanging on the outskirts of legitimate speech." This definition, though perhaps not entirely satisfactory, does stress the point that is chiefly to be considered in any discussion of slang: that slang is not in reputable use, that it always hovers "on the outskirts of legitimate speech." Without attempting to define slang, let us notice some of its characteristics.

As to origin, it may be said that perhaps the majority of

---

[1] Slang differs from provincialisms in not usually being confined to a limited region; from vulgarisms, improprieties, and colloquialisms in being, in the main, new, short-lived, and picturesque or playful in tone. Slang resembles other technical languages in being confined to a caste, a more or less exclusive order (hoboes, burglars, thieves, etc.). It is a quasi-secret lingo intended to be understood only by the initiated. Some slang — which we may call common or public slang — is different from technical slang. It is a symptom of the inventiveness of man, of the search for fresh and pungent expressions. Like all linguistic experiments, it succeeds or fails largely according to whether it is a good invention or not, whether it meets a need in the language not supplied by existing words. Another factor in its survival is that many good inventions are worn out by overuse, especially by being employed recklessly and undiscriminatingly by others than the inventor. When slang is used as a slipshod substitute for more exact expressions, when it is used as a lazy expedient to avoid thinking, it fails as a medium of expression and should be condemned.

slang expressions originate among the illiterate, vulgar, or "sporty" classes of society. Hence, it is hard for slang to free itself of this taint of birth. Other characteristics of slang are novelty and originality; the playfulness, humor, and quaintness of its metaphors; the vigor of fresh, timely inventions; and the wide currency but short life of most popular slang.

Our attitude toward slang should be neither one of undiscriminating hospitality nor one of uncompromising hostility. It should be determined largely by a consideration of the characteristics of slang mentioned above. The most ardent defenders of slang can say in its defense little more than that the best slang is original, fresh, timely, brief, suggestive, vigorous, and humorous. Unfortunately, however, the very nature of slang makes it inevitable that these, its most defensible qualities, are precisely the qualities that are dimmed and obliterated by constant use. Again, slang is so short-lived that the user of slang is constantly under compulsion to replenish his vocabulary. The popularity of slang leads to the cheapening of it and destroys whatever vigor and freshness it may have once possessed. Slang is hard to control; the habitual user of slang finds himself unable to speak readily any other language; and, since slang depends upon reference to unfamiliar and recondite subjects, it is unintelligible outside a limited group. Worst of all, the constant employment of slang robs one's vocabulary of standard words that express nice and exact distinctions of meaning, everything pleasant being *nice*, *lovely*, *bully*, *jolly*, or *perfectly fine*. The use of the first word that comes to mind thus limits one's vocabulary by removing the necessity of thinking before one speaks.

The case against slang, therefore, is much stronger than

the case for it. Does this fact mean that it should be consistently shunned? Not at all. Whenever slang is appropriate to the occasion, the audience, and the mood or context, it may be used. It is perfectly legitimate, for example, for a sport writer to use slang freely. But, it should be remembered, what is appropriate to the sporting page would be entirely inappropriate to the editorial columns; what is permissible in informal, unguarded speech may not be permissible in formal, well-considered discourse. When one uses slang, then, one should always be fully aware of the fact that one is using a type of non-standard English.

Good Use a Relative Term

Good use, it must be remembered, is a relative term. Every one has several languages, which differ from each other in many respects. He has a free and easy, somewhat unconscious colloquial language — the language of "talk." He has a more conscious, thoughtful spoken language — the language of conversation or discussion. And he has a formal, conservative written language — the language of print. Each of these has minute and delicate shadings. The time, the audience, the place, the mood, the subject — all play a part in helping him select — instinctively for the most part — that form of speech which best fits the particular occasion. This adjustment is just as much a social matter, a matter of good taste and correct manners, as the choice of dress. The man who has only one kind of language is just as handicapped as the man who has only one kind of dress. In this adjustment of speech to the occasion two extremes are to be avoided: a too rigid adherence to rules of correctness, which leads to a pedantic, artificial style; and too little regard for propriety in speech, which leads to a slangy, slovenly style. Good English avoids both these extremes.

Exercise A. Correct the violations of idiom in the following sentences:

1. He died with typhoid fever.
2. It was no other person but John.
3. This plan is not different than the one I suggested, and it is not better adapted for our needs.
4. I differ from you in this matter.
5. When Ivanhoe arrived to the place where they fought the battle, he learned what had happened.

Exercise B. What preposition or prepositions may be correctly used after each of the following words?

Adapted, agree, angry, call, change, confer, convert, dependent, independent, free, glad, part (verb), reconcile, wait.

Exercise C. Make a list of ten provincialisms heard in your own state.

Exercise D. Detect and correct the provincialisms in the following sentences:

1. The bundle I want you to pack over to the house is on the front gallery.
2. If you all don't scotch the wheels, the car will roll down the hill.
3. Are you going to carry your lady friend to the sociable to-night?
4. If I jump a rabbit, I'm going to chunk this rock at him.
5. I allowed I'd go up the road a piece.
6. He hadn't ought of done that, had he?.

Exercise E. Point out the vulgarisms and improprieties in the following sentences. Distinguish between vulgarisms and improprieties.

1. I don't see him no place. I reckon he ain't to home, but I know his folks is here.
2. I come to see about that there proposition you made a couple of us yesterday.

3. They's a real funny looking female outside of the yard wants to speak to you.
4. He might of done a lots better if he hadn't been so awfully mad.
5. I suspicioned he was going to locate in Seattle. That burg is plenty big enough for his business.
6. He received a wire that his father suicided last week because of the failure of a big combine he was trying to put over.
7. I can't get enthused over them light-complected dames. I don't think they are a bit classy nohow.
8. Lay down there and act like you was real sick.
9. These gents are fakes. They sure will get you alright. If they do, don't blame it on me.

Exercise F. Use each of the following words correctly in a sentence:

> *Fix, transpire; party, person, individual; quite; unanimous, universal; allude, elude; in, into; on, on to; love, like; female, woman; horrid, unpleasant; raise, rear; most, almost; admit, confess; proposition, proposal; deadly, deathly.*

Exercise G. Make a list of five slang expressions which are vigorous and fresh and timely. Make a list of five slang expressions that are overworked and objectionable.

Exercise H. Make a list of ten permissible colloquialisms; and a list of five homely, colloquial proverbs.

Exercise I. For each of the words below find, if possible, a slang substitute, a dignified, literary equivalent, and a poetic synonym.

> *Example: Horse,* colorless and prosaic.
>   *Plug,* slang.
>   *Nag,* colloquial.
>   *Steed,* literary.
>   *Courser, palfrey,* poetic.
>   *Automobile, meal* (dinner), *drink* (noun), *walk, miss* (verb), *fail, ocean, rustic, woman, girl, slow-thinking, head, die, fail, stubborn, proud, money.*

59   GLOSSARY OF FAULTY EXPRESSIONS

In this Glossary are listed words and expressions frequently misused. The list is intended to be a practical, workable list to which the student may add from time to time as attention is called to his misuse of other words. He should study carefully the preceding pages on Correct Diction, so that he may understand the principles underlying the comments given below.

Accept, except. These words of similar sound are often confused in meaning. *Accept* means "to receive"; *except* "to exclude."

Ad. A colloquial abbreviation of *advertisement.* Such abbreviations as *ad, auto, exam, gym, prof, phone,* and *photo* should never be used in formal speech or writing.

Affect, effect. Often confused in meaning. *Affect* means "to influence"; *effect* "to cause." As a noun *effect* means "result."

Aggravate, which properly means "to make heavy or heavier," is used in careless colloquial speech instead of *irritate, provoke,* or *annoy.* See Palmer paragraph, p. 89.

Agree to, agree with. Two different idioms. *Agree to* means "to give assent to": "He agreed to my proposal." *Agree with* also means "to be in accord with" (a person): "He agreed with me on this point."

Ain't. A vulgarism. Never to be used.

Allow. A provincial or vulgar substitute for *think, believe, say.*

Almost, most. Two entirely different words. *Most* is the superlative of *many* or *much,* and means "greatest." As a noun it means "the greatest or largest number"

255

and is often followed by *of*. *Almost* is used chiefly as an adverb meaning "nearly."

The use of *most* for *almost* is an impropriety:

Wrong: The bell rings most every hour.

Alone, only. *Alone* means "unaccompanied." *Only* means "excluding all others," "sole," "no other." The confusion of these words is an impropriety in meaning often resulting in ambiguity.

Already, all ready. *Already*, an adverb, means "previously"; *all ready* are two separate words used to form an adjective phrase meaning "all (completely) prepared, or ready." Distinguish between these words in both spelling and meaning.

All right. A phrase overworked in colloquial speech in the sense of "very well." There is no such word as *alright*. *Alright* is a vulgarism.

Altogether, all together. See **Already, all ready.**

Alumnus, alumni; alumna, alumnæ. See **Plurals, 49,** for the correct use of these frequently misused words.

Among. See **Between.**

And. See **Try and.**

And etc. Since *etc.* is an abbreviation for *et cetera*, "and the rest," "and the others," *and* is redundant in the phrase *and etc.*

Any. Vulgarism for *at all*.

Any place, no place, some place, every place. Vulgarisms for the adverbs *anywhere*, *nowhere*, etc., or for the adverbial phrases "in any place," "in no place," etc.

Anyways, someways. Provincial or vulgar for *anyway*, *some way*.

Apt. See **Liable.**

As. Do not use *as* for *that* or *whether*. Say:

I do not know *that* (not *as*) he will come.
I do not know *whether* (not *as*) he will come.

Do not use *as* for *such as* in introducing a list of examples.
Do not overwork *as* as a subordinating conjunction of time or cause.
Do not use *as — as* in negative statements. Prefer *not so — as*.

At. Redundant and vulgar in the phrase *where at*. *Where*, meaning "at or in what place," contains the idea of *at* in itself.

Auto. See **Ad**.

Awful. The correct meaning of this word is "awe-inspiring." The use of this word as a loose intensive prefix in such phrases as "awful nice," "awful pretty," is an impropriety.

Beside, besides. It is an impropriety to use *beside* for *besides* in the sense of "in addition to." *Beside* is usually a preposition.

Between, among. *Between*, connected in meaning with *twain*, refers to only two; *among* refers to more than two.

Blame it on. Colloquial or vulgar for *blame* or *blame for*.

Both. See **Either**.

Brainy. Colloquial substitute for *intelligent*.

Bully. See **Fine**.

But that. *But that* is the negative of *that*, and means *except that, that not*.

Wrong: I have no doubt but that he will come.
Right: I have no doubt that he will come.

But what. Often improperly used for *that* or *but that*. *But what* means "but (except) that which," as in

I'll say nothing but what I want to say. (Here *but* means "except" and governs the clause introduced by *what*.)

Calculate. Provincial or vulgar in the sense of "plan," "expect."

Can, may. *Can* implies ability, *may* permission.

Cannot help but. "Cannot help but" = "cannot keep from helping" (see **Double Negative, 16**); "can but help" = "can only help." (See also page 311.)

Caused by. See **Due to.**

Claim. A provincialism or an impropriety in the sense of "assert, maintain." *Claim* properly means "to demand as a right."

Clever. Colloquial synonym for "*agreeable, good-natured.*"

Combine. An impropriety when used as a noun. Never say "a combine."

Common, mutual. Webster's *New International Dictionary* distinguishes between these two words as follows: "That is *common* in which two or more share (esp.) equally or alike; *mutual* properly implies reciprocal action; as, sorrow is *common* to all; *mutual* esteem." Webster does not sanction the phrase *mutual friend. The Standard,* however, accepts this widely used expression as correct. *Common* is unobjectionable. *Mutual* may be objectionable to some readers.

Compare to, compare with. Two different idioms. *Compare with* is used when we liken two objects similar in nature; *compare to* is used when we liken two objects of a real or supposed resemblance:

> Compare this drawing with the one on page 10.
> He compared life to a river.

Complected. A vulgarism for *complexioned,* "of a —— complexion." Though correct, *complexioned* is clumsy.

Continual, continuous. *Continual* means "occurring in rapid succession"; *continuous* means "with uninterrupted continuity."

Contrast from. An unsanctioned idiom. Say "contrast to" or "contrast with."

Correspond to, correspond with. *Correspond with* means "to exchange letters with" or "to be in harmony with." *Correspond to* means only "to be in harmony with."

Could of. See *Of*.

Couple implies a pair, two objects or persons linked in some way. An impropriety for *two* unless the idea of union or bond is present.

Cunning. A colloquialism for *attractive, pleasing*.

Cute. Colloquial for *clever* or *shrewd*, and slang for the general meanings *attractive, pleasing, picturesque*.

Data. Plural of *datum*. Incorrectly used as a *singular*.

Deal. Business slang for *transaction, bargain*.

Demean. Colloquial impropriety in the sense of "debase," "degrade," "lower," "humiliate." *Demean* means "to behave" (in either a good or a bad way). Confused with *bemean*, "to lower."

Die with. The correct idiom is *die of*.

Differ from, differ with. *Differ from* is used to express unlikeness; *differ from* or *differ with* to express disagreement of opinion.

Different than, different to. Incorrect colloquial idioms for *different from*.

Do. A word overworked in colloquial speech. See any good dictionary.

Done. Colloquial for "have done," "have (am) finished."

Don't. A contraction for *do not*. Never use this contraction where *do not* would be incorrect. "He don't" is a vulgarism.

Due to. *Due to* is an adjective phrase and should be used only to modify a noun. To modify a verb use the corresponding adverbial phrases "because of," "on account of," "owing to."

Wrong: He was late, due to an automobile accident.
Right: His lateness was due to an automobile accident.
He was late on account of an automobile accident.

The same principle applies to **caused by.**

Each. See **Either.**

Effect. See **Affect.**

Either, both, each. *Either* means "one of two," "the one or the other," "each of two." It is always a singular and should never refer to more than two. Use *any, any one,* or *each* to refer to more than two. The same principle applies to *neither. Both* refers to two considered together. It means "the one and the other."

Electricute, electrocute. Regarded as a vulgarism by some authorities, but accepted by the latest *Standard* and Webster's *New International.*

Elegant. See **Fine.**

Enthuse. A vulgarism (or, according to some authorities, a colloquialism) coined on the analogy of *enthusiasm* and *enthusiastic.*

Etc. A business abbreviation undesirable in formal writing. It is unnecessary after a list introduced by *such as.*

Every. Colloquial in the expressions "every now and then," "every which way," "every bit," and vulgar in the combinations *everyplace, everywheres.*

Exam. See **Ad.**

Except. See **Accept.**

Expect. Colloquial or provincial for "suspect," "think." *Expect* means "to look forward to," "to look for," "to hope." The use of *expect* with reference to past events is therefore an impropriety.

Female. (1) An obsolete or vulgar synonym for *woman*. (2) *Female* should not be used for *feminine* unless the idea of sex is to be stressed.

Fewer, less. *Fewer* applies to number; *less* to quantity or degree.

Fierce. See **Fine.**

Fine, bully, elegant, grand, lovely, nice, splendid. Obscure or extravagant blanket synonyms for *good, enjoyable, pleasant,* etc. Use these words accurately.

First rate. A colloquialism when used as an adverb: "I feel first rate."

Fix. Colloquial and obscure when used for the noun *condition* or for the verbs *repair* or *arrange*.

Folks. Colloquial synonym of *people, relatives*.

Funny. Colloquial and slovenly synonym of *amusing, strange, odd, queer, remarkable. Funny* means "laugh-provoking."

Get. Overused in colloquial speech in the senses: "to be able to," "becomes."

Weak: That gets me.
   I hope we'll get to see the show.
   He got sick.

Found in many slang expressions, such as "And he got away with it." "Do you get me?"
See also **Got.**

Good. Incorrect as an adverb. Use *well*. "I feel well." See **Adjective and Adverb, 11.**

Got. Colloquial or vulgar in the sense of "must," "ought": "I've got to go (write *must, ought*)." In the expression *I have got* expressing possession, *got* is redundant. *Have got* means "have acquired" and stresses the completion of the process of acquiring. To indicate the result (the idea of possession) say "I have." *Gotten* is an obsolete form of the past participle. The principal parts of the verb are: *get — got — got.*

Gotten. See **Got.**

Grand. See **Fine.**

Guess. Provincialism in the sense of "suppose," "believe." *Guess* means "to conjecture," "to form a random judgment."

Gym. See **Ad.**

Had better (rather). See **Would.**

Had have. Vulgarism for *had.*

> *Right:* I wish I *had* come sooner.

Had of. See **Of.**

Had ought. Vulgarism for *ought, must.*

Has got. See **Got.**

Help but. See **Double Negative, 16.**

Here, there. See **This here, That there.**

In back of. Vulgarism for *behind, at the back of.*

Individual. See **Party.**

Ingenious, ingenuous. Two words often confused. *Ingenious* means "possessing genius," "talented," "intelligent"; *ingenuous* means "open," "frank," "naïve."

Inside of, outside of. *Of* is superfluous and should be omitted: "inside the house." Don't use *inside of* to refer to time. Say "within an hour," not "inside of an hour."

Kind of, sort of. These expressions should be followed only by a substantive used as the object of the preposition *of.* They should never be used to modify an adjective.

> *Colloquial or vulgar:* I am kind of tired to-day.
> *Better:* I am somewhat (rather) tired to-day.
> 　　　　I have a kind of tired feeling to-day.

(Remember that *kind* and *sort* are singular nouns. Never say *these* (*those*) *kind* or *sort*.)

Kind of a, sort of a. Never use the indefinite article after these expressions: "He is a strange *kind of* (not *kind of a*) man."

Last, latest. *Last* is often misused for *latest*. *Latest* refers only to order in time. *Last* means *final*.

Lay. See **Lie.**

Learn. A vulgarism for *teach*.

Leave, let. *Leave* means "to forsake," "to abandon"; *let* means "to permit." Don't say, "Leave me alone" when you mean "Don't trouble me." The confusion of these two words is doubtless due to the fact that the noun *leave* means both "permission" and "farewell."

Less. See **Fewer.**

Let. See **Leave.**

Liable, likely, apt. *Likely* means "expected," "probable," and usually refers to a favorable event. *Liable* implies the possibility of an undesirable happening. Another sense of *liable* is "responsible," "answerable." Never use *likely* alone as an adverb. *Apt* implies a natural fitness or tendency.

Lie, lay. *Lie* means "to recline." *Lay* means "to put down," "to make something lie." *Lay* is thus the causative of *lie*. The same relation exists between *sit* and *set*, and between *rise* and *raise* (or *rear*). (See *Principal Parts* under **Grammatical Terms**, p. 158.)

Like, as. See p. 141.

Likely. See **Liable.**

Loan. An impropriety when used for the verb *lend*.

Locate. Colloquial in the sense of "settle oneself," or "find." *Locate* properly means "to assign the place of."

Lose and loose. Often confused in meaning and spelling.

Lose means "to fail to keep"; *loose* means "to release," "to set free."

Lot of, lots of. Colloquial for *many* or *much.*

Lovely. See **Fine.**

Mad. A colloquialism for *angry.* *Mad* properly means "insane" or "insanely furious."

May, can. See **Can.**

Mean. Colloquial or provincial for "irritable."

Mighty. A colloquialism in the sense of *very.*

Most. See **Almost.**

Much. See **Very.**

Mutual. See **Common.**

Myself. *Myself* is an intensive or a reflexive pronoun and is not acceptable as a substitute for the personal pronouns *I* or *me.*

Near by. Usually colloquial and overworked. Prefer *adjacent, close at hand, near.*

Neither. Use *neither* to refer to one of two. For more than two use *none, no one,* or *not a one.* (See **Either.**)

Nice. See **Fine.**

No account. Undesirable colloquialism for *worthless, of no account.*

Nohow. Vulgarism for *anyway, by no means.*

No other. See **Other.**

O, oh. Two different words. *O* is used only with vocatives, *oh* in all other cases.

Of. In such expressions as *could of, would of, had of, might of, of* is a gross vulgarism. Say *could have, would have,* etc.

Off of, off from. *Of* is superfluous, for *off* and *of* (from) convey the same meaning.

O.K. A business abbreviation not to be used in formal discourse.

Only. Place this word immediately before or after the word it modifies. (See **Position of Modifiers, 93.** See also **Alone.**)

Onto. Objected to by some authorities as a substitute for *on to.* The word is growing in favor, and is now accepted colloquially.

Oral, verbal. *Oral* means "by mouth"; *verbal,* "by words."

Other. After the phrase *no other* use *than,* not *but:* "It was no other than the man I was searching for."

Outside of. See **Inside of.**

Ought. See **Had ought.**

Owing to. See **Due to.**

Party, person, individual. *Party* implies a group and should never be used in reference to one person except in legal terminology. *Individual* refers to a single or particular being. In all other cases use *person, man, woman,* etc.

Per. With English nouns, *a* (or *an*) is preferable to *per,* which is properly used only to form part of a Latin phrase. Say "a hundred," "a yard," "a dollar," but "per cent," "per capita," "per diem."

Per cent. An adverbial phrase meaning "by the hundred." Not to be confused with the noun *percentage.*

> Ten per cent of the men were absent.
> A small percentage of the men was absent.

Person. See **Party.**

Phenomena. The plural of *phenomenon.* (See **Plurals, 49.**)

Phone. See **Ad.**

Photo. See **Ad.**

Plenty. A noun. Colloquial or vulgar when used as an adjective or adverb.

> *Wrong:* There are plenty men for the work.
> The crowd is plenty big.

Principal, principle. *Principal* is an adjective except in the meanings "head (of a school)," "a sum of money." *Principle* is always a noun meaning "a governing rule or truth."

Prof. See **Ad.**

Propose, purpose. *Propose*, "to offer for consideration," should not be confused with *purpose*, "to make up one's mind," "to resolve," "to plan."

Proposition, proposal. *Proposition* is often misused for *proposal*. *Proposition* corresponds to the verb *propose*. Use *proposal* when a plan or a business transaction is referred to.

Proven. The unobjectionable past participle of *prove* is *proved*.

Quite. An adverb meaning "completely," "entirely," "wholly." Colloquial in the sense of "rather" or "very." Hence "quite a few," "quite a little," "quite a bit" are undesirable colloquialisms.

Raise, rise. See **Lie, Lay.** Do not use *raise* in the sense "to bring up" (as children), "rear." The use of *raise* as a noun is an impropriety or vulgarism.

Real. Vulgarism in the sense of "very." *Real* means "genuine," "true," "actual."

Reason is because. See **Clauses, 15.**

Reckon. A provincialism for *think, suppose, guess*. *Reckon* properly means "enumerate," "compute," "calculate."

Remember of. A provincialism or vulgarism for *remember*.

Right. Colloquial in the sense of *exactly, very, at once*. Avoid such expressions as "right tall," "right along," "right then," "right now," "right much." Do not use *right* as a synonym for *duty*.

Said. See p. 310.

Same. See **Reference, 95.**

Shape. Colloquial for *condition, manner.*

Simply. Slang or colloquial for *really.*

Sit, set. See **Lie, Lay.**

So. See **Uses of So, 13.**

Some. Vulgarism for *somewhat.* Say "I feel somewhat better to-day."

Someplace, someways. Vulgarisms. See **Anyplace.**

Sort of. See **Kind of.**

Splendid. See **Fine.**

Statue, stature, statute. These words are often confused in both pronunciation and spelling. *Statue* means "a sculptured figure"; *stature* means "height"; and *statute* means "law."

Stop. Colloquial for *stay.* "I am staying at the Gresham Hotel" (not "I am stopping").

Such. When *such* is followed by a relative clause, the proper relative is *as* (not *who, which,* or *that*):

> I shall follow such rules *as* I think are best.

In result clauses *such* should be followed by *that* (not *so that*).

> This afternoon *such* a dark cloud gathered *that* we had to postpone our trip. (Some authorities prefer *so dark a* to *such a dark.*)

See also **Uses of So, 13.**

Sure. Impropriety when used for the adverbs *surely, certainly.*

Sure and. See **Try and.**

Suspicion. The use of the noun *suspicion* as a verb is an impropriety. The corresponding verb is *suspect.*

That, this. Colloquial when used adverbially:

> *Informal:* I did not mean to go *this* (*that*) far.
> *Formal:* I did not mean to go *so* far.

These kind, those kind, these sort. See **Kind.**

This a way, that a way. Omit the glide vowel *a* in both pronunciation and spelling.

This here, that there. Since *this* and *that* are demonstrative pronouns, *here* and *there* are superfluous after *this* or *that.*

Through. Colloquial in the sense of "finished," "at an end."

Too. See **Very.**

Transpire. An impropriety in the sense of "happen." *Transpire* means "to leak out," "to become known."

Try and, sure and. Colloquial for *try to, sure to.*

    Colloquial: I want you to *try and come* early.
                I want you to be *sure and come* early.
    Better: I want you to *try to come* early.

Ugly. Colloquial or dialectic when used as a synonym of *ill-tempered, unpleasant.*

Unique. A much abused word. *Unique* means "the only one of its kind," "sole." It is often misused for *rare, odd, unusual. Unique* admits of no comparison; hence *more unique, most unique* are incorrect.

Up. In colloquial speech, this ubiquitous adverb is often used where it adds nothing to the idea of the simple verb. Thus *up* is redundant in such phrases as *wait up, fold up, open up, write up, settle up.* It is used correctly in the combinations *lay up, dig up, wake up, plow up, double up, hang up, break up, fill up, pile up, pluck up;* for in these verb-adverb combinations the combination is different from the simple verb in syntax or in meaning. *Up* often has an intensive or completive force.

Verbal. See **Oral.**

Very, too, much. *Very* — or *too* — modifies adjectives, participles used as adjectives, and adverbs. It should not immediately precede a participle used predicatively; in such a case use *much*, or *too much*, *very much*.

Right: He was very much pleased with my plan.
He was very sick.
He was very painfully wounded.
He is too much (not too) exhausted to go.
This very pleasing sight interested all of us.

Wait on. A provincialism for *wait for*. *Wait on* means "to serve," "to attend."

Way. Not permissible as an abbreviation of *away*. ("*Away* down the road.")

Ways, woods. Plurals always. Never say "a ways," "a woods."

What. See **But what.**

While. Overused as a conjunction. Use it rarely, or never, as a substitute for *but, and,* or *whereas*. *While* may be used as a subordinating conjunction to express the ideas: (1) "during the time that" and (2) "although" (when no time idea is present).

Without. Provincial or vulgar substitute for the conjunctions *except* and *without*. See **Like** and **As,** p. 141.

Woods. See **Ways.**

Would better. *Had better* (*rather*) is preferred to *would better* (*rather*).

EFFECTIVE DICTION

REMEMBER that excellence in diction involves far more than observance of what is merely permissible. Study the six entries below:

For the discussion, see pp. 32–33, 66–69.
For the exercises, see pp. 45–48, 74–76.

61 EMPHATIC DICTION

For the discussion, see pp. 32–33.
For the exercises, see pp. 45–48.

62 EUPHONY

THE word *euphony* is derived from two Greek words meaning "sound" and "well." Euphony is concerned with easy and pleasant combinations of sounds. In the writing of prose, it requires (1) the avoidance of rhymes in close succession, such as "day" and "decay," and (2) the avoidance of like sounds in close succession, as in this sentence:

> *Bad:* And she shuddered as she sat, still silent, in her seat, and he saw that she shuddered.

For further discussion, see pp. 56–57.
For the exercise, see p. 60.

63 TRITENESS

TRITE or hackneyed expressions are expressions that, like coins, have been rubbed smooth through excessive use, or, like hired horses, have worn out in service. It is by no means easy to avoid such expressions and to substitute for them fresh equivalents, for our very familiarity with these stale expressions causes them to occur to us more quickly than less common but more expressive words.

Begin at once making a kind of "black list" of the words that impress you as being trite. You will observe, as you make this list, that you are constantly enlarging it as you read more and more widely and so become more familiar with these excessively used words and expressions.

Examples:

along this line	order out of chaos
after all is said	great minds in the **same**
all in all	channel run
strong as a lion	fair sex
busy as a bee	irony of fate
white as snow	the sleep of the just
greedy as a pig	at one fell swoop
abreast of the times	fools rush in
a bolt from the blue	Old Morpheus
last but not least	where ignorance is bliss

Exercise A. Hand in a list of ten trite expressions gathered from your reading.

Exercise B. Hand in a list of expressions marked by your instructor or theme reader as trite or hackneyed.

Exercise C. Pick out the trite expressions in the exercises on pp. 45–47 and substitute more effective words.

64   ENLARGING THE VOCABULARY

For the discussion, see pp. 68–69, and Palmer paragraph, p. 89.

For the Exercises, see pp. 45–47, 74–76.

65   WORDINESS

Avoid the use of unnecessary words. Note the following types of wordiness:

   a. Redundancy, the use of a word or phrase grammatically superfluous:

      I shall never repeat *again* the experience of ascending *up* in a balloon.

      Napoleon *he* was one of the world's greatest military geniuses.

      Keep off *of* the fence.

   b. Tautology, the repetition of the same idea in different words. This sort of wordiness is due to a scarcity of ideas and a superabundance of words. Avoid especially superfluous adjectives and adverbs.

> It was a clear starry night, *and not a cloud was to be seen.*
> He was an *instrumental* factor in bringing about changes in building, sanitation, lighting, *and* etc.

See also pp. 55–56, 59.

c. *Verbosity*, a general expansiveness of style that can be corrected only by entirely recasting the sentence or paragraph.

> There were three of us who took the trip. (Say, "Three of us took the trip.")
> He was a talkative, loquacious, garrulous old man. (Needless repetition of synonyms.)
> I should like to say that these poems are all typical of the age in which they were written. (Say it; don't apologize for saying it.)

This type of wordiness often accompanies the attempt at "fine writing." (See p. 51.)

Subordination is a good remedy for wordiness. See **Subordination for Emphasis, 81.**

For the exercises, see pp. **15 ff.**

CHAPTER VI

UNITY

For ease of reading, or for the attainment of an intended effect, unity is essential. . . . Lacking [unity] any piece of writing is a failure; because, in truth, it is not a piece, but pieces. — G. H. PALMER

The body is a living organism, which must be seen as a whole if it is to be seen at all. — HALDANE, *Mechanism, Life, and Personality*

66   **SENTENCE UNITY**

A SENTENCE must contain one complete thought. This requirement has been considered from the grammatical point of view on pages 99–100, and from the logical point of view on page 5. Remember that, from the logical point of view, a sentence must (1) omit nothing that is essential to the completeness of the thought and (2) admit nothing that is not essential to the thought. It must be a unit — no less, no more. Consequently there are two fundamental tests for sentence unity:

Test I: Does the group of words express a *complete* thought? For example:

> Milton thought that man should be humble, obedient, and thankful toward God. Observing and obeying his laws.

The first group of words expresses a complete thought; the second — "Observing and obeying his laws" — does not. The first group is a sentence; the second is not.

Test II: Does the group of words contain foreign matter — does it go beyond completeness and give us something quite irrelevant to the expression of the thought? For example:

At last, on the 4th of August, England declared war on Germany, where I spent six weeks some years ago.

Here the concluding idea has no clear relation with the thought of the sentence; it is irrelevant, beside the point, and destroys the unity of the sentence.

The Remedy: When a "sentence" is incomplete, complete it — ordinarily — by linking the fragment with the body from which it has been detached. Thus, "Milton thought that man should be humble, obedient, and thankful toward God, observing and obeying his laws." When, on the other hand, a sentence is overcomplete, either omit the matter that is irrelevant or present it wherever it fits. Thus, "At last, on the 4th of August, England declared war on Germany." (The writer's sojourn in Germany, if it is to be mentioned at all, must be mentioned in another sentence.)

Exercise. Determine which of the following groups of words are not unified sentences, and then correct them. Apply the Tests and the Remedy given above: [1]

1. He works hard and keeps regular hours. His brother being a worthless spendthrift.
2. He works hard and keeps regular hours. Though his brother is a worthless spendthrift.
3. The peasants wear curiously-shaped flat caps, and grow huge crops of buckwheat.
4. In his youth he read widely among the best books. Thereby increasing both his reading and his speaking vocabulary.
5. Chaucer, the first English artist in poetry, ushered in the modern period of English literature, and had a beard the color of wheat straw.

---

[1] Unity may be obscured by faulty punctuation, either by using a period after any group of words less than a complete thought or by placing a comma between two groups of words each of which should be written as a separate sentence. See **Period Fault, 2,** and **Comma Fault, 3.**

6. I expect a note from him soon, when he reaches home after a journey he always writes to me.

7. The peasants of the little town were deformed by overwork, and on this market day they were chattering to each other as they bought and sold cattle, a business that was the chief interest of the inhabitants of the neighborhood.

8. Burns was truly in love when he wrote this poem in the woods on a summer day near his cottage, which was a typical Scotch dwelling, built with stones and whitewashed.

9. He began his trip at a small village in France and went through some parts of Italy and Spain, with occasional side trips into Germany and Holland, both of which are very interesting countries, and the trip took in all about three months.

67 COÖRDINATION

a. Avoid excessive coördination by subordinating all subordinate thoughts in the sentence.

Bad: It was a cool afternoon, and we had a fast game.
He returned home and without a moment's hesitation.
His book sold well and he now had none to blame but himself for his poverty.

Better: Since it was a cool afternoon, we had a fast game.
Without a moment's hesitation he returned home.
After his book had sold well he had none to blame but himself for his poverty.

See also **Straggling Compound Sentences, 68.**

b. Avoid illogical or obscure coördination:

Illogical: He went to visit the hermit, and he was a good man and a great doctor.
He was very fond of playing baseball, and left home at once.
The spot where he was buried was not marked with any inscription and it is now forgotten.

Logical: He went to visit the hermit, who was a good man and a great doctor.

He was very fond of playing baseball, and, since he wanted to join one of the major leagues, he left home at once.

Since the spot where he was buried was not marked with any inscription, it is now forgotten.

See also **Straggling Compound Sentences, 68, Coherence and Logical Order, 92,** and **Omissions, 75.**

c. Avoid false coördination. When two statements are logically coördinate, do not write them as separate sentences:

Wrong: Roman civilization scarcely reached the Celts. And it left but few traces among them.

Right: Roman civilization scarcely reached the Celts, and it left but few traces among them.

If, however, additional emphasis is desired for the second idea, the clauses may be separated by a semicolon, with or without a coördinating conjunction. (See **Use II** of the semicolon, pp. 182–183.) If the greatest possible emphasis is desired for each of the two thoughts write the two clauses as separate sentences.

For the exercises, see pp. 15–20.

See also pages 102–103, 109, 182.

68 STRAGGLING COMPOUND SENTENCES

UNITY is often violated by the writing of rambling compound sentences crudely joined by a string of *and's, but's, for's, so's,* or *or's.*

Examples: The book is divided into six chapters, each dealing with a different subject, and the first tells of a little boy listening to his parents' conversation, but he could not understand and then he would go off by himself and think about the conversation, and he finally reasoned out what it all meant.

He went and leaned on his father's chair and
looked down upon him, and the old man turned
about and looked up at his son, but the boy had a
most pleased expression on his face, and so I was
amazed at the way the father looked at the son.

This story shows a real knowledge of human nature,
for every man must start out in life with some occupation which doubtless he knows nothing about
at first and if he continues to work hard he will soon
reach the top.

To revise a sentence of this type, subordinate all subordinate ideas and, if necessary, divide the long sentence
into shorter, well unified sentences. Study the examples
given in the section on **Subordination, 69,** and under
Coördination, 67. See also **Variety,** pp. 51–52.

For the exercises, see pp. 15–20.

69   SUBORDINATION

Іт has been shown (pp. 8–15) that the skillful writer composes his sentences so that they abound in subordination.
By this means he gives emphasis and clearness to his main
thought and unity and compactness to his sentences. The
skillful writer avoids the following pitfalls:

a. False Coördination. Joining in coördinate constructions (with coördinating conjunctions or conjunctive
adverbs or by a semicolon between the clauses) clauses
which are not of equal importance both structurally
and logically.

Wrong: The bear made a convulsive effort *and* she raised up
her head; *so* he felt her hot breath.

Right: Making a convulsive effort, the bear raised her head
up, till he felt her hot breath.

By a convulsive effort, the bear raised her head up,
till he felt her hot breath.

In the last two sentences one idea is brought out clearly and prominently.

Wrong: Constance stayed her needle, and, without lifting her head, *gazing* motionless at her sister. (The coördinating conjunction *and* cannot join the independent finite verb *stayed* with the participle *gazing*, since these forms are neither grammatically nor logically of equal rank.)

Right: (Change *gazing* to *gazed*, or subordinate the second idea by omitting *and*, the sign of coördination.)

See also **Coördination, 67**, and **Straggling Compound Sentences, 68**.

b. *Upside-down Subordination*, which consists of putting the main idea in a subordinate construction, as in a dependent clause or a participial phrase.

Wrong: I was walking through the lane back of the house, *when* I saw the most interesting sight I have ever seen. (The main idea here is put into the subordinate *when*-clause.)

Right: *When* I was walking through the lane back of the house, I saw the most interesting sight I have ever seen.

Wrong: He mixed the two powders together, thus *causing* the fire which burned out a whole block. (The more important idea here is put in the subordinate — participial — construction.)

Right: His mixing the two powders together caused the fire which burned out a whole block.
When he mixed the two powders together, he caused the fire which burned out a whole block.
The fire which burned out a whole block was caused by his mixing the two powders together.

Wrong: He mixed the two powders together, which act caused the greatest fire the city ever had. (Relative clauses are always subordinate.)

c. *Faulty subordination — using the wrong connective.* Do

not use a subordinating conjunction between coördinate ideas.

Wrong: He was tall and slim, *while* his brother was short and stout. (*While* is usually a subordinating conjunction meaning "although" or "during the time that." Do not use it instead of the coördinating conjunctions *and* or *but*.)

Wrong: I invited him to be present, *though* he refused. (*Though* is a subordinating conjunction. Use *but* here since the ideas are coördinate.)

See **Conjunctions, 12,** and p. 98.

d. *Overlapping Subordination.* See **Overlapping Dependence, 70.**

For a further discussion of Subordination see pp. 8–15. Study carefully **Coördination, 67, Subordination for Emphasis, 81,** and **Wordiness, 65.**

70 OVERLAPPING DEPENDENCE

REWRITE a sentence containing a series of overlapping constructions, i.e., a series in which each construction depends upon the preceding, as in the "House-that-Jack-built" type of sentence. A series of overlapping, *which, who, that, for, of, so* (*that*), *but,* or possessive constructions is especially to be avoided.

Wrong: He was quite different from the other men in the party, who found that he was a youth who had never done any manual labor before.

Right: He was quite different from the other men in the party, who found that he was a youth with no previous experience in manual labor.

Exercise.

1. Let us make a real effort to do our part by abiding by the laws by saving as much material as possible.

2. He returned home at once, for he had received a message at noon, for his brother needed him.

3. He hit our boat so hard that we were driven against the pier so violently that the frail boat was wrecked.
4. Afterwards I journeyed into the oldest city in Mexico, where I found a hotel called The Gonzales, where I ordered a splendid meal.
5. I could not fail to notice the grace of carriage of the girl of listless attitude.
6. I never saw a house which had so many windows which were all on the side which faced toward the street.
7. She is Mr. Smith's wife's sister's daughter.

71   CHOPPY SENTENCES

Do not use a series of short, jerky sentences to express a thought that should be expressed in a longer, unified sentence. Such choppy sentences, aside from being monotonous and wordy, give undue emphasis to unimportant ideas. Reserve main clauses for principal thoughts and use subordinate constructions for all subordinate thoughts.

> *Lacking emphasis and unity.* He sped through the passages. He went with a very swift step. I could scarcely keep up with him. He went straight to the door of John's room. He did not wait for a summons to enter. He opened it immediately.
>
> *More unified and emphatic:* He sped through the passages with so swift a step that I could scarcely keep up with him, straight to the door of John's room, which he immediately opened without waiting for a summons to enter.

See also the examples on pp. 8 and 293. **Subordination, 69,** and **Variety, 87.**

Exercise. Combine the following groups of sentences into single complex sentences. Subordinate all unimportant ideas.

1. I went at once to my room. I sat there in great excitement.
   I listened to the turmoil of the gale. It struck full upon the
   gable of the house.
2. It was a hot summer day. Early in the morning my father
   called me. He told me I ought to learn to swim. This suggestion surprised and delighted me.
3. The lake ice melted. At once we heard the lonely cry of
   the loon. The cry of the loon is one of the most striking of
   wilderness sounds. It is a strange, sad, unearthly cry, half
   laughing, half wailing.
4. Every summer we feasted on strawberries. These grow in
   rich beds. They are found beneath the meadow grasses.
   The sunny woods also contain many strawberries.

For further examples see Exercise, p. 18.

72   INCOMPLETE THOUGHT

COMPLETE every thought you begin to express. Do not
force the reader to fill in the gaps due to your own loose
thinking.

Incomplete in thought: The piles of corn were often left in the
     field several days, and we usually killed the field
     mice.
Complete: The piles of corn were often left in the field several
     days, and when we loaded them into the wagon, we
     usually killed the field mice that we found in them.

For other examples see **Coherence and Logical Order,
92, Omissions, 75,** and **Incomplete Constructions, 73.**

Exercise. Fill the gaps in the thought of any five of the
following sentences:

1. In the English universities the students spend a large part of
   the vacations in study, whereas our students do differently.
2. The men had carried the barrel of china to the wagon, and
   were unable to explain the accident.
3. In planting, the first thing to do is to prepare the ground for
   the seed, but any seedsman can give you good advice.

4. He wanted to play professional ball and so left home at once.
5. The shifting of the gears on this car is very simple, but no machine will work well when it is new.
6. The wagons were heavily loaded, and the new road was not completed.

73   INCOMPLETE CONSTRUCTIONS

Do not leave any elements of the sentence grammatically incomplete. Do not start with one construction and shift to another before completing the first.

Wrong: With these combinations put together so well is the reason that this story is the best. (*Is* has no subject.)

Right: Since these combinations are put together so well, this story is the best.

The reason this story is the best is that these combinations are put together so well.

Wrong: The first steady job I ever had was when I was twelve years old I worked in a grocery store. (The construction "The first steady job was . . ." is left uncompleted.)

Right: The first steady job I ever had was a position in a grocery store, where I began work at the age of twelve.

See also **Omissions, 75, Coherence and Logical Order, 92, Mixed Constructions, 97, Period Fault, 2,** and pp. 53–54.

Exercise. Complete the incomplete constructions in the following sentences:

1. It was his hobby that wherever he happened to be at night for him to pitch his tent there.
2. He said that James Warren, who, pouring out his generous blood like water, saw the star of his country rise before he felt the hand of death upon him.

Because he was getting old and was going to retire from politics, though he knew that he would be glad to help if his services should be needed again by his country, for love of country was his ruling passion.

4. He said that the venerable men who had stood on that spot fifty years ago with their brothers and fathers to fight for independence, but now their children could see no smoke of battle or ruins of the city which had been bombarded.

5. Everyone who entered the room where he was imprisoned he seemed eager to be released.

6. The fact that I had never been away from home before I was at first very homesick.

7. In regard to what he was to do with the jewels I had no suggestion to make on that point.

8. The first man who saw this lake many years ago everything must have appeared remarkably quiet and peaceful.

9. Wedged between two large boulders made the pole bear the weight of two men.

10. In my last year of high school I took up English, mostly English literature and three or four themes a month, but sometimes not any.

74 COMPARISONS INCOMPLETE OR ILLOGICAL

In making comparisons a writer often leaves too much to be implied by the reader. He should take care that all comparisons are complete, consistent, and logical. Some of the most common violations of this principle are:

a. The omission of *than* or *as* in a double comparison.

Wrong: I am as tall, if not taller, than my brother.
Right, but Awkward: I am as tall as, if not taller than, my brother.
Better: I am as tall as my brother, if not taller

b. The omission of the standard of comparison.

Vague: We have learned to appreciate the greater adaptability of the American soldier. (Greater than what?)
Clear: We have learned to appreciate the greater adaptability of the American soldier as compared to the German.
Vague: He has some moderately long descriptions which can be grasped much more easily.

Clear: He has some moderately long descriptions which can be grasped more easily than shorter descriptions by other authors.

See also **Uses of So, 13.**

c. The omission of one term of the comparison.

Incomplete: I like him better than James.
Complete: I like him better than James does.
I like him better than I like James.

d. The comparison of things which are not consistent or capable of comparison.

Illogical: My profession is better than an engineer.
Logical: My profession is better than engineering.
Illogical: Stevenson was afraid to read other authors, lest his style should seem like Lamb or some other essayist.
Logical: Stevenson was afraid to read other authors, lest his style should seem like that of Lamb or some other essayist.

See **Coherence and Logical Order, 92.**

e. The careless use of *than any other, than any, of any, of all, all else, of all other,* etc., results in illogical comparisons.

Illogical: I like *Hamlet* more than any of Shakspere's plays.
Logical: I like *Hamlet* more than any other of Shakspere's plays.
Illogical: I like *Hamlet* more than all of Shakspere's plays.
Logical: I like *Hamlet* best of all of Shakspere's plays.

f. The use of a noun as both singular and plural:

Wrong: It was a very large, if not the largest, *lakes* I ever saw.
Right: It was one of the largest lakes I ever saw, if not the largest.

g. The use of the comparative to refer to more than two or of the superlative to refer to less than two.

Right: Of the two brothers he is the taller.
Of the three brothers he is the tallest.

Exercise. Correct the incomplete and illogical comparisons:

1. This bird was one of the largest, if not the largest, birds I had ever seen.
2. John was richer than all the sons.
3. John was the richest of any of the sons.
4. The lake is as large if not larger than Lake Shaster.
5. Shakspere's style is more remarkable than any other writer.
6. This book treats more fully of the labor question.
7. These rackets may be used in rainy weather as well as other days.
8. I admire Tom more than John, but, of course, John is not fair to him.

75 OMISSIONS — MISCELLANEOUS

The following are miscellaneous types of incorrect omissions. (Other types are discussed in the preceding sections.)

a. The omission of part of a verb phrase requiring a form of the verb different from that of the verb in the accompanying verb phrase.

Wrong: I always have ∧ and always will *take* an interest in painting.

Right: I have always *taken* and always will *take* an interest in painting.

Wrong: He has stayed and will ∧ for many months.

b. The omission of a copula when the verb *to be* is used both as a principal and as an auxiliary verb.

Wrong: The new country club is very pretty and ∧ praised by everybody.

Right: The new country club *is* very pretty and *is* praised by everybody.

Wrong: The novel is very interesting and ∧ read with much enjoyment by people of all classes.

Right: The novel is very interesting and *is* read with much enjoyment by people of all classes.

Note: One verb form should never be forced to perform two different syntactical functions.

c. The omission of a verb in a sentence containing a singular and a plural subject.

Wrong: About the time they were almost worn out and one of them contemplating suicide, a ship appeared in the harbor.

Right: About the time they were almost worn out and one of them *was* contemplating suicide, a ship appeared in the harbor.

If the two subjects govern one verb, the verb need be used only once.

d. The omission of an article, pronoun, preposition, or subordinating conjunction necessary to the full and accurate expression of the thought. This error is especially common with parallel sentence elements. What effect would the omission of the italicized words have upon the meaning of the following sentences?

I asked for the secretary and *the* treasurer.

Last night my barn and *my* garage burned down.

He carried a red and *a* black flag.

Tennyson once wrote a poem about a tiny flower that grew in the side of a wall and *that* revealed a great thought to those who see more than the mere surface of things.

He was praised by those who knew him best, and particularly *by* his brothers.

He congratulated the men who were faithful in their work and *who* showed a pride in work well done.

e. The omission of a preposition necessary to grammatical completeness.

Wrong: He showed a striking aptitude∧and a remarkable power in this kind of work.

Correct, but Awkward: He showed a striking aptitude *for*, and a remarkable power *in*, this kind of work.

Better: He showed a striking aptitude for this kind of work, and a remarkable power in it.

(In the first sentence given above, the two idioms require two different prepositions.)

Wrong: He tries to vindicate himself by telling everybody∧ whom he comes in contact the whole story.

Right: He tries to vindicate himself by telling everybody *with* whom he comes in contact the whole story.

Wrong: In their speech there are many peculiarities, none of which the speakers of the dialect are conscious∧.

Right: In their speech there are many peculiarities, none of which the speakers of the dialect are conscious *of*.

f. The omission of an article forming an essential part of the title of a theme, a poem, a story, a novel, etc. See **Quoted Titles, 32**, and **Manuscript Form, 38**.

g. The omission of *than* or *as* in comparisons, or the omission of the standard of comparison. See **Comparisons, 74**.

h. The omission of words essential to the logical agreement between sentence elements. See **Coherence and Logical Order, 92, Incomplete Thought, 72,** and **Incomplete Constructions, 73**.

Exercise. Supply the words necessary to the completeness of the following sentences:

1. The winter was unusually mild and fires hardly necessary.
2. The class was small and taught by an old soldier.
3. His father, brother, and sister were with him.
4. I have been reading *Old Curiosity Shop*, a novel by Dickens.
5. Maynard assured James that the girls were not making fun of him, and the speech was really very good.

6. He tried to interest those who could swim or sail and play games with the others.
7. The vision of the ideal is a vision that is forever leading one on but never overtaken.
8. The French and English troops held different parts of the line.
9. He proved that the plan was unsuitable to the upper classes as well as the nation as a whole.

CHAPTER VII

EMPHASIS

Whatever his theme he will speak as becomes it; neither meagrely where it is copious, nor meanly where it is ample, not in *this* way where it demands *that;* but keeping his speech level with the actual subject and adequate to it. — CICERO

It is not pomp or pretension, but the adaptation of the expression to the idea that clinches a writer's meaning, — as it is not the size or glossiness of the materials, but their being fitted each to its place, that gives strength to the arch; or as the pegs and nails are as necessary to the support of the building as the larger timbers, and more so than the more showy, unsubstantial ornaments. — HAZLITT

Through every clause and part of speech of a right book, I meet the eyes of the most determined of men: his force and terror inundate every word: the commas and dashes are alive; so that the writing is athletic and nimble — can go far and live long. — EMERSON

76   SUSPENSE

See pp. 37–38.

Exercise. Improve the following sentences by placing the important ideas in the most emphatic positions:

1. Jealousy is a fault he is often guilty of.
2. This is yet revenge although it is not victory.
3. However, his countenance wore a look of mingled cruelty and greed, as it seemed to me.
4. It is the great prerogative of innocence to dread no eye, to suspect no tongue.
5. We flatter ourselves with the belief that we have forsaken passions when they have forsaken us.
6. I desire intimacy with only a few though I am fond of many acquaintances.
7. Rage can make a coward forget himself and fight, as we all know, however.
8. I then surveyed the ruins carefully after having provided myself with instruments.

77   CLIMAX

See pp. 33–34.

Exercise. Arrange the words in the following sentences in climactic order:

1. I always make allowance for him when he is angry, pained, or impatient.
2. I loathe, abhor, detest, and hate a man who will not stand by his friends.
3. Jefferson's ideal for America was peace, honest friendship, and commerce with all nations.
4. Compared with death old age, pain, imprisonment, or poverty is a paradise.
5. He was stirred with the hope of living as a worthy citizen, a God-fearing man, and an honest workman.
6. All stood amazed, astounded, and surprised at the sight.
7. He was the wisest, brightest, and friendliest man I ever saw.
8. Mr. Marchand was the leading banker of the city, the donor of Marchand Park, and an enthusiastic golfer.
9. Writers of to-day are thoughtless of an immortality of fame, are exquisitely sensible to praise or blame, and write with the fear of reviewers before their eyes.
10. He was worn out, exhausted — tired.

78   BALANCE

See pp. 23, 38–40.

79   REPETITION — GOOD

For emphasis through repetition, see pp. 40–42.
For clearness through repetition, see pp. 22–23, 65, and **Parallelism, 88.**

80   REPETITION — BAD

REPETITION is undesirable unless a word or phrase is repeated either for emphasis or for clearness. Careless or awkward repetition may be corrected (1) by the use of synonyms, (2) by the use of pronouns or other reference words, or (3) by recasting and condensing the sentence. The following are the most common kinds of undesirable repetition:

a. The monotonous repetition of the same word or phrase, even if the word has a different meaning.

> *Bad:*   He believed the people would believe his story about the accident.
>
> Since I have reported on this book since seeing you, I shall now deal with the part of the book dealing with the battle of Waterloo.
>
> At first we were afraid of snakes, but soon learned that most snakes were harmless. The only poisonous snakes we saw were the rattlesnake and the copperhead. We saw only one snake of each kind. David saw the rattlesnake, and we both saw the other snake. One day, when David came in from his work, he reported that he had seen a snake that made a queer buzzy noise with its tail. This was the only rattlesnake seen on our farm, though we heard of snakes being common in the hills ten miles distant.
>
> *Better:* He believed that the people would accept his story about the accident.
>
> Because I have reported on this book since seeing you, I shall now deal with that part of it which describes the battle of Waterloo.

(Revise the third sentence for yourself, using all three of the devices listed above.)

b. The careless repetition of the conjunction *that.*

> He said *that* if there were no more heavy rains *that* we should be able to take the trip.   (Omit either *that.*)

c. The harsh repetition of similar sounds:

> *Bad:* She stood quite quietly.

See **Euphony, 62.**

d. The repetition of the same idea.   See **Wordiness, 65.**

e. The repetition of the same sentence structure, the use of monotonous series of sentences similar in length, structure, etc. See **Variety, 87, Wordiness, 65, Overlapping Dependence, 70, Choppy Sentences, 71.**

Caution: In the desire to avoid monotonous repetition do not go too far in the opposite direction. Do not strain for synonyms or construct sentences which are clumsy and awkward because they are unnatural. By avoiding one fault you may easily fall into a more serious one. Naturalness is better than an artificial variety. (See also p. 42.)

Exercise. Point out and correct the undesirable repetition in the following sentences.

1. He said that his brother said he did not believe our play would succeed.
2. Since he has had poor health since being gassed, he has not been in college since December.
3. *Hamlet* is probably the best known of Shakspere's plays. Although many of Shakspere's plays are still played very often, this play remains the most popular of Shakspere's plays, or at least the most popular of Shakspere's tragedies.
4. James Street, Pine Street, and Jackson Street have stringent parking laws. On James Street no cars may be parked on the left side beyond the point where James and Pine streets intersect. On Pine Street no cars may be parked between 8 A.M. and 11 A.M. And on Jackson Street no cars may be parked between the hours of 7 A.M. and 8. P.M.
5. He lived with his aunt since there was no other relative he could live with without quarreling.

81   SUBORDINATION FOR EMPHASIS

SUBORDINATION is a most valuable means of securing emphasis in the sentence, for by this means a writer can indicate the relative importance of his ideas and reveal the precise shades of emphasis he desires. The brevity and compactness resulting from the skillful use of subordination also adds much to the emphasis of the sentence. The main idea should be put in the main clause and all other ideas should be subordinated. These subordinate ideas may be put in the form of dependent clauses, phrases, or single words. Note the difference in compactness and emphasis in the contrasted sentences below:

1. It was against orders and it was dangerous to light the head lamp, but we had to do it.

   Although it was dangerous and against orders to light the head lamp, we had to do it.

2. We lit the lamp, and I moved to the front seat and I held my sombrero over the light and muffled most of it, but I liberated a concentrated stream of silver, and this played on the road ahead.

   We lit the lamp, and, moving to the front seat, I muffled most of the light by holding my sombrero over the lamp, but I liberated a concentrated stream of silver that played on the road ahead.

3. We came to the end of the street, and we struggled for several minutes, for we wanted to get through the crowd which had gathered to see the fight; and at last we succeeded in forcing our way through.

   When we came to the end of the street, we struggled for several minutes in the effort to get through the crowd which gathered to see the fight; and at last we succeeded in forcing our way through.

   Coming to the end of the street, we struggled for several minutes before we finally succeeded in forcing our way through the crowd gathered to see the fight.

See also **Subordination, 69, Coördination, 67,** and pp. 8–15.

82   WEAK PASSIVE VOICE

THE passive voice is properly used only when the agent is unknown or unimportant, or when the receiver of the action is more important than the agent.

Right: Four hundred men were wounded in the battle.

In all other cases avoid the passive voice, for it detracts from the smoothness, interest, and emphasis of the sentence.

Unemphatic: A delightful time was had by all.
            I was thanked by both of them with a smile.
Better: All had a delightful time.
            Both thanked me with a smile.

Avoid shifting from active to passive or from passive to active within the same sentence or in a series of similar sentences.

Wrong: A letter was then received, which he read with great pleasure.
Right: He then received a letter, which he read with great pleasure.

See also **Point of View, 99,** and **Awkward Word Order, 85.**

Exercise. Make the following sentences more emphatic:

1. Your letter of last Monday has just been received.
2. Human situations are seen more vividly by poets than by other men.
3. The end of the journey was reached by us just before night.
4. Abstractions should be avoided in the description of characters.
5. The animal was heard crashing through the bushes near us.
6. I discovered a piece of rope, and in an instant it was wound around the intruder's arms.

83   ABSOLUTE PHRASES

ALTHOUGH the absolute phrase is often a convenient means of subordinating unimportant ideas, the student should observe the following cautions:

    a. An absolute phrase is usually awkward when it contains a perfect participle or a personal pronoun.

      Awkward and Latinistic: The motor having been repaired, we set out on our journey.

Better:　　When the motor had been repaired, we set out on our journey.

Having repaired the motor, we set out on our journey.

Awkward:　*We seeing* him in daily life, it is probable that we should see nothing in him but what is ordinary.

Better:　　If we should see him in daily life, we should probably see nothing in him but what is ordinary.

Awkward:　John suddenly became ill. *He being* alone, Fender remained with him until the doctor came.

Better:　　John suddenly became ill. Since his friend was alone, Fender remained with him until the doctor came.

See *Absolute* in **Grammatical Terms, 17.**

b. An absolute phrase at the end of the sentence often detracts from the emphasis. See pp. 33–38.

c. For the punctuation of absolute phrases, see p. 170.

84　　　EMPHATIC WORD ORDER

See pp. 33–40, and **Awkward Word Order, 85.**

85　　　AWKWARD WORD ORDER

No rules can cover completely the matter of general awkwardness of expression. Some of the commoner difficulties are:

a. Faulty arrangement of words. See **Position of Modifiers, 93, Overlapping Dependence, 70,** and **Split Constructions, 98.**

b. Omission of words necessary to the smooth and clear expression of thought. See **Omissions, 75,** and **Repetition for Clearness, 100.**

c. Repetition of the same word, construction, sound, or idea. See **Repetition — Bad, 80, Euphony, 62, Wordiness, 65.**

d. Clumsy grammatical constructions:

1. The absolute construction. See **Absolute Phrases, 83.**
2. The "thus causing" participle. See **Dangling Modifiers, 94.**
3. The passive voice. See **Weak Passive, 82.**
4. The suspended preposition. Avoid the awkward separation of preposition and object:

> *Awkward:* He had no respect for, or love of, his employer.
>
> *Better:* He had no respect for his employer nor love for him.
>
> He neither respected nor loved his employer.

5. The frequent use of *there* as an expletive:

> *Awkward:* There were four buildings which were used for dormitories.
>
> *Better:* Four buildings were used for dormitories.

6. The split construction. See **Split Constructions, 98.**

Exercise. Revise the following awkward sentences:

1. This matter was attended to to the best of my ability.
2. The night was cool and comfortable, there having been a hail storm during the afternoon.
3. He smashed his car against a brick wall, thus causing a delay of several hours.
4. There were five of us who took part in the concert.
5. He had no knowledge of, nor explanation for, his strange conduct.
6. He sprang across the terrace as the bell clanged, and rushed up the hill.
7. I found him reading the book in the dining room which I gave him.
8. This room makes a very restful scene for a tired man after a hard day's work to sit by a window and look out over the lawn in front of the house at the handiwork of Nature.

86   FINE AND OVERCAREFUL WRITING

Fine Writing: Do not dress your thoughts in what may appear to be fine language, but is actually ridiculously inappropriate. Avoid the high-flown, the bombastic, the pseudo-poetic, and all other symptoms of insincerity.

> *Affected:* The present writer first saw the light of day in the year of Our Lord 1908 in that Windy City that lies by the side of the queenly waters of Lake Michigan.
>
> *Sincere:* I was born in Chicago in 1908.

Overcareful Writing: A too rigid adherence to the rules of correctness may lead to an unnatural, pedantic, bookish style, to the use of mincing, "schoolma'am" English, such as:

> I partook of all the articles of food.
> Do not abuse any one's else book.
> I bought this book very cheaply.

A mistaken striving for accuracy occasionally leads also to the use of English which is not only artificial, but even incorrect, such as:

> I feel badly.

This excess of virtue is commonest in pronunciation: *raiment* pronounced with three syllables, *ra-i-ment*, *often* with the *t* sounded, *again* to rhyme with *rain*, are examples.

87   VARIETY

See pp. 51–52, for a discussion of variety and for illustrations of desirable and undesirable variety. See also **Repetition — Bad, 80, Choppy Sentences, 71, Overlapping Dependence, 70.**

Perhaps the most objectionable sort of monotony is the series of "curt, pellet-like" sentences containing no subordination and no sense of the relative value of ideas. Note the monotony, the dead level, the absence of shading in the following passage:

> As in a mist he heard a twang. He glanced down. Denys was white and silent as death. He was shooting up at the bear. The bear snarled at the twang. But he crawled on. Again the cross-bow twanged. Again the bear snarled. And he came nearer. Once more the cross-bow twanged. The next moment the bear was close upon Gerard. He sat palsied, with hair standing stiff on end and eyes starting from their sockets.

Note the variety, the gain in force and effectiveness, when this same incident is told by a master.

> As in a mist he heard a twang; he glanced down; Denys, white and silent as death, was shooting up at the bear. The bear snarled at the twang, but crawled on. Again the cross-bow twanged, and the bear snarled, and came nearer. Again the cross-bow twanged; and the next moment the bear was close upon Gerard, where he sat, with hair standing stiff on end and eyes starting from their sockets, palsied.

Another objectionable sort of monotony consists of the constant use of compound sentences composed of clauses strung together by a series of *and's*, *but's*, *or's*, or *so's*. (See **Straggling Compound Sentences, 68,** and **So, 13**.) Divide a sentence of this sort into two or more simple, unified sentences; or change it into a complex sentence, a type of sentence the beginner would do well to cultivate. Study the examples given under **Subordination,** pp. **8–15,** and **Subordination for Emphasis, 81.**

CHAPTER VIII

CLEARNESS

As your idea's clear, or else obscure,
The expression follows, perfect or impure.
BOILEAU

Those writers who construct difficult, obscure, involved, and equivocal sentences most certainly do not know aright what it is they want to say: they have only a dull consciousness of it, which is still in the stage of struggle to shape itself as thought. — SCHOPENHAUER

I do not polish my phrase, but my idea. — JOUBERT

88   PARALLELISM

SENTENCE elements that are of the same rank — logically coördinate — should be made grammatically parallel. For a full discussion of parallelism, see pp. 21–25, **And Which, 89,** and **Correlatives, 90.**

89   "AND WHICH"

And, but, or, and the other coördinating conjunctions connect only elements of the same grammatical form and the same logical function: noun "and" noun, adjective "and" adjective, etc. "And which," "but which," and "or which" are correctly used only when another *which* clause precedes.

> *Wrong:* The house, large and roomy, *and which* was built many years ago, belonged to my grandfather.
> *Right:* The house, *which* was large and roomy, *and which* was built many years ago, belonged to my grandfather.

See also **Parallelism, 88,** and **Coördination, 67.**

Exercise. Rewrite correctly:

1. The Carnival, the most elaborate of the year and which is always held in November, afforded us an excellent opportunity for giving our play.
2. Four young ladies of exquisite beauty and who lived in the neighborhood greeted us upon our arrival.
3. The windows, large and lofty, and which open on the terrace, were covered with dark draperies.
4. He began working, with a severe headache, but which his interest in his work soon caused him to forget.
5. Joaquin Miller, a poet of the West, and who resembles Byron, is one of the authors I like best.

90 CORRELATIVES

OBSCURITY often results from the misuse of correlatives. Since correlatives always connect sentence elements of equal value — parallel elements — the words following the correlatives should always perform the same syntactical function; i.e., each correlative should be followed immediately by the same part of speech.

See **Conjunctions, 12,** and the exercise on p. 30.

91 CONNECTIVES AND TRANSITION

Connectives. In order to attain clearness, emphasis, and smooth transition, one should be thoroughly familiar with the grammatical difference between the classes of conjunctions. For a discussion of this difference see pp. 137–141. For a list of connectives see pp. 13–15, 137–141.

Transition. It is often difficult to remember that the reader cannot immediately see the relation between our sentences and paragraphs. We are so familiar with our own thought processes that we are prone to forget that the reader may not be able to follow easily and without discomfort the transition from one thought to another. The careful and thoughtful writer, therefore, takes pains to mark the exact connection between sentence elements, sentences, and paragraphs.

For transition in the sentence see pp. 64–66.

For transition in the paragraph see p. 83.

92 COHERENCE AND LOGICAL ORDER

EACH part of the sentence should be in logical harmony with the other parts. Coherence in sentences demands that the relation of the parts of the sentence be made immediately and perfectly clear. It demands (1) completeness of thought, (2) clear reference, (3) logical agreement between the parts of the sentence, and (4) logical sequence of ideas.

> a. *Logical sequence of ideas.* Arrange the thoughts of your sentence according to a logical plan. Finish one thought before you begin another, and begin the second thought where you leave off the first. The following sentences violate the principle of logical sequence:

> > He looked back cautiously after rushing wildly to the open door. (The order of time is reversed.)
> > He regained command of some of his shattered senses when he finally ventured to turn his head, and carefully commenced to examine his wound. (The first idea should be completed before the second is begun. "He regained command . . . and commenced to examine his wound . . . when he finally ventured to turn his head.")

> b. For *completeness of thought* see **Incomplete Constructions, 73, Omissions, 75, Uses of So, 13,** and **Comparisons, 74.**
> c. For *clear reference* see **Reference, 95, Agreement, 4, Dangling Modifiers, 94,** and **Connectives, 91.**

d. For *logical word order* see **Position of Modifiers, 93, Parallelism, 88, Split Constructions, 98,** and **Awkward Word Order, 85.**

e. For *logical agreement of parts of sentence* see **Agreement, 4, Clauses, 15, Point of View, 99,** and p. 63.

Exercise. Detect and correct the lack of coherence in the following sentences:

1. The strokes in golf are harder than tennis.
2. Of these applications for the position four were elected.
3. He is now studying to be a doctor, a subject I have always been interested in.
4. The story is so supported by facts that for the time the reader accepts the contents as credible.
5. The chief talent of the author is for bringing his characters into real situations.
6. I spent a most enjoyable evening last week by going to see "The Beggar's Feast," an interesting play with good characters and witty speeches, which was written by a new dramatist.
7. The tragedy of *Macbeth* is laid in Scotland.
8. He got up as I entered the room and extended his hand.
9. I was unable to go on the trip, having lost my purse.
10. If you make application, you will be given the position if your qualifications are satisfactory.
11. James has an alert manner and a clever way of talking about his business affairs which I do not like.
12. Since we sent you a copy of the book, we supposed that you intended to keep it.
13. In Defoe's and Scott's writings are found two different types of self-expression, but a common touch, the grip of human life in both.
14. The bricks are laid so that they are a perfect semicircle.

93 POSITION OF MODIFIERS

SINCE English is not a highly inflected language, word order is of supreme importance in showing clearly the relations between words in the sentence. Every modifier should therefore be so placed that the reader may connect it immediately and unmistakably with the word that it modifies. Some of the most common types of misplaced modifiers are:

a. *"Squinting"* or *"cross-eyed" Modifiers* (looking both ways at once). These are modifiers which are so placed that they may modify either the preceding or the following word or words.

> *Not Clear:* Though his style is easy and rhythmical in its structure and correctness it is not really so good as Scott's.
>
> *Clear:* Though his style is easy and rhythmical it is really not so good in its structure and correctness as Scott's.
>
> *Not Clear:* He said that if we did not pay, within a week, in spite of all our protests, he would present the note at his bank.
>
> *Clear:* He said that if we did not pay within a week, he would, in spite of all our protests, present the note to his bank.

Note that both punctuation and placing of modifiers contribute to clearness. See p. 178.

Take especial pains to place the adverbs *only, just, almost,* and *even,* so that their reference may be immediately clear.

> *Ambiguous:* I just asked one word with him.
>
> *Clear:* I asked just one word with him.
>
> *Ambiguous:* Any person who will read a good book, even the most humble, will find something of himself in that book.
>
> *Clear:* Any person, even the most humble, who will read a good book will find something of himself in that book.

b. Misplaced Relative Clauses. Whenever there is any danger of referring a relative clause to a modifier of the antecedent rather than to the antecedent itself, the clause should be so placed that its relation to the antecedent is unmistakable.

Not Clear: He rode silently down the road leading over the hill, which had been recently paved.

Clear: He rode silently over the hill, down the road which had been recently paved.

See also exercise under **Awkward Word Order, 85**.

Not Clear: In this essay Stevenson discusses the everyday things of life and also things that we have not seen in a way as simple as the way in which one friend might talk to another.

Clear: In this essay Stevenson discusses, in a way as simple as the way in which one friend might talk to another, both the everyday things of life and also things which we have not seen.

c. However, therefore, thus, then, hence, etc. Such words as *however, therefore, then, thus,* and *also* modifying the sentence as a whole or serving to mark transitions should, for considerations of emphasis, be buried in the middle of the sentence.

Unemphatic: The art of describing character is perhaps the only universal art, however.

However, the art of describing character is perhaps the only universal art.

Emphatic: The art of describing character, however, is perhaps the only universal art.

d. Other Sentence Elements.

Not Clear: He crossed the bridge under which the little stream ran, and gazed silently at the house beyond.

304

Clear: Crossing the bridge under which the little stream ran he gazed silently at the house beyond.

See also **Parallelism, 88, Split Constructions, 98,** and **Coherence and Logical Order, 92.**

Exercise. Improve the following sentences by improving the order of the words.

1. I only waited one hour.
2. A shudder passed over him. However, he thought his imagination must have deceived him.
3. The person who is wrong in most cases will stick to his opinion even after he has learned of his error.
4. These houses were seized upon by bold tramps when their dilapidation was far advanced.
5. Mr. Turley sits meditating an application to the nearest magistrate in his office.
6. At length a young lady approached the corner, adorned with a large nosegay, in which I sat alone.

94 DANGLING MODIFIERS: ELLIPTICAL CLAUSE, GERUND, PARTICIPLE

A DANGLING modifier is a modifier which cannot be connected immediately and unmistakably with an antecedent in the same sentence. The most objectionable types of dangling modifiers are:

a. *Dangling participles or gerunds.* Since verbals are not inflected for number or person, a participle or a gerund should always be so used that it can be connected logically and unmistakably with the words to which it refers.

Wrong: On approaching the island, a high cliff can be seen.
Right: On approaching the island, one can see a high cliff. As one approaches the island, a high cliff can be seen.
Wrong: In writing *Heroes and Hero-Worship* I don't think

that Carlyle's intention was to have his style imitated by college students.

Right: In writing *Heroes and Hero Worship* Carlyle never intended, I think, to have his style imitated by college students.

Wrong: The details are properly selected and well combined by the author, thus giving a better effect than mere enumeration would give.

Right, but Unemphatic: The author chooses properly and combines skillfully the details in this story, thus giving a better effect than he could attain by mere enumeration. (See **Awkward Word Order, 85.**)

Better: By properly selecting and skillfully combining the details in this story, the author gives a better effect than he could attain by mere enumeration.

A good rule for beginners is: *Never begin a sentence with a verbal in -ing unless the verbal agrees logically with the subject of the following (governing) clause; and never end a sentence with a participle unless the participle agrees logically with some word in the preceding clause.* A sentence containing a dangling verbal may be corrected either by (1) expanding the verbal phrase into a subordinate clause, or by (2) recasting the sentence so as to make the verbal agree with the subject of the governing clause. Both of these methods of correction are illustrated above. (See also p. 61.)

Note: Such words as *according to, in regard to, owing to, relating to, regarding* and *concerning* are used as prepositions, not as adjectives, and so do not constitute dangling modifiers. "Generally speaking" and "speaking of ——" are also exceptions.

See **Case 5.**

b. *Dangling elliptical clauses.* An elliptical clause is one in which subject or predicate — or both — is omitted. Such a clause "dangles" when the omitted subject and predicate are not the same as the subject and predicate of the main clause. To correct this error, expand the elliptical clause by supplying the omitted subject and predicate, or make the subject of both clauses the same.

> *Wrong:* When on the top of the ridge, the distant mountains could easily be seen.
> *Right:* When we were on the top of the ridge, the distant mountains could easily be seen.
> When on the top of the ridge, we could easily see the distant mountains.

See also p. 62.

95 REFERENCE OF PRONOUNS

AVOID ambiguity or obscurity by making the reference of every pronoun immediately clear. Some of the most serious cases of faulty reference are:

a. The use of a pronoun which may refer to any one of two or more antecedents. Often the result is a "short circuit" between the pronoun and the wrong antecedent:

> *Vague:* John told his father that he would be nominated soon.
> *Undesirable:* John told his father that he (John) would be nominated soon. (The explanatory parenthesis is a confession of inability to write a clear sentence.)
> *Right:* John told his father that he expected to be nominated soon.
> John said to his father, "I expect to be nominated soon." (Since this kind of obscurity is especially common in indirect discourse, the use of direct discourse affords a simple remedy for the obscurity.)

> *Vague:*   Nobody could tell whether this was the Italian *who* had not been there.
>
> *Clear Through Correct Position:* Nobody who had not been there could tell whether this was the Italian.

Relative and demonstrative pronouns should be placed as close to their antecedents as possible.

b. The use of *this, that, which, it,* etc. to refer to the whole idea of a preceding clause instead of to a specific noun in the clause.

> *Wrong:* Do not write on both sides of the paper. *This* is not customary.

Correct an error of this sort either by removing the pronoun from the sentence or by supplying it with an antecedent. When the pronoun refers to the whole idea of the preceding clause, express this general idea in the form of a noun like *fact, matter, process, practice, circumstance* to which the pronoun may clearly refer.

> *Right:*   Do not write on both sides of the paper. To do so is not customary.
>
> Do not write on both sides of the paper. This practice is not customary.

> *Note:* Whenever the reference of the pronoun is unmistakable, a pronoun may be used to refer to a clause.

> > While I was writing, he talked incessantly. *This* distracted my attention.
> >
> > We were all asked to remove our coats, *which* we did without hesitation.

The only reason the student is warned against using *which, this,* etc. to refer to a clause is that this practice demands the most careful attention if one wishes to avoid ambiguity.

Criticize these sentences:

> Last winter I broke my arm, which kept me out of school for three weeks.
>
> I am going to discuss the section of the book called "The Hero as Man of Letters," which is a product of recent years.

c. The use of a pronoun to refer to a word which has not been expressed, but which must be inferred from the context. This error is due to slovenly thinking.

> *Wrong:* July 14 is a national holiday in *France. They* always celebrate this day very elaborately.
>
> *Right:* July 14 is a national holiday in *France.* The *French* always celebrate this day very elaborately.
>
> *Wrong:* His father is a banker. *This* is the profession I intend to enter.
>
> *Right:* His father is a banker. Banking is the profession I intend to enter.
>
> His father is engaged in banking, a profession I intend to enter.

See also p. 61.

d. The use of a pronoun to refer to a noun which is in a subordinate or parenthetical construction. Such reference to an inconspicuous antecedent may lead to the reader's referring the pronoun to a noun which is more conspicuous in the sentence. Place the antecedent of the pronoun in an emphatic position in the sentence.

> *Wrong:* Little Mildred is the hero of "The Man Who Was," which is one of Kipling's best stories. *He* knew intimately the life of India. (Who knew the life of India? Little Mildred? Kipling?)
>
> *Right:* ... Kipling knew intimately the life of India.

Note: A pronoun should not ordinarily refer to a

following antecedent unless the antecedent immediately follows the pronoun.

Obscure: When they came to this country in search of religious toleration and to escape the narrowness of religion in England, the Puritans laid the foundations of a new order of society. (The reader does not know what the antecedent of *they* is until he has read through the long dependent clause. Such sentences must often be reread before their meaning becomes clear.)

Clear: When the Puritans ....., they .....

Right: *Who* hath ears to hear, let *him* hear.

e. The use of *same* or *said* instead of *it, this, that, the aforesaid, the above-mentioned*, etc.

Bad: I received your letter and noted contents of *same* very carefully.

The book had been lost two weeks. Then when *said* book was returned, *same* was found to be badly mutilated.

f. Inconsistency or shift in number between pronoun and antecedent.

Bad: The choir was to raise five hundred dollars for their pipe organ. (*Choir* is first regarded as a singular, the subject of *was*, and is then regarded as a plural. Use *its* for *their*.)

The Senate was considering a bill which would forbid their members from owning certain kinds of stock.

See **Agreement, 4, Point of View, 99**, and **Pronouns, 14**.

96 MIXED FIGURES

See pp. 54-55.

Exercise. Correct the mixed figures:

1. The wheels of government have stopped amid a torrent of criticism.

2. On the stage of life he patiently carried his burden of disappointments.
3. She came into his life like a little pig-headed ray of sunshine.
4. I may be up a tree, but I will fight to the last ditch.
5. In harnessing the mental forces that produce enlightenment literature is the fundamental tool.

97   MIXED CONSTRUCTIONS

Do not use two different syntactical constructions. Note the following examples of blended, or mixed, syntax:

Despite of this fact, he will agree to our proposal. (This is a blend of *despite* and *in spite of.*)

I have no room in which to work in. (*In which to work* and *which to work in* are blended.)

I told him to come as soon as he *can.* (Here the tenses of the direct and the indirect discourse are confused.)

I could *not* help *but* think that he was right. (The double negative in this sentence is due to the confusion of "I could but (= only) think" and "I could not help thinking").

See also **Incomplete Constructions, 73,** and pp. 53–54.

Exercise.   Correct the mixed syntax:

1. A child of three years old would know nothing in regarding a business matter.
2. He found that he had too little room in which to stand in.
3. Do not await for my return.
4. They should not send the kind of books which never any soldier reads.
5. The theme should be one upon which the speaker is qualified to speak to an audience upon.
6. The news went to all our hearts.

98   SPLIT CONSTRUCTIONS

Do not needlessly depart from the normal word order. (For emphatic word order see pp. 34–37.) In English, words that are logically related belong together. Any needless departure from the normal word order is likely to result in obscurity or awkwardness. Note the following cases of split constructions:

a. The split infinitive. Although the split infinitive (*to* + adverb + infinitive) is defended by some authorities and is occasionally used by good writers, the student of composition should, of course, master the rule before he experiments with the exception.

> *Dubious:*   He began to suddenly *hesitate* in his speech.
> *Certainly Correct:* He began suddenly *to hesitate* in his speech.

b. The aimless separation of such closely connected sentence elements as subject and verb, verb and object, preposition and object, word and modifier.

> *Awkward:*   He, being suddenly called home, was unable to take part in the work.
>   He saw, at one sharp glance, the open box on the table.
> *Better:*   Being suddenly called home, he was unable to take part in the work.
>   At one sharp glance he saw the open box on the table.

See also **Awkward Word Order, 85.**

c. The needless separation of the parts of a verb phrase.

> *Awkward:* There on the corner rose the great building which Summers *had* late in the spring *turned* over to the company. (*Had turned* should not be divided without good reason.)

See also **Awkward Word Order, 85.**

Exercise. Recast, avoiding the split constructions:

1. He vowed to never again interfere in another's affairs.
2. He in most of his habits was one of the most regular men I had ever seen.

3. He was, when his employer informed him of his promotion, surprised to hear the news.
4. I have never heard of, and do not care to go into, the plan you propose.
5. The mountains threw over the valley of the Broad River lying before us their long blue shadows.

99 POINT OF VIEW

CLEARNESS demands that we choose one point of view and keep it until there is good reason for changing to another point of view.

a. Avoid aimlessly shifting the subject, voice, or mode in a sentence.

Wrong: He came back to college in the fall, and all his energies were exerted in making a soldier out of himself. (Shift of subject and voice.)

Right: He came back to college in the fall and exerted all his energies in making a soldier out of himself.

Wrong: We went through a cotton mill, where the operatives greatly interested us.

Right: We went through a cotton mill, where we were greatly interested in the operatives.

See also pp. 51–52, 62–63.

b. Avoid aimlessly shifting the tense from present to past or from past to present in narration. Choose one tense and use it throughout the passage. See pp. 63–64 for example, and see **Parallelism, 88.**

c. Avoid aimlessly shifting from a formal to a colloquial style in the same passage.

d. Avoid shifting from indirect to direct discourse.

Wrong: He asked me *would I come.* (The word order of direct discourse is here incorrectly retained in the indirect discourse.)

Right: He asked me whether I would come.

Wrong: I told him to come as soon as he *can.* (Here the tense of direct discourse: "Come as soon as you can," is incorrectly retained.)

e. Avoid shifting the number, person, or class of pronouns.

Wrong: If *one* determines to avoid all misspellings, *he* (*you, they*) can learn to spell correctly. (*One* is a singular indefinite pronoun. *He, you,* and *they* are personal pronouns.)

Right: If one determines to avoid all misspellings, one can learn to spell correctly.

Wrong: Take pains with spelling and one can avoid all misspellings.

Right: Take pains with spelling and you can avoid all misspellings.

Wrong: We examined the trees that had been cut down and which were to be used for the walls of the cabin. (Needless shift from *that* to *which.*)

See **Pronouns, 14,** and **Agreement, 4.**

100   REPETITION FOR CLEARNESS

THE omission of words necessary to completeness of thought is discussed in sections **72, 73, 74,** and **75.**

To attain perfect clearness it is often desirable to repeat prepositions, auxiliary verbs, subordinating conjunctions, and other connectives between parallel sentence-elements. Study the examples under **Omissions, 75.** See also **Overlapping Dependence, 70,** and **Parallelism, 88.**

Exercise. In the following sentences supply the words that should be repeated for clearness:

1. My friend and brother went with me.
2. You should ask what laws cover the case and carefully study the evidence.

3. He was informed that his application blank was not in proper form and he must fill out another.

4. They would remain out of doors to enjoy the view and generally keep in the shade of the large trees near the house.

5. There are people of another fashion, who have agreed to cast a glamour of romance over this world and keep down its stern realities.

6. Since he might be seen at any hour of the day strolling through the village, where he had lived all of his life, and he knew every house in the county, he was well qualified to judge of the value of my property.

7. The story deals with the trials of a young couple who live beyond their means in order to keep up appearances and invite disaster thereby.

8. These dramas were composed during the fourteenth and fifteenth century.

INDEX [1]

All numbers refer to pages.

A and *an*, 149.

Abbreviations, 215; period after, 190, 215.

Absolute phrases, definition, 148; punctuation of, 170; wrongly used for sentence, 106; awkward, 294–95.

Accept, 255.

Ad, 255.

Adjective, defined, 149; distinguished from adverb, 135–36; punctuation of series of, 165.

Adjective clause, 149.

Adjective modifier, comma with, 172 ff.

Adverb, 149; punctuation of series of, 165; distinguished from adjective, 135–36.

Adverbial clause, defined, 149; misused for noun clause, 147.

Adverbial modifier, comma with, 171.

Affect, 255.

Aggravate, 255.

Agree to, *agree with*, 255.

Agreement, of pronouns, 115, 144; of subject and verb, 112 ff.; illogical, 63.

Ain't, 255.

Alliteration, 156–57, 270.

Allow, 255.

Almost, 255; position of, 303.

Alone, 256.

Already, *all ready*, 256.

All right, "alright," 256.

Also, position of, 304.

Altogether, *all together*, 256.

Alumna, *alumnæ*, 256.

Alumnus, *alumni*, 256.

Among, 256.

And etc., 256.

And not, subject not plural with, 113; subject plural, 112; comma before for emphasis, 168.

And which construction, 299.

Antecedent, defined, 149; agreement of pronoun with, 115; reference to, 61, 307–10.

Any, 256, reference of pronoun to, 115.

Anybody, singular verb with, 112; reference of pronoun to, 115.

Any one, singular verb with, 112.

Any place, *no place*, etc., 256.

Anyways, 256.

Apostrophe, uses of, 196–97; abuse of, 197.

Appositive, defined, 149; case, 119; comma with, 172; no comma with, 173; colon with, 187; dash with, 194; confused with sentence, 106.

Apt, 256.

Archaic words, 245.

Articles, defined, 149; omission of wrong, 209, 286; repeated, 314–315; in quoted titles, 209, 219.

As, omitted in comparisons, 283; case after, 117; punctuation with, 174; for *that* or *whether*, 256; for *such as*, 257; overworked as conjunction, 257; *not so ... as* in negative comparisons, 257.

As well as, subject not plural with, 112.

At, 257.

Auto, 257.

Auxiliary, defined, 149; double use of wrong, 285; repeated for clearness, 314.

[1] The citations do not include the spelling lists on pages 237–242.

317

INDEX

Awful, 257.

Awkward, omissions, 282–87; passive, 293–94; word order, 294–96, 304–05, 311–12.

Badly for *bad*, 135–36, 297.

Balance, 23, 38; and parallelism, 23; correlative conjunctions and balance, 24, 300; for emphasis, 38–39; types of balanced sentence, 38–39.

Barbarisms, 248.

Because clause wrong, 147.

Beside, besides, 257.

Between, 257.

Bible, capitals for books of, 213; reference to, 188.

Blame it on, 257.

Both, 257.

Brackets, uses of, 199–200.

Brainy, 257.

Bully, 257.

But, double negative with, 148; comma before for emphasis, 168; singular subjects joined by, 113.

But that, 257.

But what, 257.

But which construction, 299.

Calculate, 258.

Can for *may*, 258.

Cancellations in MS., 218.

Cannot help but, 258.

Capitals, uses of, 212 ff.; after colon, 188, 214; misuses of, 214.

Caret, 218.

Case, defined, 116 ff.; errors in use of: nominative, 116; objective, 117; possessive, 118; of appositive, 119.

Caused by phrase, 258.

Causing, thereby causing, thus causing construction unemphatic, 306.

Cede, ceed, sede, words in, 226–227.

Change in point of view, 51–52, 62–63, 313–14.

Choppy sentences, 280, 297–98.

Claim, 258.

Clauses, defined, 101 ff., 146; independent, 102, 146; dependent, 101–02, 146; uses of, 101; overlapping, 279; misplaced relative, 304; adverbial for noun, 147, wrongly used for sentence, 107; dangling elliptical, 62, 306–07; essential and non-essential, 132–33; punctuation, 162–78, 181–84.

Clever, 258.

Clearness, 61 ff.; in reference: of pronouns, 61, 307–10; of verbals, 61, 305–06; of elliptical clause, 62, 306–07; in diction, 66–68; in point of view, 51–52, 62, 313–314; in transition, 64, 300; in order of sentence elements, 301–04, 311–12; in punctuation, 163, 183; repetition for, 41–42, 66–68, 286, 314.

Climax, 33–34.

Coherence, between sentences, 65, 300–01; within sentences, 65, 301 ff.; between paragraphs, 83; within paragraphs, 81, 300–01.

Collective noun, agreement with verb, 113; agreement with pronoun, 115; definition, 154.

Colloquialisms, 249.

Colon, uses of, 186–88; capital after, 214.

Combine, 258.

Comma, uses of, 162–78; one comma to separate, 163–69; two commas to group, 169–76; unnecessary, 176–78.

Comma fault, 5, 108, 202; methods of correction, 109–10.

Comma unnecessary, 176–178.

Commands with *shall* and *will*, 128.

Common, 258.

Common noun, 154; not capitalized, 214.

Compare to, compare with, 258.

Comparison, of adjective and adverb, 150; incomplete or illogical, 283–285; *than* or *as* omitted in, 283; inconsistent, 284; illogical, 62–63, 284; one term omitted, 284; comparative or superlative misused, 284–85.

Complected, 258.

Complement, 150.

Complex sentence, defined, 150; punctuation of, 163–178, 184.

Compound adjective. See Compound words.

Compound personal pronoun, 143–144.

Compound predicate, comma with, 167.

Compound sentence, defined, 9, 102, 150; straggling, 9–10, 276–77, 298; contracted, 168; comma with, 167; semicolon with, 181 ff.; colon with, 187.

Compound-complex sentence, 150.

Compound words, plural of, 233; hyphen with, 234–35; written solid, 235.

Concrete diction, 33.

Conditions, *should* and *would* in, 131; subjunctive to express, 120–121.

Confusion of similar forms in spelling, 225.

Conjugation, 150.

Conjunctions, defined, 137–39; distinguished from other parts of speech, 140; classes of, 137–39; lists of, 13–15, 137–139; repeated for clearness, 41–42, 65–66, 314.

Conjunctive adverb, defined, 138; distinguished from other conjunctions, 140–142; punctuation with, 142, 182.

Connectives, types of, 65, 98; lists of, 13–14, 137–39; and transition, 80, 300–301; repeated, 41–42, 65–66, 314; of purpose, result, manner, cause, etc., 13–15, 22–23.

Construction defined, 150; incomplete, 282–83; split, 311–12; mixed, 53, 311; shifted, 282; awkward, 295–96, 311–312; *because* clause, 147; *due to, caused by*, 259; *owing to*, 260; *when* and *where* clauses, 147; sentence as clause, 146; clause as sentence, 5, 105–107, 274.

Continual, continuous, 258.

Contracted compound sentence, punctuation of, 168.

Contractions, apostrophe with, 196–97; when wrong, 215; verbs, 114.

Contrast, marked by comma, 168; by semicolon, 183.

Contrast from, 259.

Contrasted sentence elements, comma with, 175; semicolon with, 183.

Coördinate, defined, 150; coördinate conjunction, 137.

Coördination, 150, 275–76; excessive, 9–10, 275; illogical, 275; false, 276.

Copula, copulative verb, defined, 151; adjective after, 135–36; omitted, 285.

Corrections in MS., 218.

Correlatives, defined, 140, 300; lists of, 140; position of, 24, 300; in parallel and balanced constructions, 24, 300.

Correspond to, correspond with, 259.

Could of, 259.

Couple, 259.

Cunning, 259.

Curves (parentheses), uses of, 197–200.

Cute, 259.

Dangling modifiers: elliptical clause, 62, 306–07; gerund, 305–06; participle, 61, 305–06.

Dash, uses of, 194–195.

Data, 259.

Dates, punctuation of, 174; writing of numbers in, 216–217.

Days of week, capitalized, 212.

Deal, 259.

Declension defined, 151.

Definitions, *when* and *where* misused in, 63, 147.

Degrees, capitals with, 213–214; comma with, 174.

Deity, names of, capitalized, 213; pronoun referring to, 213.

Demean, 259.

INDEX

Demonstrative pronoun, defined, 143; vague reference of, 145, 308.

Departure from normal word order, emphatic, 34–35; awkward, 296, 303–305, 311–12.

Dependent clause, 101, 146; wrongly used for sentence, 107; comma after preceding, 164–65.

Derivatives associated in spelling, 226.

Determination, future of, 128.

Dialogue, quotation marks in, 200–203; paragraphing of, 203; punctuation before, 187–188, 202; punctuation of, 202–203; capitals in, 214.

Diction, importance of, 243. Effective, 269–272; affected, 51, 297; emphatic, 32, 270–72; exact, 32; fresh, 32; concrete, 33; specific, 32; clear, 66–68; economy in, 55–56; euphony in, 56–57, 270; wordiness, 55–56, 271–72. Correct, 243–269. Good use, 244–45; archaic, 245; barbarism, 248; colloquialism, 249; idiom, 246; impropriety, 248; obsolete, 245; provincialism, 246; slang, 250–252; vulgarism, 248; technical, 246; glossary of faulty diction, 255–269.

Diction faulty, glossary of, 255–269.

Die with, 259.

Differ from, differ with, 259.

Different to, different than, 259.

Direct address, comma with, 170.

Direct quotation, 200–204.

Division of words into syllables, 210–211.

Divided reference, 307.

Do, 259.

Done, 259.

Don't, 259.

Double negative, 148; double reference, 307–08; use of same word, 285–07.

Doubling a final consonant, 228 ff.

Due to, 259–260.

Each, every, either, etc., singular verb with, 112; reference of pronoun to, 115.

Each and *either*, 260.

Economy, a social, not a private matter, 52–53; tangled constructions, 53; misplaced modifiers, 54, 303–305; mixed figures, 54–55; unnecessary words, 55, 271–72; unpleasant sounds, 56–57, 270.

Effect, 260.

Effective diction, 32–33, 51, 66–68, 269–272, 297.

E.g., punctuation with, 174, 182.

Ei, ie, spelling, 227–228.

Either, 260.

Either, neither, each, every, etc., singular verb with, 112; reference of pronoun to, 115.

Electricute, electrocute, 260.

Elegant, 260.

Ellipsis, defined, 151; improper, 209, 220, 281–87.

Elliptical clause, dangling 62, 306–07; *than* or *as* in, 283.

Elliptical sentence, punctuation after, 189; distinguished from period fault, 189–190.

Emphasis, and accurate representation of thought, 30–31; by italics, 31; by subordination, 292–298; by improving words, 31; climax, 33; word order, 34–35, 295, 304; suspense, 37; balance, 38; repetition for, 22–23, 40–41, 290–292. Punctuation for, comma, 168; semicolon, 183; dash, 195.

Emphatic adverbial modifier, comma with, 171.

Emphatic diction, 32, 270–272.

Endorsement of theme, 219.

Enlarging the vocabulary, 68–69, 89.

Enthuse, 260.

Erasures in MS., 218.

Essential and non-essential modifiers, defined, 133; tests of, 133–34; punctuation of, 134, 171–72.

320

INDEX

Etc., 260.

Etymology a guide to spelling, 226.

Euphony, 56–57, 270.

Every, 260.

Every, *each*, etc., singular verb with, 112; reference of pronoun to, 115.

Exact diction, 32, 66–68.

Exactness in use of connectives, 13–15, 278–79, 300–301.

Exam., 260.

Examples, comma before series of, 174; comma between, 165–68; colon before, 187.

Except, 260.

Excessive coördination, 9–10, 275; punctuation, 176–78.

Exclamation point, when used, 192; comma instead of, 170, 192; position relative to other marks, 202–203; with sentence in parenthesis, 195, 199.

Expect, 260.

Expletive, defined, 151; agreement of verb with, 114; overuse of *there*, 296.

Expression and thought, 1.

False coördination, 276.

Faulty subordination, 278–280.

Female, 261.

Fewer, 261.

Fierce, 261.

Figures, when used to represent numbers, 216–217.

Figures of speech, mixed, 54–55; trite, 270–271.

Final consonant, doubled, 228–29.

Final *-e*, 229–230.

Final *-o*, plural of words in, 232.

Final *-y*, before suffix, 231; plural of words in, 232.

Fine, 261.

Fine writing, 51–52, 297.

Finite verb, 99–100, 151.

First rate, 261.

Fix, 261.

Folks, 261.

Footnotes, 218–219.

For, comma before, 165, 168.

Foreign words, plural of, 232–33; objectionable use of, 246; italics with, 206.

For example, punctuation before, 174, 182.

Fractions, hyphen with, 217, 234; numbers for, 216.

Fragment of sentence mistaken for sentence, 5, 105–107.

Funny, 261.

Future tense, with *shall* and *will*, 128–130; misused, 123.

Gender, 151, 154; shift in, 62–63, 314.

Geographical expressions, comma with, 174.

Gerund, defined, 100, 151; distinguished from participle, 100; with possessives, 119; dangling, 305–06.

Get, 261.

Glossary of faulty diction, 255–269; of grammatical terms, 148–161.

Gnomic present, 124.

Good, 261.

Good Use, defined, 244–45; a relative term, 252.

Got, 261–262.

Gotten, 261–262.

Government, defined, 152.

Grammar, 97–161; relation to composition, 97; agreement, 112–16; case, 116–120; gender, 62–63, 154; mode, 120–121; number, 112–115; parts of speech, 155–156; person, 112–116; tense, 121–132; voice, 62–63, 160. Grammatical terms defined, 148–161.

Grand, 262.

Guess, 262.

Gym, 262.

Hackneyed expressions, 270–271.

Had better, *had rather*. See *Would better*, 269.

Had have, 262.

Had of, 262.

Had ought, 262.

INDEX

Handwriting, 217–218.
Hardly, double negative with, 148.
Harsh sounds, 56–57, 270.
Has got, 262.
He for *he or she*, 115; *he* for *one*, 144–45, 314.
Help but, 148, 262.
Hence, position of, 304.
Historical present misused, 63–64, 313.
However, position of, 304.
Hyphen, in compounds, 210, 211, 217, 234–35; between syllables, 210–211; placed at end of line, 210.

Idiom, 246.
Idiomatic question, comma with, 169.
Ie, ei, spelling, 227–28.
I.e., punctuation with, comma, 174; semicolon, 182.
Illogical, comparisons, 62–63, 284; construction, 63, 301, 311–313; coördination, 275; connectives, 13–15, 98, 300; thought, 273–74, 301, 313.
Impersonal constructions, 114, 296.
Implied reference of pronoun, 61, 309.
Improprieties, 248.
In back of, 262.
Incomplete comparisons, 283–85; constructions, 282; thought, 281–82, 285–87, 301.
Indefinite pronouns, defined, 144; *one* (not *he*), 144; *you*, 145; *they*, 145; use of *this, that, which, it* as indefinites, 308.
Indention, of paragraph, 218, 221; of outline, 85; of verse, 220–221.
Independent clause, defined, 102, 146.
Independent element, defined, 152; punctuation of, 170.
Indirect discourse, no quotation marks with, 201; no punctuation before, 176, 201; shifted to direct, 313–314; *shall* and *will* in, 130.
Indirect question, no comma be-

fore, 177; no quotation marks with, 201, 207; no question mark after, 193.
Individual, 262.
Infinitive, defined, 100, 152; syntax of, 100, 152; tense of, 124–25; case with, 118; subject of, 118; split, 312; repetition of sign of, 314.
Inflection, defined, 152.
Ingenious, ingenuous, 262.
Ink, 218.
Insertions in MS., 218.
Inside of, 262.
Intensive pronoun, 143.
Interjection, defined, 152; punctuation of, 170.
Interpolations, brackets for, 199–200.
Interrogative pronoun, 143.
Interrogative sentence, question mark after, 193; in parenthesis, 195, 199.
Intransitive verb, defined, 152–53.
Introduction of theme independent of title, 220.
Introductory, adverbial modifier, comma with, 171; phrase, comma with, 171; no comma with, 177.
Inversion of words, emphatic, 34–35; awkward, 294–96, 303–305, 311–312.
It, agreement of verb with, 114; as indefinite, 145; vague reference of, 308.
Italics, for emphasis, 31; foreign words, 206; literary titles, 206–207, 209; ships, 206; misuse of, 207, 219.

Kind of, 262; *kind of a (an)*, 263.

Last, 263.
Latest, 263.
Lay, 263.
Learn, 263.
Leave, 263.
Legibility, 217–218.
Less, 263.
Let, 263.

322

INDEX

Letters and figures italicized, 206; plural of, 233.

Liable, 263.

Lie, 263.

Like as conjunction, 141.

Likely, 263.

Lists, colon before, 187.

Literary titles, capitals in, 209, 214; italics with, 206, 209; quotation marks with, 207, 209; article omitted in, 209, 220.

Loan, 263.

Localisms, 246–247.

Locate, 263.

Logical agreement, 63; arrangement of sentence elements, 296, 303–305, 311–312; sequence of ideas, 282, 301.

Loose, 263–64.

Loose sentence, 37–38.

Lose, 263.

Lot of, lots of, 263.

Lovely, 264.

Mad, 264.

Main clause, defined, 102, 146; main idea in, 11, 22, 275–76; 278, 298.

Manuscript form, 217–221; legibility, 217; paging, 218; spacing, 218; indention, 218; erasures, 218; corrections, 218; footnotes, 218; endorsement, 219; title, 219–220; verse, 220.

Margins in MS., 218–219.

May, can, 264.

Me, "It is me," 117.

Mean, 264.

Mechanical form. See Manuscript form.

Metaphors mixed, 54–55.

Mighty, 264.

Misplaced modifiers, 54, 302–305; unnecessary punctuation because of, 178.

Misreading prevented, by comma, 163–165; by semicolon, 183–184.

Misspelling, 223–242; recording, 223.

Mixed constructions, 53–54, 311; figures of speech, 54–55.

Modal auxiliary, defined, 153.

Mode, defined, 153; subjunctive, 120–121; shifted, 313.

Modification, 154.

Modifiers, defined, 154; dangling, 305–307; misplaced, 54, 303–305; squinting, 303; relative clause, 304; *however, therefore, thus, then*, etc., position of, 304; punctuation of, 171 ff.

Monotony in sentence structure, 8–10, 51–52, 276, 280, 290–292, 297–98.

Most, 264.

Much, 264.

Mutual, 264.

Myself, 264.

Namely, punctuation with, comma, 174; semicolon, 182.

Names of persons, capitalized, 212–213.

National use, 246–247.

Naturalness, 51–52, 292, 297.

Near by, 264.

Negative, double, 148; comparisons, *so* in, 142, 257.

Neither, 264; agreement of verb and pronoun with, 112, 115.

Newspapers, correct form for title of, 206–209.

Nice, 264.

No, modifying whole sentence, comma with, 170.

No account, 264.

Nohow, 264.

Nominative absolute, defined, 148; punctuation of, 170; awkward, 294–5; unemphatic, 295.

Nominative case, 116–117.

Nominative of address, 154; comma with, 170.

None, agreement of verb with, 112.

Non-essential modifiers, defined, 133; distinguished from essential, 133–34; punctuation of, 134, 171–72.

Non-finite verb, 99–100.

323

Non-restrictive modifiers. See Non-essential modifiers.

No other, 264.

No place. See *Any place*, 256.

Nor, double negative with, 148; subjects joined by, 113.

Not, comma before for emphasis, 168.

Notes in MS., 218–219.

Noun clause, defined, 154; sentence used as, 146; adverbial used as, 147.

Nouns, classes of, 154; agreement with verb, 112–114; agreement with pronoun, 115; collective, agreement with verb, 113; with pronoun, 115; case, 116–119; plural of, 232–33; plural form with singular verb, 113–114; proper, capitalized, 212; to be repeated, 22–23, 65–66, 284, 314.

Number, 155; agreement of subject and verb, 112–114; pronoun and antecedent, 115; collective, 113; shift in, 314.

Numbers, figures used for, 216–17; apostrophe with plural of, 197; not repeated in parenthesis, 198, 216.

O, oh, 264.

Object, defined, 155.

Objective accusative, predicate objective, defined, 155.

Objective case, uses of, 117–118.

Obsolete words, 245.

Of, 264.

Of-phrase denoting possession, 118.

Off, off from, 264.

O.K., 264.

Omissions, marked by apostrophe, 196; of article in literary titles, 209, 220; of article, possessive, preposition, conjunction, 286, 314; of noun, 22–23, 65–66, 284, 314; part of verb *to be*, 285; part of verb phrase, 285; auxiliary or copula, 285; of sign of parallelism, 22–23; of sign of transition, 300–301; of part of thought, 281–82;

285–86, 301; in comparisons, 283–84; of punctuation marks, 163–65.

One, singular verb with, 112; as indefinite, 144–45, 314.

Only, 265; *only, just, even, almost,* position of, 303; double negative with, 148.

Onto, 265.

Or, comma before for emphasis, 168; confused with *nor*, 148; subject not made plural by, 113.

Oral, verbal, 265.

Order, of words, awkward, 54, 294–296, 303–305, 311–312; coherent and logical, 303–305; emphatic, 33 ff. Of sentence elements, 301, 304–305, 311–312.

Other, 265.

Ought, 265.

Outlines, sentence, making of, 84–86; proper form for, 85, 221–222.

Outside of, 265.

Overcareful writing, 297.

Overlapping dependence, 279; overlapping thought, 301.

Owing to, 260.

Paging, 218.

Paragraph, purpose of, 81, 221; summary sentence in, 77 ff.; topic sentence in, 77, 81; methods of developing, 81–82; transition in, 83; indention, 218; length, 81–82; relation to whole theme, 81, 83; first paragraph and title, 220; dialogue, 203; quotation marks with, 201; paragraphs for analysis, 88–96.

Parallelism, when to use, 21, 299; false, 25; faulty, 22, 24; after correlatives, 24, 300; and balance, 23; in summary sentences, 26–27.

Parentheses (curves), uses of, 197–200; punctuation within, 198–199; punctuation after, 198–199; parenthesis within parenthesis, 194, 200; numbers in, 198, 216.

INDEX

Parenthetical matter, defined, 155; set off by comma, 169 ff.; by dash, 194; by curves, 197–200; by brackets, 199–200.

Parenthetical sentence, set off by commas, 170; by dashes, 194; by curves, 199–200; punctuation after, 199.

Parsing, 23, 155.

Participle, defined, 100, 155; distinguished from verb, 100; from gerund, 100; dangling, 61–62, 305–306; tense of, 124–25; weak use of, 294–295.

Parts of speech, 23, 155–156.

Party, person, individual, 265.

Passive voice, weak, 293–94.

Past perfect tense, 123–24.

Past tense, 122–123.

Per, 265.

Per cent, 265.

Perfect infinitive for present, 125.

Period, after declarative sentence, 189; after abbreviations, 190, 215; position relative to quotation marks, 202–203; in combination with other marks, 190; after a parenthetical sentence, 199.

Period fault, 5, 105–107, 274.

Periodic sentence, 37–38.

Person, 265.

Person, defined, 156; agreement in, 112–115; shift in, 62, 313–314.

Personal pronoun, 143.

Personifications, capitals with, 214.

Phenomena, 265.

Phone, 265.

Photo, 265.

Phrases, defined, 101, 156; mistaken for sentence, 5, 106; functions of, 101; absolute, comma with, 170; awkward, 294–95; punctuation of introductory, 171, 176–77.

Pivotal words, position of, 35; repetition of for emphasis, 40–41.

Plenty, 265.

Plurals, of nouns, 232–233; of letters and figures, 197.

Poetry, capitalizing first word of line in, 212; writing of, 220–221.

Point of view, shifted, 51–52, 62–63, 313–314; subject, 51–52, 62–63, 313; tense, 63, 313; number, 314; mode, 313; voice, 313; in comparisons, 63.

Position of modifiers, 54, 302–05.

Position of Words. See Order of words.

Possessive, formation of, 118; uses of, 118; with gerund, 119; apostrophe with, 196; spelling of, 118, 197; of inanimate objects, 118; *whose* and *of which,* 118; undesirable as antecedent, 309.

Preceding event in past time expressed by past perfect tense, 123.

Precise diction, 32–33, 66–69.

Predicate, defined, 99, 156; predicate adjective, 156; complement, 156–57; pred. nominative, 156; noun, 157; objective, 157.

Predication, defined, 99–100, 157; reduction of, 10–11, 275–277.

Prefixes, distinction between, 226–227; hyphen with, 211.

Preposition, defined, 157; idiomatic use of, 246; omitted, 286–87, 314; repeated, 22–23, 286–87, 314; suspended, 296.

Prepositional phrase, 117, 306; case after, 117–118.

Present use, 245.

Principal, principle, 266.

Principal parts of verb, 125, 157–159.

Principal verb in double capacity, 285.

Prof, 266.

Promise, future of, 128.

Pronoun, definition and classes, 143–145; syntax of, 144; agreement of, 115, 144; case, 116–119; reference, 61, 307–310; shift in number, person, class of, 143; possessive, spelling of, 118; repeated, 22–23, 286, 314–15.

INDEX

Pronunciation and spelling, 224; words mispronounced, 224.

Proper names, capitals with, 212–213.

Propose, purpose, 266.

Proposition, proposal, 266.

Proven, 266.

Provincialisms, 246–247.

Punctuation, 162–205; purpose of, 162; at beginning of line, 221; ex-·cessive, 176–178; for clearness, 163–165.

Question mark, with direct question, 193; not to label humor or irony, 193; to indicate uncertainty, 193; position in relation to other marks, 203; after parenthetical sentence, 195, 199.

Questions, *shall* and *will* in, 129; indirect, 177, 193, 201; comma after idiomatic, 169.

Quite, 266.

Quotation marks, with technical, slang, or coined words, 207; with translations or definitions, 207; with literary titles, 207, 209; for dialogue, 200–203; position relative to other marks, 202–203; quotation within quotation, 201.

Quoted matter, punctuation before, 202 (comma), 187 (colon); punctuation of, 200–203; direct, 200–203; indirect, 201, 207; paragraphing of, 203; quotation marks with, 207.

Quoted titles, capitals with, 209, 214; quotation marks with, 207, 209; italics with, 206–07, 209; article in, 209; incorrect omissions from, 220.

Raise, rise, 266.

Rapidity of movement checked by semicolon, 182–83.

Real, 266.

Reason is because, construction wrong, 147.

Reciprocal pronoun, 144.

Reckon, 266.

Redundancy, 271.

Reference, of pronoun, 61, 307–310; ambiguous, 307; indefinite, 307, 309; to possessive or parenthetical antecedent, 309; to unexpressed antecedent, 309; elliptical clause, 62, 306; gerund, 305–306; participle, 62, 305–306.

References and footnotes, 218–219; colon with, 188.

Reflexive pronoun, 143.

Related words together, 54, 296, 301–04, 311–12; related ideas together, 301.

Relative clause misplaced, 304.

Relative pronoun, 138, 143; agreement of verb with, 114; agreement with antecedent, 115; reference of, 307–310; confusion of *who, which, that,* 145.

Remember of, 266.

Repetition bad, how corrected, 290–291; monotonous repetition of words, 42, 291; of syntactical constructions, 42, 280, 292, 297–98; similar sounds, 56–57, 291; same idea, 271–272, 291; careless repetition of conjunction *that,* 291.

Repetition good; for emphasis, 22–23, 40–41; for parallelism, 22–23; for clearness, 41–42, 65–66, 285–86, 314.

Reputable use, 247–252.

Resolved, capitalized, 214; italicized, 206.

Restrictive and non-restrictive. See Essential.

Rhetorical rules, purpose of, 7–8.

Rhyme in prose, 56–57, 270.

Right, 266.

Said, 310.

Salutation of letter, comma after, 185; colon after, 188.

Same, 310.

Scarcely, double negative with, 148.

Seasons, names of not capitalized, 214.

Semicolon, between independent

326

INDEX

clauses not joined by coördinate conjunction, 181–82; between independent clauses joined by conjunction, 182–84; before conjunctive adverb, 182; for clearness, rapidity of movement, emphasis, 182–83; misuse of, 184–85; position relative to quotation marks, 202–203.

Sentence, defined and distinguished from sentence elements, 5–6, 8, 98 ff., 106–107; simple, complex, compound, 8–9, 150, 159; unity in, 5–6, 273–74, 287; emphasis in, 30–42; clearness in, 61–69; variety in, 51–52, 291–92, 297–98; subordination in, 8–15; parallelism in, 21–27; economy in, 51–56; summary, 77–80; sentence and paragraph, 80–83; and outline, 83–86; used for subordinate clause, 146. See also Awkwardness, Coherence, Elliptical, Exclamatory, Fragment, Loose, Omissions, Repetition, Order of Words, Periodic, Reference, Stringy, Choppy, Monotony, Topic, Transition, Weak ending, etc.

Sentence element, defined, 159.
Sentence summary, 77–80.
Separative comma, 163–69.
Sequence of tenses, 124; of ideas, 282, 301.
Series of examples, colon before, 187; comma between, 165–67.
Series of words, comma between, 165–67; comma wrong before or after, 176–177; semicolon between, 184.
Shall and *will*, 128 ff.
Shape, 266.
Shift in construction, awkward, 53, 282, 311; dash for, 194.
Shift in point of view, change of subject, 62–63, 313; tense, 62–63, 313; logical agreement, 63, 314.
Ships, names of italicized, 206.
Should and *would*, 130–131.

Sign of infinitive repeated, 22, 286, 314.
Similar forms or sounds confused in spelling, 225.
Simple future, with *shall* and *will*, 128; simple sentence, 8, 159; simple subject, 160.
Simply, 267.
Sit, set, 267.
Slang, term vaguely used, 250; defined by Greenough and Kittredge, 250; attitude towards, 251; distinguished from other forms of non-standard English, 250; origin of, 250–251; case against, 250; case for, 251; quotation marks with, 207.
So, punctuation before, 142, 182; in negative comparisons, 142; *so* and *so that*, 142; misused for *very*, 142; excessive use of, 142, 276.
Some, 267.
Some place, someways, 267.
Sort of, 267.
Sound of words, 56–57, 270.
Spacing, of letters and words, 217–218; of titles, 219–20; of outlines, 83–85, 221–222; of verse, 221–222.
Spelling, rules, 223–242; list of misspelled words, 237–242.
Splendid, 267.
Split, construction, 311–312; infinitive, 312.
Squinting modifiers, 303.
Standard of comparison, not expressed, 283; illogical, 284; shifted, 63, 314.
Statue, stature, statute, 267.
Stop, 267.
Straggling compound sentence, 9–10, 276–77, 298.
Stringy compound sentence, 9–10, 276–77, 298.
Strong close in sentence, 35–38; thwarted by absolute phrase, 295.
Strong verb, 160.
Structure of paragraph, 80–83.

INDEX

Style and personality, 4–8.

Subject, defined, 99, 160; agreement of verb with, 112 ff.; shift in, 51–52, 62, 313; repeated for clearness, 41–42, 284.

Subjunctive mode, 120–121.

Subordinating conjunction, defined, 137–38; list of, 13–15, 137–38; repeated for clearness, 22–23, 41–42, 65–66, 314.

Subordination, when used, 12 ff.; 277–279; for clearness, 8–12; for emphasis, 8–12, 292–93, 298; upside-down, 278; overlapping, 279; faulty, 278–89; improper, 22.

Substantive, defined, 160; substantive clause, 160. (See also Noun clause.)

Such, 267.

Such as, punctuation with, 174.

Such . . . . . that, 267.

Suffix, hyphen with, 211.

Summarizing adverb or adv. phrase, comma with, 171.

Summary sentence, writing of, 77–80; in paragraph, 82–83; in outline, 83–84.

Sure, 267.

Sure and, 267.

Surely, modifying whole predication, set off by commas, 170.

Suspicion, 267.

Suspended preposition, 296.

Suspended sentence element, punctuation of, 175; awkward, 175, 296.

Suspense, 37–38, dash to indicate, 194.

Syllabication, 210–211.

Syntax, defined, 160.

Tangled construction, 53–54, 311–312.

Tautology, 271.

Technical terms, undesirable, 247; quotation marks with, 207.

Tense, defined, 121; present, 122; historical present, 63–64, 122, 313; past, 122–23; time modifier with, past, 122; future, 123; present

perfect, 123; past perfect, 123; future perfect, 124; shall and will, 126 ff.; of subjunctive, 121–122; of verbals, 124–25; sequence, 124; shift in, 63–64, 313.

Terseness, in structure, 292–93; in wording, 55, 271–72.

Than, case after, 116–117; omitted in comparisons, 283; than any other, vaguely used in comparisons, 284.

That, this as adverbs, 267; careless repetition of, 291; vague reference of, 308.

That-clause mistaken for sentence, 106.

That a-way, this a-way, 268.

That is, punctuation with, 174 (comma), 182 (semicolon).

Then, position of, 304.

There, agreement of verb with, 114; overused as impersonal, 296.

Thereby causing construction weak, 306.

Therefore, position of, 304.

These, loose reference of, 145, 308; these kind, those kind (sort), 268.

Thesis sentence, 84–86.

They as indefinite pronoun, 145.

Thinking and writing, 1–8.

This, vague reference of, 308.

This here, that there, 268.

Those, loose reference of, 145, 308; those kind, those sort, 268.

Thought and expression, 1–8.

Thought incomplete, 281; obscure, 53–54, 311–312.

Through, 268.

Thus, position of, 304; thus causing construction weak, 306.

Time modifier with past tense, 122.

Title of theme, correct form, 219–220; capitals, 219; spacing, 219–220; without quotation marks or italics, 219; punctuation after, 219; omissions from, 220; reference to, 220.

Titles of persons, abbreviation of, 215; capitals with, 213–214; set off by commas, 174.

328

INDEX

Titles quoted: capitals in, 209, 214; quotation marks with, 207, 209; italics with, 206, 209; articles in, 206–209, 220; incorrect omissions from, 220.

To be, case after, 118; used in double capacity, 285.

Together with, subject not plural, 112.

Too, 268.

Topic sentence, 77, 81.

Transition, marked by connective, 65, 80, 300; by reference word, 65; by repetition, 65, 314; in paragraph, 83.

Transitional expressions, set off by commas, 171.

Transitive verb, defined, 160.

Transpire, 268.

Transposed sentence elements, punctuation of, 175–176; awkward, 294–96.

Triteness, 32, 270–271.

Try and, sure and, 268.

Ugly, 268.

Uncompleted, comparisons, 283–84; constructions, 282–83; thought, 281–82, 285–87, 301.

Undeveloped thought, 281–82.

Unique, 268.

Unity, in sentence, 273, 287; in the paragraph, 80–83; in whole composition, 83–84; and punctuation, 103, 187.

Unnecessary punctuation, 176–178; words, 55–56, 271–72.

Unrelated ideas in same sentence, 273–277.

Up, 268.

Upside-down subordination, 278.

Usage good, 244–55.

Vague diction, 32, 66–68; reference, 307–309.

Variety in sentence structure, 51–52; 297–98; mechanical undesirable, 51, 291–92, 297.

Verb, defined, 100, 160; distinguished from verbal, 100; agreement, 112 ff.; principal parts, 126, 157–159; tense, 121 ff., mode, 120–121, 153; voice, 160; omission of, 185–86.

Verbal, 100, 268.

Verbal, distinguished from verb, 100, 160, 268; misused for verb, 105–106; tense, 124–25.

Verbosity, 272.

Verb phrase, defined, 101, 160; separation of parts of, 312; omission of part of, 285–86; written as sentence, 106.

Verse, writing of, 212, 220–221.

Very, too, much, 268–269.

Viz., punctuation with, 174, 182.

Vocabulary, size of, 68–69, 89.

Vocatives, set off by commas, 170.

Voice, defined, 160; shifted, 51–52, 62, 313.

Vulgarisms, 248.

Wait on, 269.

Way, ways, woods, 269.

Weak, close of sentence, 35–38, 295; passive, 293–94; word order, 33 ff., 296, 304–05, 311–313; reference of *this, that, which, it,* etc., 145, 308; verb, 161.

Well, modifying whole predication, commas with, 170.

What. See *But what,* 257.

When clause misused as predicate nominative, 63, 147.

Where, misused for *that,* 147; *where* clause misused as predicate nominative, 63, 147.

Whereas, capitalized, 214.

Which, confused with *who,* 145; vague reference of, 308.

While misused as coördinating conjunction, 137, 269, 279.

Who, confused with *which,* 145; with *whom,* 116.

Whom, for *who,* 117.

Whomever for *whoever,* 117.

Whose, as impersonal possessive, 118, 145.

Will and *shall,* 128 ff.

INDEX

Without as conjunction, 263, 269.

Woods, 269.

Word grouping, by comma, 163–65; by semicolon, 183–84. See also Word order.

Word order, awkward, 54, 296, 304–305, 311–313; logical, 304–305; emphatic, 33–38.

Word used in double capacity, 285–86.

Wordiness, 55–56, 271–72.

Words. See Diction, Omissions, Order of Words, Repetition Good, Wordiness, Spelling, Good Use, Glossary of Faulty Diction, Barbarism, Impropriety, Slang, etc.

Would better, 269.

Yes, modifying whole predication comma with, 170–71.

You as indefinite, 145.